THE PRACTICAL GUIDE TO
KAYAKING
& CANOEING

THE PRACTICAL GUIDE TO
KAYAKING & CANOEING

BILL MATTOS
Consultant Andy Middleton

LORENZ BOOKS

This edition is published by Lorenz Books

Lorenz Books is an imprint of Anness Publishing Ltd
Hermes House, 88-89 Blackfriars Road, London SE1 8HA
tel. 020 7401 2077; fax 020 7633 9499
www.lorenzbooks.com
info@anness.com
© Anness Publishing Ltd 2002

Published in the USA by Lorenz Books, Anness Publishing Inc.
27 West 20th Street, New York, NY 10011
fax 212 807 6813

Published in Australia by Lorenz Books, Anness Publishing Pty Ltd
Level 1, Rugby House, 12 Mount Street, North Sydney, NSW 2060
tel. (02) 8920 8622; fax (02) 8920 8633

This edition distributed in the UK by Aurum Press Ltd
25 Bedford Avenue, London WC1B 3AT
tel. 020 7637 3225; fax 020 7580 2469

This edition distributed in the USA by National Book Network
4720 Boston Way, Lanham, MD 20706
tel. 301 459 3366; fax 301 459 1705; www.nbnbooks.com

This edition distributed in Canada by General Publishing
895 Don Mills Road, 400-402 Park Centre, Toronto, Ontario M3C 1W3
tel. 416 445 3333; fax 416 445 5991; www.genpub.com

This edition distributed in New Zealand by David Bateman Ltd
30 Tarndale Grove, Off Bush Road, Albany, Auckland
tel. (09) 415 7664; fax (09) 415 8892

A CIP catalogue record for this book is available from the British Library.

Publisher: Joanna Lorenz
Managing Editor: Judith Simons
Senior Art Manager: Clare Reynolds
Project Editor: Sarah Ainley
Text Editors: Richard Rosenfeld and Paul Grogan
Photographer: Helen Metcalfe
Designer: Nigel Partridge
Illustrator: J. B. Illustrations
Indexer: Helen Snaith
Editorial Reader: Richard McGinlay
Production Controller: Stephen Lang

1 3 5 7 9 10 8 6 4 2

DISCLAIMER
The author and publishers wish to stress that they strongly advise the
use of a helmet and flotation aid in all paddling situations. There is no
legal requirement to wear either, but paddling is all about taking
responsibility for your own decisions, actions and personal safety.

CONTENTS

If you were to ask me, "Mr Nealy, I'm an expert. Should I paddle flooded rivers?" I would say, "No. But if you do, you should read this and learn from my mistakes."
William Nealy,
Kayak (1986)

You must dominate the boat while submitting to the river. You must tune to the shape of the river while persistently focusing the boat's energy. Tough moves require unbending intent.
Jim Snyder,
Squirtboating (2001)

The features you need to check out from a "How do I get out of that?" point of view are the same ones you need to understand in order to make the most of the hole's freestyle potential.
To quote a jet fighter test pilot: "Never put your body where your mind hasn't been first".
Franco Ferrero, British Canoe Union coach,
White Water Safety & Rescue (2000)

"There is nothing — absolutely nothing — half so much worth doing as simply messing about in boats." That's what Ratty said to Mole in Kenneth Grahame's beloved 1908 novel, *The Wind in the Willows*. "In or out of 'em, it doesn't matter. Nothing seems really to matter, that's the charm of it", Ratty continued.

Open canoeing is everything from a chilled-out day on the lake, through hammering down a raging torrent, to throwing some ends in a hole... Open boating never fails to satisfy. James Weir, 2001 European OC1 Freestyle Champion

1 INTRODUCTION

Taking Up Paddling

The words kayaking and canoeing describe two distinctly separate variants of small boat paddling. Together, they represent an activity that has a much longer history than most people imagine, predating the invention of the wheel.

Thousands of years ago, ancient tribesmen hollowed out logs to make vessels for fishing. As they carved out crude seating places, they could have had no idea that they were designing cockpits for today's paddlers, or that their heavy craft would one day be made from lightweight, manmade materials. How could they know that these boats would demand exceptional levels of skill from paddlers racing on white water or performing acrobatic feats on the crest of a wave?

In fact, it was only during the recreation explosion of the late twentieth and early twenty-first centuries that paddle sport has experienced a meteoric rate of growth. It soon touched the lives of the thousands and thousands who enjoy the outdoors and, in particular, the great pleasure of messing about in boats.

Spirit of Adventure

There is something about the simplicity of paddling a boat with a free blade – that is, a paddle unattached to the boat – that captures the imagination. Few who have tried paddling can deny that it is amazing fun, and that you can get a real sense of freedom even if it is your very first day on the water. Best of all is the

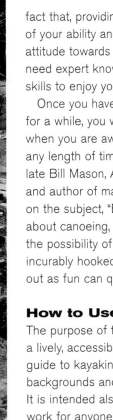 *Two sea kayakers enjoying bright sunshine and calm seas – the perfect conditions for a day on the water.*

A group of kayakers and canoeists prepare to get afloat at a launching spot on a white water river.

fact that, providing you know the limits of your ability and have a responsible attitude towards personal safety, you don't need expert knowledge or any specialist skills to enjoy yourself.

Once you have dabbled at paddling for a while, you will start to get restless when you are away from the water for any length of time. In the words of the late Bill Mason, American canoe guru and author of many inspirational texts on the subject, "Before you get serious about canoeing, you must consider the possibility of becoming totally and incurably hooked on it." What first starts out as fun can quickly become addictive.

How to Use This Book

The purpose of this book is to provide a lively, accessible and comprehensive guide to kayaking and canoeing, their backgrounds and likely future directions. It is intended also as a seminal reference work for anyone who cares about making the most of their time on the water in a kayak or a canoe.

◓ *An expert kayaker playing on white water. He is paddling a freestyle kayak, designed especially for surfing waves on white water.*

For beginners, we look at the best way to prepare yourself for paddling in order to have the most fun and avoid taking risks. There is advice on getting the best from your gear and your body, and the essential clothing and equipment that is needed for comfort, safety and performance. All the paddling skills are covered in enough depth to enable you to master them with practice. The emphasis is on helping you make decisions safely and responsibly.

Later sections of the book look at white water and open water paddling, and at the different disciplines in which kayakers and canoeists specialize. There is an introduction to the various forms of competitive paddle sport that the progressive paddler might choose, and a chapter that visits some of the best paddling locations in the world. Finally, and crucially, there is detailed information on all the key safety and first aid issues that the modern paddler needs to know.

If you are new to kayaking or canoeing, you will benefit hugely from reading right through the book before you take to the water. This way, you will be aware of the

scope of the sport and of the safety issues involved that may affect you. But do not let the theory put you off. In the words of Richard Fox MBE, five times World Slalom Champion, "If there is paddling to be done, go and do it – you can read about it another time!"

If you are an experienced paddler already, there should be plenty here to inspire and interest you, so that you can extend your paddling skills and develop your knowledge. This book will examine every aspect of kayaking and canoeing, from the gentle to the very extreme, presenting in all its diversity the face of twenty-first century paddle sport.

The Origins of Paddling

The design and appearance of kayaks and canoes have undergone a revolution since trees were first hollowed out by early tribesmen. Today's models are fast and lightweight, and tough enough to survive the most extreme water conditions.

Kayaking and canoeing share the same goal – to propel a craft over water by the simplest and most versatile means possible. Unlike rowing, there is an almost unbroken tradition in which the paddler faces the direction of travel, and this has helped make paddling a more versatile way of negotiating difficult water and overcoming changeable conditions. Rowing, on the other hand, is often a more efficient way of powering your way across water but, except in a race or a long journey across open water, power is worth little without the control provided by a free blade and a clear view ahead.

◔ *Canoe design developed out of need. Here, Native Americans use a dugout canoe to transport fresh fruit to store.*

◔ *This painting shows an English ship meeting hostile natives on land and in kayaks in the waters off Greenland.*

Early Boats

The first canoes were logs, paddled by hand or propelled with makeshift poles made from strong, stout branches. It can not have taken early tribes long to realize that a better and more stable alternative was a hollowed-out log. Depending upon the type of trees and tools available, the log was either scraped out or had a fire lit on top, burning out a hollow. There is archaeological evidence of both techniques. The one big problem with a craft fashioned from a solid log was the difficulty of transporting the heavy craft over land for any distance.

Kayak and Canoe Design

Eventually, people acquired the necessary tools and skills to construct a more manageable boat from scratch, using a variety of smaller components, and this is when the now distinct and quite separate forms of kayak and canoe first appeared.

The kayak was invented by the aboriginal Inuit peoples of the Arctic and sub-Arctic regions, probably because a single blade could not generate enough power in the rough seas in which the Inuit hunted and travelled. The kayak paddler, who always sits, uses a paddle with a blade at each end. A shortage of large pieces of wood or bone meant that ancient kayak paddles would have been shorter and thinner than they are today.

The canoe was developed in response to the needs of the native peoples of North America several thousand years ago. The boat is propelled using a single-blade paddle or a pole that is not attached to the boat, in which the paddler sits or kneels facing the direction of travel.

Inuit kayaks and North American canoes were first made from wood bark and bone frames with animal skins stretched over them. In other parts of the world, canoes resembled dugouts made from solid wood, except in South-east Asia, where bamboo was sometimes used.

Recreational Boats

Both kayaks and canoes were conceived out of necessity, and their form continued to follow their intended function. One of the first examples of a boat created purely for recreation was that of John MacGregor, nicknamed Rob Roy, a nineteenth-century English adventurer. MacGregor built his kayak in order to tour the inland waterways of Europe. His book, *A Thousand Miles in the Rob Roy Canoe*, may be the prime reason why many people still use the word "canoe" as a generic term for kayak or canoe. He designed his boat to fit in a railway carriage for easy transportation – modern kayaks are often small enough to fit into a family car!

⊙ *John MacGregor's kayak, the Rob Roy. The boat was made using the clinker construction of traditional boatbuilding.*

⊙ *MacGregor encounters a herd of cattle swimming a river.*

⊙ *A Thousand Miles in the Rob Roy Canoe by John MacGregor. The illustration shows the author seated and using a two-bladed paddle: his craft is therefore a kayak, despite the book's title.*

⊙ *MacGregor gets a rapturous welcome from the Swiss town of Bremgarten.*

The Evolution of Kayaks and Canoes

For thousands of years the basic form of kayaks and canoes changed little, but 200 years ago came the introduction of modern materials, including mass-produced woven fabrics and smooth-planed wood. While there are still a few Inuit hunting boats made from sealskins, the traditional boats have now been superseded.

In an effort to create lighter boats in the nineteenth and twentieth centuries, boats were given a canvas skin over a wooden frame. Light fold-up frames, such as the Klepper, were designed for easy transportation. While some canoes from the Victorian era made from wood construction methods, such as clinker (overlaying planks and/or woodstrip), have survived, the more common canvas boats of that time have not. Further changes came when the skins of kayaks and canoes were replaced by newer manmade fabrics, such as plywood.

❍ *The Klepper folding kayak mimics the construction style of skin-on-frame boats but now uses modern materials.*

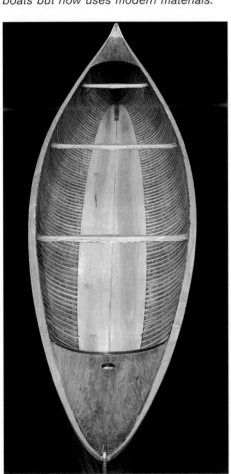

Plastic Fantastic

During the latter half of the twentieth century, kayaking and canoeing received a dramatic boost from new technology. In the 1950s, the prevalent form of construction was still canvas over a wooden frame, and the paddles were made exclusively from wood. But, within 20 years, fibreglass (or glass-reinforced plastic) had totally revolutionized boat construction, and most boats were now made this way. For the first time it was possible to make more rounded shapes, and countless new designs soon flooded the paddling world.

In the 1980s, fibreglass and even more advanced composites, such as carbon fibre and Kevlar™, were dramatically overshadowed by plastic. The advent of plastic suddenly made it possible to mass-produce cheap and durable kayaks or canoes whose performance could almost rival the more expensive and fragile composite boats.

❍❍ *This beautiful woodstrip boat is a traditional Victorian courting canoe, dating from the late nineteenth century and used for recreational purposes only.*

The Percy Blandford Kayak, or PBK, is an example of a wood and canvas boat from the 1950s. The construction method used is similar to the early Inuit kayaks.

Wooden battens line the floor of the PBK to protect the boat's fragile canvas skin when the paddler steps in.

The first fibreglass kayaks were not so different from their wood and canvas forebears. This 1960s example is more manoeuvrable because of its shorter length.

The next progression in general-purpose kayak design was to make the boats slightly wider behind the cockpit and higher in front, for better rough-water handling. This boat was used on extreme white water during the Descent of Everest Expedition in 1975.

For steep descents in heavy white water, boats became rounder, to give more control, and bigger in volume, with end grabs and foot rests.

Introducing the Kayak

The modern general-purpose kayak is so strong and versatile that even moderately experienced practitioners can tackle difficult feats. That is one reason why kayaking has recently become so popular, with many disciplines that provide all the thrills and spills of surfing.

Changing Shape and Form

Canoes might have remained largely unchanged while they were used primarily as a means of transport, but the design of kayaks for sport gradually deviated from their original look. Those used for recreation have become unrecognizable from the original Inuit style, which is now only retained by sea kayaks designed for open-sea use.

The kayak became a recreational and sporting boat in the twentieth century, and quickly adapted two forms. The flat water touring and racing kayak shape has derived from the rowing shell or skiff and, as the rowing boat became narrower and more rounded, so did the kayak. By the 1930s, the general-purpose and white water kayak had settled into a fairly widely accepted form, about 4m (13ft) long and 60cm (2ft) wide across the beam. The ultimate derivatives of these boat designs were seen in slalom and

white water racing competitions, and for most of the late twentieth century they were the driving force behind the new look of the kayaks and decked canoes.

At about the same time, slalom racers realized that the boats performed much better if they were very low in volume, with thin pointed ends that could dip under the hanging poles, and slice better through the water to save time as they raced down the course. This development resulted in the invention of many of the techniques that have shaped the sport as it is today, and changed the way kayaks and decked canoes look forever.

The Influence of Plastic

The widespread introduction of mass-produced plastic boats in the 1980s brought further changes, both to the look of kayaks and the way in which they were used. Before then, boats belonged either to the high-performance competitive market and featured sleek, low-volume craft handmade from space-age composite materials, or they were recreational designs, typically more rounded, general-purpose boats made of plastic. Then, technological developments began to produce plastic boats that had many of the performance

characteristics of the handmade models, combined with greater durability, and because they were cheaper to make, they were relatively inexpensive.

This change marked the end of slalom and river racing as the pinnacle to which every white water paddler aspired; both now became marginalized by the very different activities that the new plastic boats had made possible.

New Disciplines

The plastic revolution enabled even paddlers of intermediate ability to attempt white water descents that would have been impossible even for the most skilled paddler in the older, composite boats. This was partly because the new boats were more likely to bounce off rocks without mishap, and because they were shorter and more manoeuvrable.

Front deck
The top of the whole front half of the kayak (or decked canoe).

Bow or end grab
This can be used for carrying the boat, tying it to a roof rack or trailer, recovering the boat in the water, and in rescue situations. On a white water kayak this would be strong enough to hold 1000kg (2200lbs) or more.

Footrests
Kayaks should always have some kind of footrest; pressing on this with the feet is an important part of the paddling technique. Most footrests are adjustable.

Cockpit rim
This raised, moulded flange is there to stop any water flowing over the decks and into the cockpit. It is also the part of the kayak to which the spraydeck (spray skirt) is attached.

Back deck
The top of the whole back half of the kayak (or decked canoe).

Stern or end grab
As with the bow grab, this can be used for carrying the boat, tying it to a roof rack or trailer, recovering the boat in the water, and in rescue situations.

Hull
The underside of a kayak (or any boat) is called the hull.

Rail or edge
Some boats are quite rounded, but many have sharp corners between the deck and side, and the side and hull. These are called rails or edges, and can be used to hydrodynamic effect by a skilled paddler.

Initially, short boats were frowned upon by the more conservative, traditional paddlers, but the designers kept creating even shorter models. The stage has now been reached whereby the boats cannot get any shorter because the paddlers' feet are so close to the end of the boat. This development, more than any other, has altered white water paddling for ever. It has also meant that many of the skills and strokes practised today are unique to the newer boats now in common use.

Plastic boats made descents of extreme white water possible for the first time, and enabled white water

boaters to perform demanding, high-energy manoeuvres that would previously have smashed a lightweight competition boat. In short, plastic led to the sport of freestyle kayaking, where paddlers perform acrobatic tricks on white water and create complex routines to be judged on style and technical ability.

Meanwhile, the flat water touring and competition scene continued largely unaffected by the plastic revolution. The competitive side is best seen at the Olympics, and features very long, narrow and unstable sprint boats. They, and other similar boats, can also be used for fast

inland touring. Touring boats with better rough water handling have been designed for less sheltered conditions and coastal use, while the Inuit-style sea kayak is extremely popular for more demanding estuary and ocean paddling.

Paddling on the sea taught kayakers how to handle their craft in surf and waves, which in turn led to the popular sport of kayak surfing. A number of kayak styles can be used to ride waves like surfers do, and to perform tricks and manoeuvres. Competitions for kayak surfing judge paddlers on the style and quality of their rides, as with freestyle kayaking.

Introducing the Canoe

Many canoes today look remarkably similar to their traditional Native American ancestors. Some, such as those used for racing, slalom and freestyle, look entirely different. All have benefited from the advances in materials technology that changed kayaking forever, but there are still many canoe paddlers who prefer to adhere to tradition.

The canoe remained largely unchanged in shape and concept while it was used as a means of transport. Apart from the Polynesian canoes and outrigger boats that were used for fishing and inter-island sailing, the prevalent form has always been the open boat with an upswept bow and stern associated with the North American hunters and trappers. Once the canoe became a recreational and sporting boat in the twentieth century, new developments began.

Open Canoes

Many of today's open canoes look much like the traditional models. Materials and construction techniques may have altered, but in form and function they remain virtually unchanged. While these boats are unsuitable for open sea touring, there is and always will be a tradition of using open boats for inland touring. There are many traditionalists who prefer to paddle an open canoe, using air bags or buoyancy tanks to stop the boat sinking in heavy water. For the family and recreational user, the relatively low purchase price and durability of the open canoe make it an extremely practical choice of boat for general-purpose use.

Decked Canoes

Decking in the top part of the boat is a logical move to keep the paddler dry in rough water conditions. Decked boats were initially designed for performance and the more extreme disciplines.

Decked boats were best seen in action in slalom and white water racing competitions, and for most of the latter part of the twentieth century the needs of these disciplines were the driving force behind much of the commercial development in canoes. The single-seater competition canoe, known as the C1, became, for all intents and purposes, like a kayak in design, except for the kneeling position and the smaller cockpit. The two-seater competition canoe, or C2, had cockpits at either end, although competitive racing meant that the cockpits were moved as close to the centre of the boat as possible, to provide sharper manoeuvrability.

At about the same time, slalom racers realized – as with kayaks – that the boats performed much better if they were less buoyant (very low in volume), with thin, pointed ends that could pass underneath the vertical hanging poles of the slalom course, and carve a quicker passage through the water. The move towards low-volume boats led, in turn, to the development of many of the handling techniques seen in the sport today.

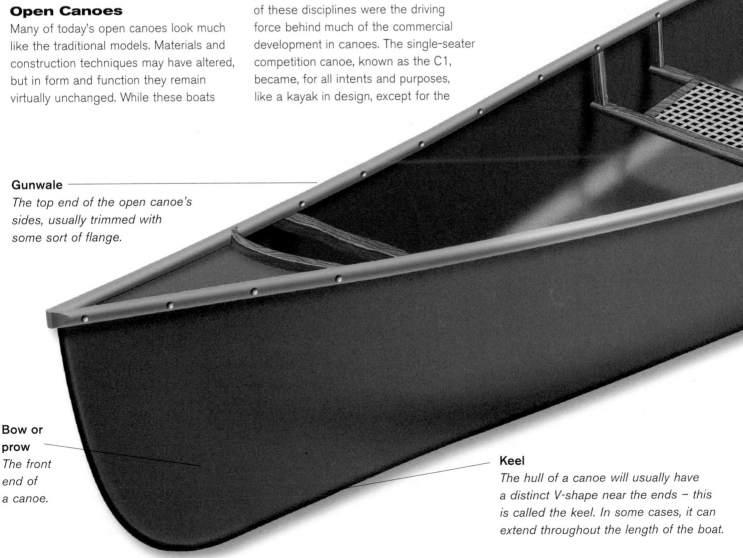

Gunwale
The top end of the open canoe's sides, usually trimmed with some sort of flange.

Bow or prow
The front end of a canoe.

Keel
The hull of a canoe will usually have a distinct V-shape near the ends – this is called the keel. In some cases, it can extend throughout the length of the boat.

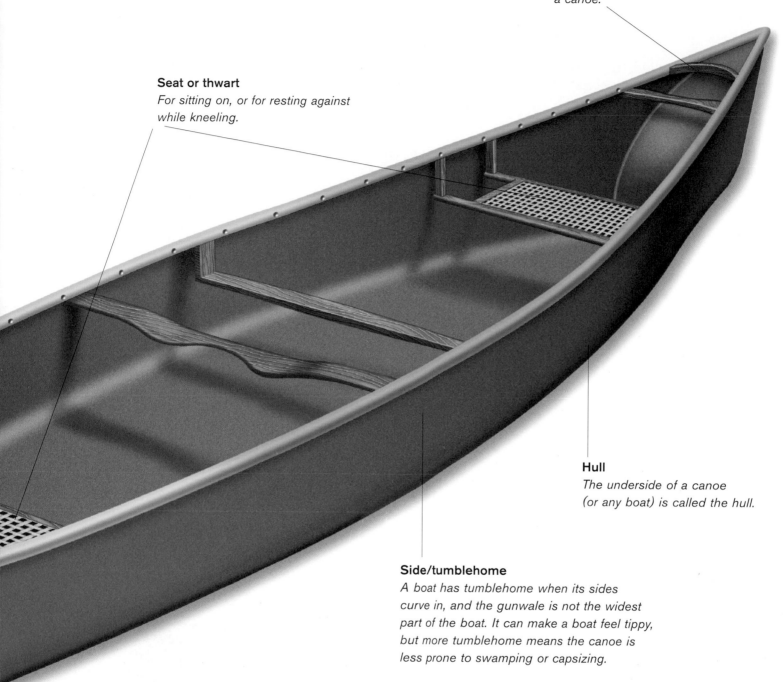

Stern
*The back end of
a canoe.*

Seat or thwart
*For sitting on, or for resting against
while kneeling.*

Hull
*The underside of a canoe
(or any boat) is called the hull.*

Side/tumblehome
*A boat has tumblehome when its sides
curve in, and the gunwale is not the widest
part of the boat. It can make a boat feel tippy,
but more tumblehome means the canoe is
less prone to swamping or capsizing.*

Modern Materials

The arrival of plastic boats in the 1980s had huge repercussions on the sport. Before then the canoe world had two very distinct groups. At the top end of the scale were the expensive low-volume decked boats used by the high-performance competitive scene, which were handmade from the latest materials. Meanwhile, the recreational scene was still dominated by general-purpose open boats made of fibreglass or wood. By the 1970s, technological developments led to plastic boats that could rival the handmade ones; they were tougher and less expensive, and allowed white water paddlers to have bigger aspirations than slalom and river racing. The plastic boats of the 1980s gave an extra edge to the competitive world of canoeing, changing it completely.

The new plastic canoes, like the new kayaks, were becoming so manoeuvrable they could perform increasingly aggressive moves. This led to the sport of freestyle canoeing, where paddlers take turns to perform elaborate tricks on white water.

The plastic revolution enabled paddlers of intermediate ability to attempt descents (not always safely) that would have been beyond even skilled boaters in the older, composite boats. The new boats were tough and could withstand knocks against rocks, and they were highly manoeuvrable. While there were dramatic developments in white water canoeing, flat water touring, slalom and competitions continued largely unaffected. The Olympic Games is still the focus for long, narrow and unstable sprint canoes.

2 GETTING STARTED

GOING PADDLING FOR THE FIRST TIME

There are a wide variety of paddle sports, ranging from the placid to the frankly insane, and it pays to be sure that you know what you are getting into. Most people take the gentle approach, and learn to paddle on completely safe, flat, sheltered water. Even so, most kayaks and canoes seem initially unstable, and for most people that is exactly what distinguishes these craft from more solid dinghies and rowing boats.

The possibility of being capsized means that you have to take certain precautions. Being able to swim at least 50m (170ft) in clothing is a prerequisite, and wearing a buoyancy aid (personal flotation device, or PFD) is important, particularly when you start because you might fall into the water quite often. What is more often overlooked is the need to think through what will happen if you do end up in the water. Will the boat float? Will you be able to get ashore quickly? Is there land close by?

These considerations are covered in this chapter. The important point when starting out is to think about your personal safety; do not just jump into a boat and paddle off. Canoeing and kayaking are not dangerous, but a cavalier approach most certainly is.

◀ *Two kayakers in traditional boats cruising up a beautiful estuary.*

◆ *Paddlers getting organized in plastic general-purpose boats.*

Where and When to Paddle

Boating is great fun, but it pays to be careful. Stick to the elementary rules and always put safety first. A few minutes' careful checking before you get into the water is all that is required.

Suitable Waters
Until you have achieved the level of self-sufficiency that sets a kayaker or canoeist apart from someone just "having a go", it is best to seek out safe, predictable environments to paddle in, where there is help at hand if required.

You should learn to paddle on still water, although this is often surprisingly hard to find. Non-tidal rivers and lakes in calm weather, or reservoirs where public access to the water is allowed, would be suitable, but make sure there is good bank access in case you have to swim ashore. Beaches are generally safe for beginners as long as the waves are less than 2m (6½ft) and the wind is not blowing offshore. Find out about the character of the stretch of beach you plan to use in advance, and make sure there are no strong currents you cannot see.

◓ The points to consider on a beach are wave size, wind and water currents.

◐ Sheltered inland waterways such as this river are ideal for safe paddling.

◓ For novices in search of trouble-free water, inland lakes are best of all.

Where Not to Paddle

There are a number of situations that are unsuitable for paddling. Some situations can present difficulties, while others are dangerous. It pays to know what to avoid.

Do not paddle where the wind or current can carry you away faster than you can paddle or swim. In fact, avoid fast currents when learning; it is far easier to learn if the conditions are in your favour.

Do not paddle where it might be difficult to get out of the water. Remember that you might be cold and tired after capsizing. Avoid any obstacle that might present a problem, such as steep banks, deep mud and slippery rocks, which can be a nightmare to the tired paddler with a boat full of water.

If there is a current, avoid paddling where there are rocks, trees, pontoons or obstructions in the water. A barely visible current can be enough to pin a boat or a person against the upstream side of an obstruction, and this is a common cause of paddling accidents.

Always stay away from weirs. Do not approach them either from above or below. Not all weirs are dangerous, but it takes experience to be able to tell a friendly weir from a dangerous one, and even friendly weirs have minor hazards. The only safe policy is to give them a wide berth unless you are an experienced and confident white water paddler who chooses to accept the risk. To beginners, weirs represent a genuine threat to safety and should be avoided at all costs.

Beware of water flowing beneath low bridges, such as this. Although the water here is fairly slow-moving, it could easily pull you along with it. If your boat were to jam under the low bridge, you could find yourself in trouble very quickly.

Do not paddle on fast-flowing water until you have learned a range of skills.

Weirs can be extremely dangerous for paddlers, and it is always advisable to stay away from them.

Serious Hazards

Some situations can and do prove fatal. It is imperative that you are aware of the dangers involved with any of the following.

River Levels

Be aware that river levels can rise and fall very suddenly. This might only affect your access to or exit from a river, but it could turn a friendly stream into a lethal one.

Rivers rise because of the amount of rainfall or because of snow melt. Many mountain rivers rise very dramatically in the afternoon because the sun melts the snow or ice, and the water produced reaches the river a few hours later.

⌃ The mud banks and reeds here would make it very difficult to get out of the river with your boat.

◂ Compare these two pictures, taken on the same day. The water level has risen 1m (3½ft) and turned a meandering stream into a potentially lethal torrent after several hours of rain.

⌄ Beware when paddling upstream of any obstruction in the river, especially if the water can flow through or under it, as in the case of this log-jam. The current could very easily force you into or under such an obstruction.

In addition, many very steep rivers are dammed for hydro-electric power. When the turbines are required, the dam will be opened and a lethal wall of water can be sent hurtling down the valley.

Strainers and Siphons

These are usually found on white water rivers, but they can occur anywhere the water is flowing at a significant speed.

A barrier through which water flows, such as a fallen tree or log jam is called a strainer because it lets water pass through but will catch anything solid. These are very dangerous. Do not risk being swept into the upstream side of one.

Even more dangerous is the siphon, where water disappears underground. Get too close and you will be sucked down too, and possibly jammed stuck.

Preparing to Paddle

When first learning to paddle, it is best to practise in a familiar area, within sight of a reliable launching and landing place, instead of attempting any kind of journey. As you build up your experience, and become more familiar with the boat and the basic manoeuvring techniques, you will be able to go further afield and use your boat to explore.

Once you have become hooked on boating, it is very easy to become complacent and to imagine that you are more experienced and more capable than you really are. Beware of asking too much of yourself too soon. Remember your own limitations and, just as importantly, those of the other members of your group. A failure to do this can seriously compromise your safety, and no amount of fun will justify this risk.

Are You Up To It?

It is vital that you have a realistic idea of the kind of distance you can paddle, and that you know your own limitations in terms of ability, fitness and strength: some people are surprised at how quickly they become tired in a boat out on the water. Remember, too, that you could get hot, cold, tired, hungry or dehydrated according to the weather conditions. While this might not be any different from when going for a long walk, if any of

CHECKLIST

If the answer to any of the following questions is "No", reassess your plan before you set out on the water.
• Is everyone in the group capable of looking after themselves? If not, will some be able to look after the others?
• Do you have all the appropriate equipment for today's trip?
• Does everyone know how many hours they will paddle for?
• Are you sure that you can get to where you intend to go in that time?
• Does someone on land know where the group is going and what time they are expected to finish?

these conditions affect you severely while you are on or near the water, the consequences can be far more serious. Consider this before you set out, and make sure that you are properly equipped.

Advance Planning

It always pays to be prepared for likely eventualities. Make it a key part of your preparation routine to plan the route of your journey, using an up-to-date Ordnance Survey 1:50,000 map. If your group can all do this together, so much the better. Listen to a detailed weather report for the area on the day of your trip and consider how the weather is likely to affect the water conditions. If you know what to expect, you will be able to make an informed choice to continue with the

◔ *Paddlers will often "raft up" to give themselves a rest if anyone in the group is feeling tired.*

trip, to resort to the contingency plan or to put the whole thing off for another day in order to avoid anything too severe that might cause you problems. Check that you have the right type of clothing and equipment for the conditions, and enough food and drinking water to see you through to the end of your trip. Finally, consider the needs of the weakest member(s) of the group and adapt your preparation plan accordingly, allowing more time for the journey and more provisions as necessary. Your plan must take account of all levels of expertise if everyone is to have an enjoyable time.

Exposure to the Elements

Whether you are boating on an inland stream or out at sea, you are generally more exposed to the elements than when you are on land. It is necessary to take precautions since the effects of heat and cold, and sudden changes of wind direction, can strike very suddenly.

Sun

When you are out on the water, the effects of the sun are greater than normal, and ultimately these may dictate how long you can stay out. It is quite possible to get severe sunburn in as little as 30 minutes on the water on a day when you could sunbathe on the shore for much longer. It is extremely important that you always take with you an adequate sunscreen for your face, neck, arms and legs. If you are not wearing a helmet, protect your head and the back of your neck with a sunhat or baseball cap to minimize the risk of sunstroke.

Wind

The effects of wind are also much more pronounced when you are on the water. A light breeze ashore, which necessitates no more than a thin summer shirt, might cause serious wind chill when you are afloat. As a general guide, there are few days when you will not need a windproof top plus at least one thermal layer, even when the sun is out and the weather is hot. If you are wet after a swim, these potential problems will all be magnified.

Always take with you a selection of clothes that allow you to adjust your level of insulation during the course of the trip.

Never go paddling during a gale. High winds make it almost impossible to control a kayak or canoe, and you will struggle to hang on to your paddle. In addition, the water will become rough and unpredictable. You won't be able to make forward progress against anything more than a stiff breeze but, bizarrely, it is a following wind or a crosswind that make the boat hardest to control. Accept that strong winds and paddling just don't mix, unless you are equipped to sail your boat.

Rain

It can be very pleasant to paddle in the rain if you are sensibly dressed. On the other hand, it can be a miserable experience if you aren't. Being cold and wet at the same time is uncomfortable and it can become a real problem if the temperature is low. If rain is likely, make sure you pack a waterproof garment. A woollen hat or a hood on your jacket or cagoule can make a huge difference to how you feel. Reducing the heat loss from your head is an effective remedy when you are cold, and in the rain, headgear will stop water constantly running down your face, which can become very uncomfortable.

Lightning

Although it is a lot more rare than a situation involving strong currents or a sudden change in the weather, lightning is one of the most dangerous weather phenomena for paddlers. On the land you are unlikely to be struck by lightning. On open water, it is a different matter. Anything sticking up out of the water is in danger, and that means you. You also have a long pole (your paddle) in your hands to add to the effect. On land, the people most likely to be struck by lightning are golfers because they stand in the middle of open spaces holding golf clubs that serve as

◀ *Paddlers out at sea are exposed to sun, wind chill and salt spray.*

conductive objects. As a boater, you are taking the lightning attractor concept several stages further because lightning is more likely to strike a solitary object on water than on land. If the weather report suggests storms, don't go out at all; if a storm blows up while you are on the water, get ashore as quickly as possible.

Extreme Hot and Cold

Luckily, you are unlikely to experience extreme heat and cold in the same location. However, if you go paddling in an extreme climate, your usual paddling clothing may not be appropriate, and you will need to consider other safety issues.

In hot climates, apart from the dangers of sunburn and sunstroke, there is a real danger of dehydration and heat stroke. The most important thing is to keep drinking water. If you feel thirsty, you are already dehydrated. If you cannot quench your thirst, or have a limited water supply, you need to get into the shade and cool down. One of the problems with very hot, tropical environments is the humidity. The air is so saturated that the process of sweating does not cool you down, although your body doesn't realize and carries on sweating. This is why you get dehydrated even though you may be soaking wet the whole time.

● *Make sure you are equipped for all weather conditions before you set out.*

● *Taking a rest in the hot midday sunshine. This paddler would be at risk without his drinking water, sunscreen and protective hat.*

In very cold air or water, the key is to dress to be both warm and dry. If you get soaked in a freezing environment you only have a few minutes to get warm and dry before you start to suffer from hypothermia. For practical reasons, then, a dry suit is needed for severely cold conditions. This will ensure that you don't get wet from immersion. Wear gloves or mitts on your hands: they will prevent the pain of frozen fingers.

Managing Body Temperature

By far the best way to control your body temperature is to wear good quality thermal base layers, which will work with your body's inherent control mechanism. A versatile cagoule with adjustable seals will allow you to adjust your temperature by opening and closing the neck or rolling up the sleeves. If you wear conventional manmade fabrics, you will find yourself endlessly putting on extra clothes and taking them off as your body heats and cools down too rapidly.

Basic Safety and Rescue

It might be tempting to think that you are quite experienced, and can cope with any potential danger, but the rule is, always, "Beginners beware!" Make sure you and your group are up to the challenge.

Safety in Numbers

When out on the water, there should always be at least three people in the group. In the event of an accident or a medical emergency, one person can stay with the victim and the other can go for help. It is even better if there are four or five people, so that no one has to deal with emergencies alone, but if there are too many in the group then other logistical problems arise, even when things are going smoothly. Experienced paddlers may choose to ignore this basic safety rule, but they only do so when they feel totally confident about taking risks. Beginners should always stick to the rule.

Assessing your Group

You must be sure that the group is capable of taking care of itself as a unit, and can sort out any problems as they arise. Everyone should be able to swim 50m (170ft) in their clothing, and flotation aids should always be worn when afloat. But what if a boat has filled with water? Will the group be able to empty it and get the paddler back in? Or tow the victim back to shore? And what if the location turns out to be trickier than imagined, or the distance greater? Will the group have the skills required to get a tired paddler back to safety if they cannot paddle alone?

These are crucial questions. If the answers to any of them are "No", then you should restrict your paddling to safe locations, such as a beach or small lake, where everyone could make it ashore, and there are no significant safety threats.

Rescue Procedures

Although you may be unfamiliar with paddling a canoe or kayak, let alone rescuing one, it is a good idea to know what to expect if you find yourself in need of a tow because of tiredness or injury, or if you are swimming in the water after a capsize. If you are already an accomplished paddler, these techniques can be used to help a fellow boater in the event of a mishap.

What to do in the event of a capsize is covered in detail at the beginning of the chapters on kayaking and canoeing skills. If you are unable to roll your boat, your priority is to get out. Once out, you can be carried back to shore on the front or back of another paddler's boat, or you can be helped back into your own boat while it is still afloat, using a X-rescue or, for a larger boat, a H-rescue. If you need a pull because of tiredness or injury, your fellow paddlers can use a husky tow or an assisted tow to help you back to shore.

Practising basic rescue skills is an important part of becoming a competent paddler. If everyone in your group is familiar with the rescue skills shown opposite, the group will be self-sufficient, as well as safer and more confident.

◐ *The husky tow, in which one paddler is pulled by two, is used for long distances.*

◐ *Assisted tow. A tired paddler is helped and towed by two companions.*

X-rescue

1 Drag the boat across the rescuer's deck, and rock it to and fro to empty it of water. Constantly reassure the victim, who may be in shock.

2 Put the empty boat back in the water, the right way up and alongside, and with the stern next to, the rescuer's bow. Place both paddles across the decks.

3 The victim can lift his legs up out of the water and over the paddles, keeping an equal amount of body weight on each boat. Keep reassuring the victim.

4 The rescuer holds the victim's boat to stop the two boats floating apart. The victim shuffles forward until he is able to put his feet into his boat.

5 Shifting the weight across, the victim is now entirely back on his own boat, and is ready to climb back in. The rescuer can hold his boat steady as he does this.

6 With the rescued paddler now securely back in his boat, he can take his paddle and push off from the rescuer's boat to continue the trip.

Alternative Rescue Techniques

◁ ◥ *One paddler tows the empty boat, while another paddler carries the tired swimmer on the back of their boat.*

◁ *Heavier larger boats can be difficult to empty using the X-rescue. Some paddlers use a H-rescue, which involves two boats, as shown here.*

▷ *Another way to transport a swimmer is on the front of the boat like this. It is slower than on the back deck, but the rescuer can see and reassure the victim.*

EQUIPMENT AND PREPARATION

From a sport that, in the 1980s, had little in the way of specialized equipment, kayaking and canoeing have certainly come a long way. The clothing and safety equipment, and the boats and paddles, are now quite sophisticated and high-tech. This is thoroughly appropriate because sport on water is physically quite demanding.

When you first start boating, you will not need much in the way of specialist gear. If you only intend to splash about on flat water near to land, and never go far or encounter difficult conditions, the bare minimum may be perfectly adequate. If, on the other hand, you decide to progress, and try more demanding water conditions, you will find that there is an ever-increasing array of equipment that you must consider.

⊙ Sea kayakers wearing comprehensive paddling gear and in well-equipped boats.

⊙ A kayaker stretching in preparation for a session out on the water.

Kayaks

A huge range of kayaks are now available, and it is important that you check the following features. When buying a kayak, talk to the sales staff: ask the right questions, based on the following criteria, and make sure you are happy with the answers. If you are unable to find out what you want to know, you could contact kayak manufacturers for more information about their products.

• A kayak must have sufficient buoyancy to float when full of water, and provide you with something to hold on to if you are swimming alongside after capsizing. The buoyancy should be distributed so that the kayak floats level when swamped.

• It must have a seat, and a footrest to brace against, otherwise you will not be able to paddle it properly.

• Not advisable the first time out because it makes entry and exit more difficult, but beneficial thereafter, is padding either

⊙ *This touring kayak is an all-round boat and a good first time buy.*

◐ *This boat has been fitted out to a high standard with hard foam padding to hug the hips and legs, and make the paddler an integral part of the kayak.*

⊙ *Adjusting the backrest. This kayak has a modern fit system that allows you to fine-tune your position while you are seated in the boat.*

side of the hips. Without this, your body movements will not be transmitted to the boat and the boat's movements will not be felt by you. Much of your body's energy is also delivered to the boat by your knees, so it is particularly important that the knees are held firmly in position. This is usually achieved by some sort of built-in grips or mouldings to hold the legs in place under the deck. Without these, the boat will not respond well to you or you to it.

TIPS

• The basics for going paddling are a kayak – which can be used with a spraydeck – or canoe, flotation aid, paddle, suitable clothing, helmet and safety and rescue equipment.

• Try out as many different pieces of equipment as you can before deciding which is for you.

• Before buying any equipment, make sure that you know exactly what you are going to do on the water. Only when you know how you want your equipment to perform can you make informed choices.

• All kayaks, except those used for competition or the more specialist disciplines, need to have end grabs, which give you something to hold on to if you need to tow the boat, or a capsized paddler in the water, to the shore.

• Be confident that you can get out of the kayak easily before you agree to use it on the water. Your paddling will not be very good if you are constantly worried that you will not be able to free yourself if the boat capsizes.

Spraydecks

A spraydeck (spray skirt) fits around your waist and over the cockpit to stop water getting into the boat. Spraydecks are not generally needed on flat water, where the water is calm, with little or no splashing.

Nylon spraydecks are commonly used for teaching beginners, but these can let in water because they are only really designed to be splash-proof. Neoprene ones are much drier and warmer, but they are more expensive and more difficult to fit and detach. You may not use a spraydeck at first, but if you do it is important that you can attach and remove it easily, without help. This can take quite a bit of practice.

Fitting a Spraydeck

Whichever type of spraydeck you use, you should be wearing it around your waist before you get in the kayak. Once you are sitting comfortably, and have made sure that you are not sitting on any part

of the spraydeck, reach back with both hands and put the shock cord, or other attachment, under the cockpit rim at the back. Now feed the hands outwards, keeping some tension on the spraydeck, until you can pull forwards with both hands and fit the spraydeck over the front of the cockpit. Make sure that the release strap is outside and not trapped within. Familiarize yourself with where it is: you will need to find it quickly if you capsize.

To release the spraydeck, take the release strap in your hand and pull firmly upwards. It is usually better to pull a little

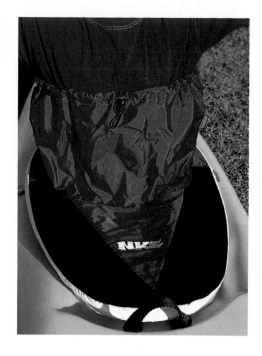

◔ *A nylon spraydeck (skirt) that might be used by a beginner on flat water.*

forwards at the same time, rather than back. Once the spraydeck has been released from the front of the cockpit, run your hands under it right the way round to make sure it is totally free. It is annoying to start getting out of the boat and then come to an abrupt halt as the spraydeck pulls tight.

As a beginner you need a spraydeck that is easy to put on and release. It may not be very waterproof compared to other models on the market, but it will keep the kayak from filling up, and this is as much as you will need on flat water.

Fitting your Spraydeck

1 Get into the kayak wearing the spraydeck (skirt). Fit the spraydeck under the cockpit rim at the back of the boat.

2 Feed the hands forward, keeping the spraydeck under tension so that it stays hooked under at the back.

3 Hook it over the front of the cockpit, making sure the release handle is outside and can be reached easily.

Canoes

There are some basic features that you should check for when choosing a canoe.
• Make sure you know which end is the front. Some models are symmetrical at both ends but all have a bow and a stern.
• Consider whether you want to sit or kneel in your canoe and choose a suitable model accordingly.
• Solo and double open canoes are available, as well as boats for three or more people. Doubles can be paddled by one person, but putting two people in a solo canoe is a recipe for a swim.
• End grabs may not be necessary because you can hold the seat or even the gunwale (upper edge of the deck).
• Padding around the seat is rarely needed because your legs can brace against or under the seat and on the inside of the boat, making your position more secure.

❯ The design of the open canoe has changed very little since its invention.

❯ An open canoe fitted with suitable equipment for use on white water.

⬆ *These lightweight white water paddles are extremely strong, and superior to heavier models.*

⬆ *Laminated wooden paddle. The wooden paddle can still compete with paddles made from man-made materials.*

Some expensive paddles have bent shafts, which apply less stress to the wrists by loading them in a way that is more anatomically sound. Many paddlers used to straight-shafted paddles find that this feels a bit strange at first, but the concept is gradually gaining acceptance across all paddling disciplines.

Whichever type of paddle you first learn with, you will probably find that your personal style and anatomy, and your preferred type of paddling, dictate that you will soon want a longer or shorter paddle than these guidelines suggest.

Boaters will often be fiercely protective of their paddles, but if you are able to borrow the paddle of a friend before you buy your own, it will give you a better idea what differences a longer or shorter paddle, and the wide choice of shapes and constructions, can make to your paddling. If you are a member of a paddling club that supplies equipment, take the opportunity to test out different models. The sooner you can identify what works well for you and have a paddle that is exactly what you need, the faster your stroke skills will progress. But don't rush

⬆ *Split (break-down) paddles can be stored inside the kayak as spares in case of loss or breakage.*

into it. Make sure you are comfortable with a paddle before you buy. Paddles can be expensive, and it is a good idea, if you can, to put off buying one for as long as possible. When you are sure what kind of paddling you want to practise, and have learned the basic strokes, you will be in a much better position to choose.

⬆ *A replica of a traditional Greenland paddle, based on the Inuit style.*

⮕ *Traditional wooden canoe paddles. One has a reinforced square tip; the other is more suited to deep water.*

Transporting your Boat

Most people need to move their boat about on land before they can use it on the water. How you do this will depend on the type of craft and how far you have to carry it. Broadly speaking, there are two options: carrying the boat manually, or mechanically.

Carrying the Boat

Many beginners will carry a boat between two people, using the end grabs. Two boats together can also be carried in this way. However, once you have become more familiar with carrying your boat, you might find it easier to carry a kayak or a light canoe on your shoulder. Carrying boats by holding on to the ends is the usual method for heavily laden craft.

When carrying a boat on your shoulder, you can either carry the paddle in your free hand, or you can put the paddle in the cockpit and carry the boat and the paddle together.

Boats that are too heavy to lift, such as a loaded sea kayak, can be moved short distances using a trolley. The trolley can be dismantled and transported in the boat while afloat.

⬦ *A fold-up trolley is useful for moving large boats from the car to the launching point. The trolley can be dismantled and stowed on the boat during the trip.*

❱ *Kayaks and canoes are now made from such lightweight materials that most adults are able to carry their boat on their back for short distances.*

⬦ *Two paddlers carry their loaded sea kayaks down to the water. Hold the boat's end grabs, one in each hand.*

Transporting your Boat

Over longer distances, you may have to transport your boats by car or van, boat or aeroplane. The key here is to be sensible, and to think about whether your boat will get damaged, or could cause damage to other people's property.

A cockpit cover will allow you to put additional gear inside your boat. This is by far the best way to carry paddles and bulky safety and rescue equipment.

You will need a good roof rack if you are going to carry your boat on top of your car. Make sure the roof bars are securely attached to the car; if in doubt, tie the boat to the car as well.

Pad your roof rack with pipe lagging or proper pads bought for the purpose, and tie down the boat, using webbing roof straps with metal buckles. If you plan to carry more than two boats, it is worth getting upright bars to attach to the roof rack to enable you to carry up to six boats.

Don't be afraid to take your boat on a commercial flight or passage. Most companies will carry one piece of sports equipment per passenger free of charge. You just have to check the boat in with the rest of your luggage, and then take it over to the oversized baggage area. Always make sure it is well wrapped.

⊙ (Top right) Kayaks are best transported on their side, strapped firmly to the bars and uprights. It is much better to use proper roof straps than to tie the boat on with rope.

⊙ A strong roof rack is essential. This one has uprights bolted to it, which are ideal for transporting kayaks.

⊙ Do not tie kayaks on to roof racks right side up. They are unaerodynamic this way, and they will quickly fill with water if it rains.

⊙ The roof bars and uprights can be padded with proprietary roof bar pads or with pipe lagging, to protect the boats from damage during transit.

⊙ The correct orientation for a single kayak if you are not using uprights on the roof rack. If carrying more than one boat, store them sideways.

⊙ More than one boat can be transported on either or both sides of the uprights. Make sure both boats are central between the roof bars.

Essential Clothing

The right clothing is vital when you are on the water, not least because if you fall in and the conditions get cold, you could suffer remarkably quickly.

Before you get into a boat, you must consider what you should be wearing, some of which might be provided by your instructor. This will, to an extent, depend on the weather, but as a general rule you need to think about thermal insulation, in addition to footwear and flotation.

Insulation

Your insulation requirements will depend on the weather conditions you can expect to experience on the day you are boating. Always check the weather forecast before you set out, and adapt your level of clothing accordingly.

• If the climate is tropical and the water is warm, you do not need any insulation. You could paddle in a swimming costume, but some degree of sun protection is recommended. If the weather is balmy, you should have a T-shirt and shorts, and something warmer in case you capsize or swim, and get drenched. Whatever you wear should not get heavy when soaked; items made of polyester or polypropylene

⊗ *Tight-fitting thermals are the best base layer in cold weather.*

⊗ *A thermal top worn with board shorts is ideal for warm weather.*

⊗ *A correctly fitting cagoule: close-fitting but allowing full upper body motion.*

⊗ *This cagoule is too big. It would be cold and difficult to swim or paddle in.*

⊗ *A flotation aid worn over the top of a cagoule and board shorts.*

⊙ *A correctly fitting wetsuit. The suit should fit close like a second skin.*

⊙ *An incorrectly fitting wetsuit. The baggy suit will not feel comfortable.*

⊙ *Wear waterproof trousers and a cagoule over thermals as an alternative to a wetsuit.*

are better for warmth when wet than cotton. Board shorts, popular with surfers, are ideal for boating because they are durable for sliding in and out of the kayak or canoe, but do not soak up much water.
• If the water temperature is less than pleasant for dangling your fingers and toes in, or the air is a little too chilly for a T-shirt, then a thermal base layer is necessary. Choose one made from polyester fleece or polypropylene thermal

material, or wear a wetsuit over your thermal layers. The wetsuit should be as close fitting as possible without being restrictive.
• If wind chill is an issue, you can add a wind- and spray-proof shell top over your thermals for upper body warmth. There is a wide variety available from water-sports suppliers, including wind-tops, spray-tops, paddling jackets or cagoules (also known as cags); different manufacturers give

their products different names. The features to look for are waterproof fabric, neoprene cuffs, comfortable neck seal and an adjustable or elasticated waist.

Protective Headgear

Helmets are not a legal requirement but they should be worn whenever your experience and the conditions dictate that they are necessary. You are always safer wearing a helmet: if in doubt, wear one.

⊙ *A correctly fitting helmet sits snugly on the head without sliding forward.*

⊙ *A helmet that is too small exposes the temples, giving no protection.*

⊙ *A helmet that is too big will expose the base of the skull and can impair vision.*

⊙ *Technical sandals: lightweight and comfortable, and widely available.*

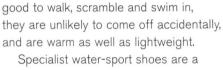

⊙ *Wetsuit boots make ideal footwear and will keep feet warm even when wet.*

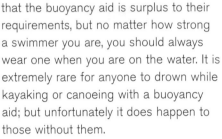

⊙ *Specialist water-sports shoes make a good alternative to wetsuit boots.*

Footwear

You cannot paddle well if you are wearing heavy, cumbersome footwear, although bare feet are not ideal either.

In most water environments it is a good idea to wear something on your feet. Old trainers (sneakers) or running shoes are often recommended, but they can be bulky and the rubber soles can jam on the inside of the boat.

If the weather is warm, technical sandals may be appropriate. These are comfortable, and are light enough to swim in should you capsize. They are also relatively inexpensive.

Otherwise, wetsuit boots are best, although they will add to the cost of kitting yourself out. Wetsuit boots are

⊙ *A correctly adjusted flotation aid should fit snugly to the body.*

good to walk, scramble and swim in, they are unlikely to come off accidentally, and are warm as well as lightweight.

Specialist water-sport shoes are a good alternative to wetsuit boots. These have non-slip soles that are ideal for wet surfaces, and are padded and reinforced in all the right places. They often have straps to keep them firmly on the feet during a swim. Again, though, this is specialist footwear and not necessary for beginners starting out.

Flotation

A buoyancy or flotation aid (personal flotation device, also known as a PFD) is a vital piece of paddling equipment. Over-confident beginners might think

⊙ *Check the flotation aid cannot come off accidentally by pulling firmly upwards.*

that the buoyancy aid is surplus to their requirements, but no matter how strong a swimmer you are, you should always wear one when you are on the water. It is extremely rare for anyone to drown while kayaking or canoeing with a buoyancy aid; but unfortunately it does happen to those without them.

There are many different styles on the market, but the important thing is that it should be a buoyancy aid and not a life jacket, and that it should allow you to wave your arms about freely. It should fit well enough so that it does not pull up and off when you are in the water – check this does not happen by pulling up, or getting someone else to pull up, the shoulders. Also check that all the straps and fasteners do up properly.

In many countries there are stringent standards for what may be sold as a buoyancy aid. In Europe, look for the CE EN393 Approved Buoyancy Aid, and in the United States, the US Coastguard Approved Personal Flotation Device.

Flotation Maintenance

It is worth remembering that a buoyancy aid that is a few years old may not provide the expected level of flotation. It really does pay to look after your buoyancy aid correctly. Whether you are using your own buoyancy aid or one belonging to your paddling club, do not stand on it, sit on it or do anything else that might compress the foam, and make it less effective. Although wearing a buoyancy aid is never an absolute guarantee of your safety, it is essential that the buoyancy aid you wear will perform exactly as you expect it to.

◔ *A reinforced neoprene spraydeck (skirt) for white water paddling. It has a tight-fitting body tube that is pulled right up to prevent water getting in.*

◔ *A nylon spraydeck suitable for flat water paddling, but not rough water.*

◔ *A cagoule is worn over the spraydeck to prevent water from splashing up and entering down the body tube.*

◔ *A nylon spraydeck worn over a light sweater and board shorts is perfectly adequate for flat water paddling.*

TIP
Spraydecks (skirts) are not needed on flat water because you are not likely to get a soaking from splashing water. However, if you do use one, it is essential that you know how to attach and remove it without help.

Fitness and Personal Skills

As with most sports, the fitter you are the more success you will have. When it comes to boating, being relatively fit and a competent swimmer are even more important for the sake of personal safety. You must also be able to set yourself clearly defined, achievable goals.

You need very little in the way of skills when you first begin to paddle, but the one essential is the ability to swim. You should be able to swim at least 50m (170ft) in the clothing you will be wearing when you paddle the boat. Only if reliable, trained rescue cover is forewarned and constantly at hand should a paddler who can not meet these basic standards go paddling, unless practising in the shallow end of a swimming pool.

Personal Fitness

One of the important activities most commonly overlooked by paddlers is their physical preparation for the demands of the sport. The demands will obviously be to a much higher degree if you are doing white water freestyle, but even if you are paddling around gently you need some kind of preparation. It will dramatically enhance the amount of fun you get from paddling, while simultaneously reducing the likelihood of injury and tiredness. After all, why tend aching muscles and stiff joints the day after you paddle, when you can so easily avoid them?

As you attempt more and more demanding kinds of paddling, or paddle further and in more exposed situations, you should have a level of strength and fitness commensurate with the challenge you are undertaking. This can only be acquired by practice and experience. Even extremely strong and athletic people find that they struggle when attempting to use their strength and fitness in unfamiliar ways or conditions.

Mental Fitness

Sportsmen and women now realize that their state of mind is as important as their physical condition. It does not matter what level they are at, whether professional or amateur, they still want to perform to the best of their ability.

The secrets of a good state of mind are feeling confident and positive, and clearly visualizing yourself realizing a set of achievable goals. Unless you believe you really can realize these goals, you will make it much harder for yourself to do so. Have a clear picture in your mind of what you plan to do. And having achieved those goals (or not!), set the next ones with an equal degree of realism.

The final stage of mental fitness is remembering to listen and be receptive. That does not just mean listening to your instructor. The most important thing is to listen to your body, and to be aware of yourself and the water. Never become so obsessed with what you have been told, or what you have read, that you focus on that more than upon vital, first-hand experience.

⬆ *The ability to swim 50m (170ft) in the clothing you paddle in is essential.*

Special Needs Paddlers

Paddlers with disabilities (mental or physical) have particular needs that must be met if they are to realize their potential on the water with minimal risk and full enjoyment. The aim is to enable the special needs paddler to participate as far as possible with the same equipment and the same objectives as anybody else, with any modifications being made as required for that person. The key factor is good communication between the experienced paddler(s) leading the group, the paddler with special needs, his or her parents, and any medical and care staff. This will produce a paddling programme tailored to meet the needs of the individual.

Out of Water Training

Knowing the ins and outs of keeping fit, and avoiding injury, apply as much to paddlers as to any other sportsmen and women. Being fit also enables you to achieve your goals; you cannot paddle if your muscles are aching and tired.

All-body Workouts

Many people use paddling as their main form of exercise, and paddling vigorously or over a long distance is certainly an excellent, all-body workout. Despite the fact that your legs do not appear to be doing much, they are actually contributing quite a lot of the power, provided you have a good paddling technique. If you want to progress with your boating skills, however, you may want to do extra, non-paddling exercises to tone your muscles and increase body strength.

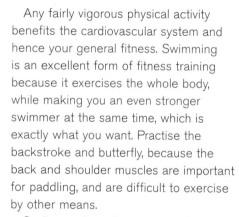

⊘ *Cycling is good training for the quads, the large, powerful muscles in the thighs.*

⊙ *Running is good cardiovascular exercise, but beware of impact.*

⊙ *Swimming provides an excellent body workout without straining muscles.*

Any fairly vigorous physical activity benefits the cardiovascular system and hence your general fitness. Swimming is an excellent form of fitness training because it exercises the whole body, while making you an even stronger swimmer at the same time, which is exactly what you want. Practise the backstroke and butterfly, because the back and shoulder muscles are important for paddling, and are difficult to exercise by other means.

Cycling and running are good for improving all-round fitness, and are especially good for the quadriceps (the big thigh muscles), which are used a surprising amount when paddling. Much of the torso rotation in a forward paddling stroke comes from the quadriceps.

Many paddlers favour either climbing or snowboarding as a second sport, whether because of a love of the outdoors or because they are extremely complementary disciplines. Whatever cross-training you choose to do, use it in moderation and aim for a good all-round level of fitness. Regular gentle exercise – every day, if possible – will help you avoid illness and injury.

Targeted Action

If you have access to a gym, then a professionally planned regime can target the muscle groups you need to exercise.

Avoid concentrating too much on the arm muscles because the quadriceps, abdominals, shoulder and back muscles do most of the work when you are in the boat. The arms mainly provide fine motor control, and gain more from activities such as juggling than from lifting weights.

Press-ups, pull-ups and crunches are the best simple non-gym exercises to prepare you for paddling, and these are all something you can do at home.

Avoiding Injury

Whichever exercises you do, remember that it is vitally important to warm up first, and then to stretch, or you might strain or pull a muscle. It is also important to make sure that your posture is correct when exercising. Kayakers, in particular, are prone to lower back problems if they fail to keep their spinal curvature correct.

After any form of exercise you must also stretch again and warm down. This helps keep injuries at bay. It might seem

◉ *The press-up is an exercise to build short, powerful muscles in the pectoral, bicep and tricep areas of the body.*

◉ *You may find that by supporting your weight with your knees, you will find it easier to do more repetitions.*

wholly unnecessary, but it pays dividends. It also gives you time to focus on how you have performed, and how you can improve next time. Mental visualization is extremely important, and will make more difference to your paddling than almost any other single factor.

Good Habits

If you can integrate exercise into your daily life it will save you a lot of time and money that you might otherwise spend on fitness clubs and sports equipment. Simply being more aware of your body will help you enormously. For example, by knowing which muscle groups are

working to perform different actions, you may find yourself doing a mini workout just walking up the stairs.

Maintaining a good body posture at all times, whether exercising, at work in the office or watching television at home, will also make a difference. Your posture can affect both your performance as a paddler and your overall well-being. Not only will you find it easier to make more effective strokes in your boat, you will also reduce the risk of injury, particularly damage to your back.

◉ *Diagonal crunches (elbow to knee) are excellent training for paddling.*

◉ *Pull-ups mimic paddling exceptionally well and help to promote arm strength.*

Warming Up

You should always warm up before you do any kind of strenuous activity. Warming up is essential to prepare your body for sudden exertions and to minimize the risk of injury. Your body will then be much more flexible and able to absorb shocks and over-extensions. Even stretching should not be attempted until you have warmed up thoroughly.

Establish a Routine

It is important to formulate a pre-paddling routine for yourself, and to make a habit of following it as a precursor to going out on the water.

Start with some light warm-up exercise for at least 15 minutes. Depending on how often you go out paddling, you might want to include a selection of activities in your routine, so that you don't become bored with the same one.

Once you have warmed up, it is time for some gentle stretching. This can improve the performance of your muscles and tendons enormously and, at the same time, it will dramatically reduce the likelihood of injury.

Practise the body stretches given over the following pages to achieve a good all-round level of flexibility. Do not bounce to increase your range of movement, but

extend yourself gently to the limit of comfort and hold each stretch for about 15 seconds before relaxing.

Next, get into your boat, still on land, and continue with the boat stretching exercises. You can then take the boat stretches one step further by going out on to the water. This will ensure that everything has been stretched in the right way, and that there are no problems with your range and freedom of movement.

After paddling for a while, it is often beneficial to stop your boat and repeat the in-boat stretches. Remember, too, that it is important to warm down and stretch once again after you have finished paddling and are back on land.

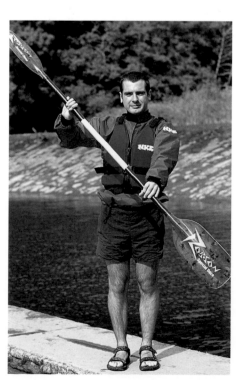

Simulated paddling action on land can make sure everything is moving properly without any undue strain.

Gentle jogging, especially through water, is a great way to warm up.

How to Warm Up

The best way to warm up is with gentle exercise. This could take the form of walking briskly, particularly uphill, with your arms swinging. If the water is warm, then you could have a warm-up swim. Some people like to play with a frisbee, and this sort of group activity can be a lot of fun, and adds to the enjoyment of the whole occasion.

In fact, any activity is fine, provided you actually feel yourself getting warm, and your heart rate is raised significantly. You should be able to sense this without taking your pulse. Do not go for a fast run to warm up though, or do anything that involves impact because it could be counter-productive.

Body Stretches

Light stretches are a vital part of your warm-up routine. They help fine-tune the body, can be done in the home or on the river bank or beach, and are a good way of building up team spirit when done in a group. There are a variety of simple stretches you can do to ensure that you have extended every muscle group in your body, and you will not require any props or assistance to do them.

◗ *Gentle neck rotation to the left and to the right is a good way to start off your stretching routine.*

⬆ *Neck flexion. Bend the head forward from the neck, but do not rotate or roll the head, which is bad for the spine.*

⬆ *Spine extension.*

⬇ *General arm and shoulder stretch.*

⬆ *Hamstring, tricep and shoulder stretch.*

⬇ *Trunk rotation stretch.*

⬆ *Quadriceps and hamstring stretch.*

⬇ *Side stretch.*

Stretching in the Boat

After your initial stretches on land, it is time to get seated in the boat and continue your warm-up routine with exercises that simulate more closely your movements while out on the water.

Before Getting Afloat

Exercises performed in the boat while you are still on land serve a dual purpose. First, you will be getting all the usual benefits of stretching, but specifically geared to the range of motion you have in the boat. Second, you are checking that you have good freedom of movement in the boat and in your paddling kit. If something is hurting, chafing or digging into your ribs when you do these stretches, get out now and solve the problem immediately.

On the Water

Once you have warmed up, stretched, and are afloat, it is a good idea to go for a bit of a paddle to settle into your boat, and then do some more stretching, perhaps using the paddle as an additional prop. There are a number of useful exercises that anyone can do without risk of capsizing, and they are all good confidence-building tools for new or nervous paddlers.

Having done all this preparation, you are now ready to paddle more skilfully and effectively than someone who jumps straight into the boat without first warming up and stretching. Typically, the whole process would take about 30 minutes, but it is time well spent. Without this pre-paddling routine, you probably would not be able to spend as much time on the water, and your skill and fitness levels might well stagnate.

TIPS

• Always stretch gently and progressively; never bounce.
• Only use your muscles to stretch; do not use weights or external forces, which will cause muscle strain and possible injury.
• If you stretch to the point that it hurts, you have over-reached yourself and should stop the stretch.

Boat Stretches on Land

1 Make sure you can reach the right-hand side of the stern with your left hand.

2 Repeat the same stretch on the other side of the boat, using your right hand.

3 Extend fully backwards, so that you are stretching over the back deck.

4 Then, extend fully forwards, so that you are stretching over the front deck.

Boat Stretches on Water

1 Press the left blade against the right-hand side of the bow and vice versa.

2 Press the left blade against the right-hand side of the stern and vice versa.

3 Stretch forward in the boat as far as you can and hold for a few seconds.

4 Stretch backwards in the boat as far as you can and hold for a few seconds.

KAYAKING SKILLS

Kayaking and canoeing are accessible to most people because the skills required to get in the boat and have fun are not specialized. If, however, you want to progress in one area of the sport, or want to paddle for longer distances or look after friends and family while they, too, enjoy their paddling, you ought to acquire some new skills.

This section outlines the basic skills and strokes that will help you to use the boat in a skilful manner. The exercises are described in approximately the order in which they tend to arise, although some instructors may prefer a different order.

When you are learning how to do each technique, try not to progress too fast. Make sure you have the right skills in place before you move on. Equally, though, it is a bad idea to practise a technique badly. If something is not working and you do not know why, change to a different skill until you can find out how to deal with your problem. Sometimes just going away and trying again much later is all it takes.

Choose a sheltered piece of flat water near to the shore to try out these skills. Put safety first, and make sure you are confident that you can swim to a safe landing place and rescue your equipment. This is a simple point, but so often overlooked.

A group of paddlers under instruction, using short general-purpose kayaks.

Practising a reverse sweep stroke. Head and body rotation are part of good technique.

Getting into the Kayak

The first thing to learn is how to get into the kayak while it is afloat. It is one skill that you may be able to practise on dry land, if you are sure that the boat is strong enough to take your weight on its hull. Sooner or later, though, you will have to try it at the water's edge.

Find a place to launch where the bank or jetty is not too much higher than the gunwale of your kayak. Place the boat on the surface of the water here, making sure that the water is sufficiently deep that you will still be afloat after you get in! If it is deep enough to capsize, ensure that it is also deep enough to get out of the boat when upside down.

Don't be tempted to tether the boat to the bank, which would make things very difficult if you capsized. It may be possible to step into the boat while holding on to

the bank, simply pick up your paddle, and paddle away, but this can often be tricky. A useful technique is to place your paddle across the boat at the back of the cockpit, and hold on to it and the cockpit rim at the same time. The paddle blade will then be resting on the bank, and this will stop the boat floating away, as well as supporting the back deck of the boat – this is not always an issue, but some kayaks are not strong enough to be sat on without a little reinforcement.

Don't attempt this if the bank is much higher than the kayak, or you just will tip yourself in: find another launch place.

Now that the boat is afloat and you are holding on to it and the paddle, place one foot in the bottom of the boat, and make sure it is right in the middle before you put any weight on it. Transfer all your

weight on to that foot and, still holding on to boat and paddle with one hand, place your other foot right inside the footwell of the boat and sit down on the back deck. Take a moment to get settled.

You may now need to change hand positions, but from here you should be able to lift yourself up again and move forward to sit down on the seat. With luck or practice you are still holding the paddle behind you, and have your other hand free to help you stabilize your position without being cast adrift. Sit centrally on the seat and arrange your clothing and equipment in an orderly fashion.

Finally, get your legs into position in the cockpit. Now you are ready to use your free hand to hold on to the bank, and can bring your paddle around in front of you ready to paddle away.

Getting into the Kayak

1 Place the boat in the water as close to the river bank as possible. Keep hold of the cockpit to stop the boat drifting off.

2 Place the paddle across the back of the cockpit. Continue to hold on to the front of the cockpit with your left hand.

3 Put one leg at a time into the boat. Steady yourself and the boat by holding on to the bank and the boat.

4 Slide forward into the cockpit and get both legs in. You should still be holding on to the paddle and the river bank.

5 Bend your knees to get both your legs stretched out beneath the front deck. Continue to hold the paddle and the bank.

6 Adjust your position so that you are sitting comfortably on the seat. Bring the paddle to the front and you are ready.

Seating Position

Sloppy posture is bad at any time, but doubly so when paddling because it puts a strain on your back, and can lead to all sorts of problems, some of which can mean long-term damage. The following tips spell out exactly how you should sit to avoid injury.

In most kayaks there will be a seat, which, with the position of the backrests and footrests, will dictate which way you are supposed to face. What is not so obvious is the correct posture.

Maintaining good spinal posture means keeping your back straight and shoulders back, so that your spine is curved like the letter S: imagine you were sitting on an upright chair. If you do not, you will not be able to paddle properly. If your kayak is equipped with a back strap, the strap will give support and will encourage you to sit up properly. Even without this support though, you should be able to maintain a good, upright posture.

A common mistake is to slouch against the back of the cockpit. New paddlers often do this from the start, and even after you know how to sit there is a tendency to do this when tired. But if you cannot sit up properly in the boat, it is time to get out. By slouching, you make every stroke more difficult and less effective, and it is very bad for your back.

In most kayaks you will sit with your knees under the deck and your legs bent, so that pressing the feet against the

◔ *Correct seating position in a kayak. The knees are under the deck, and the body is upright and central.*

footrest will push your knees up and out to maintain a firm grip on the boat. In some racing and fast touring boats the paddler will sit with the knees straight up, but in the majority of kayaks this does not afford good control.

Sometimes people worry that they will not be able to get out of the boat if they capsize because their legs are under the deck. This is not actually a problem, but worrying about it is, so practise getting out until you have allayed your fears.

◔ *Correct seating position for a narrow, racing kayak, which is designed to be paddled with the knees up.*

◔ *Incorrect seating position. The knees should not be bent up in this particular type of kayak.*

◔ *The release handle of the spraydeck (skirt) should be visible and within reach.*

◔ *Correct posture. The body is upright, maintaining a well-defined spinal "S".*

◔ *Incorrect posture. Slouching backwards may cause spinal injury.*

Capsize Drill in a Kayak

You cannot get into a boat unless you accept that you may capsize. Hence, you also need to learn the escape drill. It is a simple skill, but the sooner you learn it the better. Losing the fear of capsizing means you will enjoy paddling a lot more.

Most people realize that a kayak, by its very nature, is prone to capsize. Although this can be avoided, the beginner will not know how, and that is why everyone should know how to capsize.

If you try to get out of a kayak while it is in the process of capsizing, you run the risk of injuring yourself or ending up in a position where your head is underwater, but you cannot free yourself. It is better to wait until the boat has capsized and stopped moving, and then get out. It is quite hard to visualize what you will do when you are upside down, but do not worry. When you are in the water you will not be aware of being upside down.

Everything will look and feel exactly as it does when upright, except, of course, that you will be holding your breath.

First, remove your spraydeck (spray skirt), if you are wearing one, by pulling up the release handle and letting go. Then, bang on the bottom or sides of the boat to attract attention. Lean forwards and push yourself out by placing your hands either side of the cockpit. You will naturally do a somersault in the water, breaking surface in front of the cockpit.

If you come up directly under the boat, do not worry because kayaks are so narrow that there is no way you will be stuck underneath. If you can open your eyes it helps, but you can easily escape blind. If possible, try to keep hold of your paddle, but this is often difficult. As soon as your head breaks surface, take hold of the boat and paddle or swim to the bow or stern. From there you can swim the

boat ashore. Alternatively, someone may rescue you and help you back to land, or put you back in your boat so that you can continue paddling.

You should practise the capsize drill every time you go kayaking, until you are extremely confident. Most people do it at the end of a session because emptying a boat is tiring, and you need to be fully warmed up before you do it. If you get cold doing a capsize drill at the end of a session, imagine what it would have been like to capsize at the beginning.

With practice, you may be able to keep hold of the boat with one hand, and the paddle with the other. This can be very useful to rescuers, or if you need to try to get back in the boat on your own. In practice, however, a paddler with these skills will be ready to learn how to roll as an alternative to capsizing, and will be determined to stay in the boat.

Capsize and Get Out (underwater view)

1 Locate the spraydeck (skirt) release handle and pull off the spraydeck.

2 Bring your knees together, place your hands on each side and tuck forwards.

3 Push firmly away with your hands and you will fall out of the boat easily.

4 From the cockpit, turn to one side. Hold on to the boat and paddle if you can.

TIPS
• Wait until the boat has capsized completely before you try to get out of the boat.
• Pull off your spraydeck (spray skirt) as a matter of urgency, using the handle at the front of the boat.
• Make sure your spraydeck has been released all the way around the cockpit before you attempt to move, or you risk getting caught up in it.
• Free both of your knees from under the deck at the front of the boat.
• Tuck your body forwards, with your knees pulled up to your chest in a foetal position; don't try to lie across the back deck.
• Aim to keep hold of your boat with one hand as you come up to the surface of the water.
• Don't try to get your head above the surface of the water until your legs are completely out of the boat because you risk getting into a tangle that could prove dangerous: learn the stages of a capsize in one sequence and keep to it.

Capsize and Get Out (above water view)

1 You are on flat water and are ready to begin the capsize drill. Keep your hands by your sides and take a deep breath.

2 Lean over to one side and capsize. At first, you may have to resist your body's natural instinct to right itself.

3 Remain sitting upright, at 90° to the boat, as you go over. It may help to place your hands on the sides of the boat.

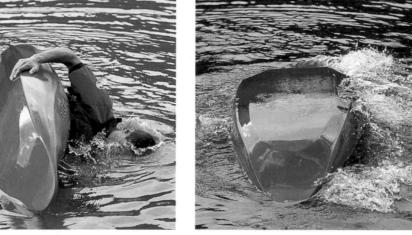

4 It will help to keep hold of the sides of the boat as your head hits the water and goes under.

5 Wait in this position until the boat stops moving. You will feel it settle when you are completely upside down.

6 Once completely inverted, bang on the bottom or sides of the boat. This makes a loud noise and attracts attention.

7 ◗ Once out of the boat, go to one end and hold on to the grab handle. Swim the boat to the shore or towards the rescuer.

TIPS
• Only practise the capsize drill when there is an instructor or experienced rescuer on hand to help you in case you get into difficulties.
• Make sure the water is at least 1.2m (4ft) deep. It is tempting to stay in shallow water, but this can lead to entrapment or injury.

Holding the Paddle

How the paddle is held is critical if you are going to use it properly. This is because the correct grip enables the paddler to apply the maximum amount of force with the minimum effort. It is also important to hold the paddle in the same way every time you pick it up. Reacting to the signals the paddle sends you from the water is an important part of paddling, and you can only learn to interpret that feedback if you have a consistent grip.

Almost all kayak paddles are feathered (one blade at an angle to the other), which means that with each stroke you will turn the paddle to put the other blade in the water. One hand will be your control hand and will grip the paddle at all times. Allow the paddle shaft to turn in the other, non-control hand, gripping it only as you make the stroke on that side.

Find your best hand position by putting the middle of the paddle shaft on your head and shuffling your hands until your elbows make 90°, making sure that your hands are still equidistant from the blades when you have finished.

Hold the paddle out in front of you with your arms straight and horizontal, knuckles up. Grip the paddle with your control hand so that the blade on the control side is vertical, and the drive (concave) face is forward. If it is your paddle, you can mark the hand positions with tape. Now you are ready to paddle.

Never be tempted to change your grip on the paddle once you've got it right. There are no significant advantages to shifting your grip, and you will find that any changes hamper the learning process. Learning is feedback related. You do something, you feel the effect; you do it a bit differently, and you feel a different effect. Changing your grip means you have to start out all over again.

You will get used to the feather angle of your paddle. Beginners often ask why kayak paddles can't be flat: the reason is so that the blade that isn't in the water doesn't give wind resistance as it goes through the air. Once you are used to it, a change in feather will feel strange to you. This is one reason why you should try to use the same paddle if you can.

⌃ *To find your correct grip, hold the paddle so that, with the wrist of the control hand straight, the drive face (the concave side of the blade) faces down towards the water.*

TIPS

• The control hand's grip on the paddle never changes during a stroke; instead, the wrist of the control hand is flexed.
• The slip hand loosens between strokes to allow the shaft to rotate.

⌄ *With the centre of the shaft on the head, the elbows make 90° and the control side drive face (here, on the paddler's right) is correctly orientated.*

⌃ *Incorrect hold. You should never hold the paddle shaft off-centre.*

⌄ *Incorrect hold. Here, the hands are too close together on the shaft.*

Using the Paddle

There is more to paddling than building up a fantastic set of arm muscles, and thrashing about. Good paddling is an art, and that means following certain rules.

With all paddle strokes you should aim to put the whole of the blade in the water, but no more. There is no advantage to the blade being deeper in the water, and it will not work properly if it is only half in. The whole blade should be just immersed.

When you make a stroke, you should always try to rotate your shoulders to give you as much reach as possible. This also means that much of the power for the stroke will come from your leg and torso muscles, leaving your relatively smaller arm muscles to provide control and react to feedback during the stroke. It is a misconception to think that kayaking is exclusively about using your arms. In fact, with good technique, a vigorous workout is much more likely to leave you with tired and aching legs and stomach muscles.

The other point that a kayak paddler should concentrate on is head rotation. Before making a stroke you should make sure your head is facing in the direction you want the boat to move in. So, for forward paddling, you must be looking at the horizon. If you want to turn the boat to the left or right, you should first turn your head to look that way. This helps the whole of your body make the strokes. It also tends to inhibit various bad practices, such as looking at the paddle blades or the end of your boat, neither of which are any help and will encourage bad posture, which can lead to injury.

💿 *Using the paddle properly is essential to make each of your strokes count.*

💿 *Correct technique: the paddle blade is submerged just deep enough to start a forward stroke.*

💿 *Blade too deep in the water – the paddler's hand is too low.*

💿 *Blade too shallow in the water – only half the blade would come into play.*

Forward Paddling

A good forward paddling stroke is a basic requirement, but it is not the easiest stroke to master. The main aim is to propel the boat forward while applying as little turning force as possible. Normally, if you make a stroke on one side, the boat will move forwards while turning away from the paddle blade that made the stroke. In order to minimize this effect, you should make the stroke as close to the boat as possible, with the paddle shaft as upright as possible.

Reach forward as far as you can, leaning from the hips but without bending your spine forward. You should be able to put the blade in the water about 2.5cm (1in) from the boat, near your feet, and drive face back. When the blade is fully immersed, pull it back using your shoulders and torso, straightening up

your top arm to push the "air blade" to the side of the boat that the stroke is on. This will make the paddle vertical and a lot more comfortable for you.

Continue to pull the paddle blade through the water until it is level with the back of the seat. Try to resist the urge to pull with your bottom arm for as long as possible. When your arm finally does bend at the elbow, it will be time to extract the blade from the water. Keep this blade the same distance from the boat throughout the stroke.

As soon as the blade is out of the water, rotate your body the other way to make the next stroke on the other side. As you do so, you will have to rotate the shaft with your control hand; drop in the blade with the drive face pointing the same way as before.

Forward Paddling Technique

1 Begin the forward stroke by placing the blade as far forward in the water as you comfortably can do.

2 Drop the whole of the blade into the water and start to push away from you with your top hand.

3 The blade in the water follows the side of the boat, and the bottom arm stays fairly straight.

4 As the water blade passes your body, the top arm should be coming across in front of your face.

5 Finally, as you reach the end of the stroke, the air blade starts to come down towards the water.

6 Continuing this motion recovers the water blade, and you are ready to place the opposite blade in the water.

⬆ *Excellent body rotation, as the paddler is about to place the left blade in the water for another stroke.*

⬇ *Forward paddling on flat water in a general purpose kayak.*

⬆ *About to make a stroke. Note that the top arm is bent, ready to punch the top blade forward.*

⬆ *Good forward paddling technique. The paddle is quite vertical and the blade is submerged.*

Backward Paddling

Paddling backwards is in principle no different to paddling forwards, but it is more difficult to get the hang of.

Do not change your grip on the paddle: this is a classic mistake made by most beginners. Always back-paddle using the back of the blade. There is no need to turn the paddle around since its curvature actually helps you to make the back stroke, and because it is bad practice to change your grip.

It is not possible to keep the paddle shaft as vertical as you do for forward paddling, or to keep the blades so close to the boat, but this is what you should aim for. Make a big effort to rotate your shoulders as far as you can to place the blade behind you – this also helps you to glance behind and see where you are going. Push your paddle forward through the water with your arms fairly straight, and make the stroke as long as you can.

Most boats will turn during the back stroke so that you zig-zag a little. Find somewhere where you will not crash into anything, and see how long you can keep going backwards in a straight line. It will teach you excellent control over the boat.

> *Incorrect method. Do not turn the paddle around like this.*

TIPS

- Think before you back-paddle: it may be quicker and easier to turn your boat and paddle forwards.
- Look over your shoulder at least every other stroke to avoid a crash.
- Pick out a feature behind you in the direction of travel, and focus on it whenever you turn around.

Backward Paddling Technique

1 Rotate as far as you can to one side, and place the blade quite far back in the water behind the boat.

2 Drive the blade forwards through the water using your torso; do not use your arms for strength.

3 As you come around to face the front, straighten your arms, keeping the blade as close as you can to the boat.

4 Try to keep looking behind you as you finish the stroke. This may seem difficult at first but it will come with practice.

5 The stroke should end with the bottom arm straight and the blade in the area of the boat next to your feet.

6 As the blade comes out of the water, you can continue rotating to place the blade behind you on the other side.

Stopping

Learning how to stop the boat quickly is important. Use this stroke if you are in danger of hitting something.

Begin by moving the boat forwards at a good pace. To stop, jab one blade into the water next to your body, as if to paddle backwards. The drive face should be pointing backwards with the shaft perpendicular. Resist the force on the blade, but as soon as you tense against that force and the boat begins to turn, jab the other blade in quickly on the other side. Repeat on the first side, and by the time you make your fourth jab, the boat should have stopped. Do the jabs quite aggressively, and switch sides when you feel the pressure on the back of the blade.

❯ *Stopping quickly in a fast racing kayak requires sharp jabs in the water.*

Stopping Technique

1 Jab the paddle in on one side, at 90° to the kayak rather than as you would for a normal stroke.

2 Pull the paddle out again as soon as you feel the pressure of the water on the blade and the boat begins to turn.

3 Drop the opposite blade in on the other side. Resist for a little longer this time, until the boat is pointing straight again.

4 Back on the side of the boat on which you started, make a longer back stroke this time.

5 Moving backwards this time, make a final stroke to straighten up the boat.

6 At the finish, you should be pointing in the same direction you were at the previous step, except with the boat still.

Forward Sweep Stroke

The forward sweep is the most useful turning stroke in the kayaker's repertoire. It will turn the boat on the spot, and can be used to turn the boat through 180°. By inserting just one sweep stroke, you can also change or correct your direction while paddling forwards, without breaking your rhythm.

Start by placing the blade in the water as far forward as possible, with the shaft fairly low and the drive face pointing away from the boat. Rotate your head and shoulders, so that they are facing the direction of travel. Keeping your bottom arm straight, sweep the paddle in as wide an arc as you can. When you have turned as far as you need to, or the blade is coming close to hitting the back of the boat, lift the blade straight out of the water – don't let it hit the boat.

It helps considerably if you can "edge" the boat slightly, so that the side opposite your stroke is raised a little for the first half of the stroke. Level the boat again as the paddle passes perpendicular to the kayak, or you may catch the paddle.

TIPS
- Practise edging the boat by lifting up one of your knees.
- The bigger the arc, the more effectively you will turn the boat.
- Think about the difference between a forward paddling stroke (vertical paddle, close to the boat) and a sweep stroke (low paddle, wide arc).
- Use the forward sweep if you want to turn while travelling forwards.

⬆ *The forward sweep stroke is the most valuable turning stroke. It can be used to spin or to change direction.*

Forward Sweep Technique

1 Place the paddle in the water as far forward as you can reach, with the blade facing away from the boat.

2 Keeping your lower arm straight, swing your paddle blade away from the front of the boat.

3 Looking in the direction you want to turn, continue to sweep the blade in the widest arc you can make.

4 Still looking where you want to go, continue to sweep until the blade is swinging in towards the stern.

5 At this point, quickly flip the blade up out of the water before it catches on the back of the boat and trips you up.

6 If you keep the boat stable and the blade out of the water, you'll carry on turning even after the stroke is finished.

Reverse Sweep Stroke

As the name implies, the reverse sweep stroke is the exact opposite of the forward sweep. It is a much more powerful turning stroke, but it should not be used while moving forwards unless you want to turn and head back in the other direction because it will arrest all forward motion.

Start with the paddle blade as far back as you can reach, on the side you want to turn towards. Rotate your head and shoulders in this direction. Drop the blade into the water with the drive face towards the boat, then sweep the blade forwards in the widest arc you can, until you are pointing the right way, or until the blade is about to hit the front of the boat. Lift the blade straight up out of the water.

Keep your bottom arm as straight as you can throughout the stroke, and try to keep the boat level in the water.

⏶ *Incorrect technique: don't turn the paddle around. Use the back of the blade for all reverse strokes.*

It should be easy to turn most general-purpose boats through 180° with one reverse sweep. Once the blade is out of the water, the kayak will continue to spin for further rotations. Practise spinning

using alternate forward and reverse sweep strokes. Go forward on the left and reverse on the right to turn clockwise. Go forward on the right, then reverse on the left to spin in the opposite direction.

TIPS
• Use the back of the paddle blade and don't change your grip.
• Use a reverse sweep stroke when you need to make a powerful turn.
• Keep the boat fairly level in the water for a reverse sweep stroke.
• Remember, a reverse sweep stroke will arrest forward progress.
• Practise combining forward sweep strokes and reverse sweep strokes on opposite sides of the boat.

Reverse Sweep Technique

1 Rotate your body and look where you want the boat to be pointing. Place the blade in the water close to the stern, with the drive face towards the boat.

2 Sweep the blade out and forward, keeping the bottom arm straight. Note how the body hasn't actually moved but the boat has.

3 Complete the arc, leaning your body forward over the front deck to extend your reach as far as you can at the front of the boat.

4 Lift the paddle blade out of the water before it reaches the boat, or you will risk catching your paddle under the boat.

5 Keep the boat level and the blade out of the water, and keep looking where you want to go!

6 The boat continues turning on its own. It is usually possible to complete a 180° turn like this in general-purpose boats.

Draw Stroke

This stroke moves the boat through the water sideways, and although you can get by without being very good at it, learning to do it well will help you to improve many of your other skills. The draw stroke is, curiously, a fairly obscure technique that many paddlers never learn to do properly.

Place the blade in the water as far from the side of the kayak as you can reach, with the drive face pointing towards the boat. Push your top arm out as far as you can, so that the paddle shaft is as vertical

as possible. Lift the edge of the kayak with your knee on the stroke side, and pull the blade towards your body. This should pull a general-purpose boat about 50cm (20in) sideways.

As the blade approaches, cock your wrists back quickly to rotate the blade 90°, then slice it back to where it started. If you do not, and the blade hits the boat, you may be knocked off balance or fall in. If you try to stop the stroke before it hits the hull, the same may happen.

From the starting position, straighten your wrists so that the paddle is pointing towards the boat, and repeat the stroke. If the boat turns rather than moves sideways, the stroke is being made too far towards the front or the back of the boat. If the bow starts to turn towards the paddle, move the stroke back a little, or vice versa for the stern. It can be very useful to make this happen deliberately though, so practise doing draw strokes towards the bow or stern.

Draw Stroke Technique

1 Rotate your body to face the way you want to move. Place the blade as far out to the side as you can, with the drive face towards the boat.

2 Pull the blade towards the boat, keeping the paddle as vertical as you can. Lifting your knee on the paddle side of the boat will help you achieve this.

3 Continue to pull smoothly until the paddle blade is just about to reach the boat at a point level in the water with your hip.

4 Turn your wrists sharply through 90° to change the angle of the blade before it hits the boat.

5 Move the paddle away from the boat by slicing the blade out sideways to where it first started.

6 Flick your wrists back to their original position, so that the drive face is towards the boat. Repeat as required.

Sculling Draw

Like the draw stroke, the sculling draw will move the boat sideways. It has the advantage, however, of being more useful in a confined space. For instance, when you are close to a jetty and want to move closer, the draw stroke may be difficult to execute. The sculling draw is also a lot less likely to tip you in, although it is more difficult to do effectively.

Start with the paddle blade next to your hip, 20cm (8in) from the boat, with the shaft vertical and the drive face towards the hull. Cock your wrist so that the blade rotates 20°, opening out towards the bow.

Keep the shaft vertical and move the paddle forwards as far as you can. Keep the paddle 20cm (8in) from the boat, resisting its tendency to slice away from the hull. If anything you will be pulling it inwards, which is where the sideways

motion of the boat is generated. When the blade is as far forward as you can get it, keep the shaft vertical and rotate your wrist the other way to angle the drive face 20° towards the stern. Then pull the blade back through the water as far as you can. At this point, quickly rotate again to push forward, maintaining enough pressure on the blade face to keep it the same distance from the boat at all times.

As you push and pull the paddle to and fro, the boat will move towards the side where you are paddle stroking. It helps to lean towards the paddle and to edge at the same time, so that the leading edge (the one nearest the paddle) of the boat is lifted. It is also possible to do this with the blade angles reversed, so that the pressure is on the outside (back) face of the paddle. The boat will then move

● *A sculling draw. Note how the boat moves quickly sideways, creating a wave.*

sideways away from the paddle. This is a sculling pushover. In this case the leading edge is the one opposite to the paddle.

Sculling further forward will move the boat sideways with the bow ahead of the stern, while sculling behind will mean the tail leads. In this way, sculling can move and turn the boat at the same time.

Sculling Draw Technique

1 Start as for a draw stroke, but with the blade only 20cm (8in) from the hull. Bend your wrists back so that the drive face is facing slightly towards the bow.

2 Move the blade forwards as far as you can reach without leaning, keeping it vertical and exactly the same distance from the side of the boat.

3 Quickly cock the wrists so that the paddle blade is pointing slightly towards the stern. (Note: the paddle is shown partly out of the water for teaching only).

4 Move the paddle back, keeping the pressure on the blade so that it stays equidistant from the hull.

5 When the paddle is as far back as is comfortable, cock the wrists back again to open the drive face towards the bow.

6 Move the paddle forwards as before, keeping the pressure on at all times. Repeat as necessary.

Stern Rudder

Sometimes it is desirable to make subtle direction changes, or to keep a kayak running in a straight line while in readiness for a turn. For this the stern rudder is extremely useful.

As the name of the stroke suggests, the paddle blade is used as a rudder at the stern of the boat. Place the paddle in the water, with the drive face towards the boat and the paddle shaft at a low angle. The back arm will probably be fairly straight. If the boat is not moving this will have no effect at all, but if you have some forward momentum the boat will probably turn slightly towards the paddle. If you move the paddle away from the hull, the turn will become more pronounced; closer to the hull and there will be less effect. If you bring it really close to the boat you may even start to turn the other way, away from the paddle.

● *Textbook stern rudder. The body is rotated to help place the blade as far back as possible, while the paddler looks ahead to where he is going.*

A good exercise involves getting the boat up to speed, and then placing your stern rudder in the water, letting you experiment with pushing and pulling, and getting the boat to veer to and fro until it runs out of momentum, without taking the blade out of the water. This is a useful way to get used to feedback from the paddle.

A handy technique is to approach a landing place perpendicular to the shore, using a stern rudder to keep the boat pointing straight at the spot where you want to land. At the last moment, before the bow touches the bank, sweep your stern rudder forward in a reverse sweep to turn the boat 90° and kill your speed. You will finish up stationary and parallel to the shore, close enough to get out.

When deciding to use a stern rudder, ask yourself why. If you want to go forwards and turn, use the forward sweep, which will not slow you down. If you want to stop and turn, the reverse sweep may be better. The stern rudder does not propel you, and has little effect on speed except for interrupting your paddling.

It is possible, when paddling backwards, to do a sort of stern rudder at the bow of the boat, with the paddle placed as for the beginning of a forward sweep, the drive face pointing away from the hull. This is sometimes called a front rudder, and should be regarded as a rudder for going backwards.

TIPS

• Use a stern rudder sparingly. Think of it as a stroke to control steering, rather than to change direction.
• A stern rudder will impair forward movement, so you may prefer to use a forward sweep instead.
• Always have the drive face of the blade pointing towards the boat.
• Remember that your blade is acting as a rudder to steer the boat, and not as a brake to stop it.
• The stern rudder is used most when surfing waves, but practise it anyway, even if you don't need it just yet.

Bow Rudder

Expert paddlers seem to use bow rudders for everything, and can make complex manoeuvres while appearing just to stick in a bow rudder and lean on it. The bow rudder is in fact the fastest and most attacking turning stroke of them all, and it is the signature stroke of demanding white water paddling for this reason.

The bow rudder, unlike the stern rudder, can be a very difficult stroke to learn. It seems appropriate to mention it now, but you may find it difficult to make it work until you have mastered all the other strokes in this section. It relies on an excellent feel for what the paddle is doing in the water, as well as the draw stroke skills already covered.

The bow rudder is a compound stroke, which is to say it is a collection of smaller movements rather than one single stroke. It can make the boat spin dramatically, or it can turn the boat in a long, powerful sweep. It is applied when the kayak has started to turn with the current. Where there is no current, the energy needs to be generated by a good forward swccp.

While moving forwards, place the paddle vertically in the water 30cm (12in) from the side of the bow, about level with your feet, with the drive face of the blade towards the boat. Experiment with rotating your wrists to turn the blade out slightly, but resist any forces that act on the blade in the water. You will find that there is a position with the blade face almost parallel to the side of the boat when the boat does not tend to slow or turn, and you cannot feel any pressure on the blade. Roll your wrist back and turn the blade out to face the bow, and the boat will start to turn towards the paddle. The more you roll your wrist back to open out the blade, the more you will turn, but there will be a lot of force on the blade and the boat will quickly stop.

You can increase the effect by letting the pressure take the blade away from the boat, then pulling it back towards the bow in a modified draw stroke. There are many ways in which you can control the boat with the paddle blade in this mode, so experiment, noting what happens when you go with the water or oppose it.

⬤ *It is not easy to see how the bow rudder works until you have spent a lot of time practising it. The boat should swing around the vertical paddle by 180°, while the paddle itself remains pretty much motionless in the water.*

Don't be discouraged by your first attempts to perform the bow rudder. You will need a lot of practice to build up the strength, mobility and feel for the water that is necessary to execute the stroke properly and to make full use of it when you are paddling, and this can be very demanding on your strength and patience. But once you have it, you'll love it.

TIPS

• In manoeuvrable kayaks the bow rudder is very versatile.

• Familiarize yourself with how it feels when you rotate the blade in the water while the boat has some speed.

• Imagine running along a street and grabbing hold of a lamppost. You would swing around it, wouldn't you? This is how the bow rudder works.

• Most boats have a turning centre somewhere near your calves. Next to or slightly in front of this is where the bow rudder works best.

Low Brace

A low brace is a support stroke on the back of the blade, and it is used to keep you upright when you find yourself side-on to a wave that is trying to capsize you. All bracing or support strokes require quite a leap of faith. It is difficult to believe that you can trust your weight to your paddle blade, but this is exactly what you must do. The force that you commit to the paddle is exactly how much support you will get from it in return.

Place the blade on the surface with the drive face up. If you are moving, you must angle the leading edge up to stop it diving. It is easier to low brace with the blade behind you, but the further the blade is from the boat while flat on the surface, the better the technique will work.

Committing your weight to the blade will support you and stop you capsizing until the blade sinks too far into the water to keep it flat. If using the low brace to avoid a capsize, you must use your legs to level the craft before the paddle sinks. If the boat is moving, a low brace can be used to turn the boat, while giving some support. This is called a low brace turn.

◔ *The low brace is the best way to support your weight while leaning over, thereby preventing a capsize. If you are moving forwards, it will also make the boat turn towards the paddle.*

◔ *The low brace is an important stroke that should be practised regularly when you are learning to paddle. It can help you to regain your balance, and avoid getting into further trouble.*

High Brace

The high brace works on the same principle as the low brace, but with the drive face of the paddle downward, and the bracing blade in the water rather than flat on the surface. This a support stroke, used to keep you upright – for instance, when a wave threatens to tip you in.

A high brace is more powerful than a low brace, and should be avoided if the latter is possible because of the huge force it exerts on the shoulders, which can lead to injury. However, as the paddle is already in the high position as you stroke, it can be more convenient to turn that stroke into a high brace when a wave is about to turn you over, rather than change your paddle position for a low brace.

Because the drive face is pointing down, high bracing demands that your elbows are below the paddle shaft. This usually means that the water is higher than the boat, either because of a wave or because you have tipped over a long way.

Keep your weight on the paddle until you can right the boat with your legs and hips. Move the weight of your body back over the boat to regain your equilibrium.

TIP
• Do not use the high brace in any powerful water feature, including river rapids. The blade may get jerked down without warning, and if the opposite arm is held too high it can be forced even higher, increasing the likelihood of a shoulder dislocation.

⬆ *When taken to the extreme, the high brace over-extends the shoulders and there is a significant risk of dislocation or other, often very serious, injuries to the shoulders and upper back.*

⬇ *The high brace is more powerful than the low brace because you can reach further out for more leverage, and use the drive face of the paddle.*

CANOEING SKILLS

Canoeing is accessible to most people because the skills for getting in and out of the boat, and having fun, are not specialized or demanding. If, however, you plan to progress to a specialist area or want to paddle longer distances, or look after friends and family while they, too, enjoy their paddling, it is time to acquire new skills.

This section outlines the basic skills and strokes that will help you use the canoe in an effortless and skilful manner. The exercises are tackled in approximately the order in which they tend to arise, although some instructors may prefer a different order.

When you are learning the following skills, choose a suitable place to practise them, and try not to progress too fast. Make sure you have mastered them before you move on. If something is not working and you do not know why, take a break and then have another go. If there is still a problem, get expert advice. Also remember that until you can do most of the strokes, you will not be able to paddle the boat to the desired location, and that is why it is vital that you know you can swim to a safe landing place.

◁ *Two paddlers charging along a flatwater river in a tandem open canoe.*

▽ *Swimming with an upturned canoe after a capsize, keeping hold of the boat and paddle.*

Getting into the Canoe

The first key lesson while the canoe is floating on the water is to get into the boat. It is much trickier than it looks, but it will come with practice.

It is best to start by finding a launching site where the river bank or jetty is low enough to let you step into the canoe without having to jump or climb in. Place the boat on the surface. The water should be deep enough to keep the craft afloat with your weight. If the water is deep enough to capsize in, make sure that it is deep enough for getting out of the boat when it is upside down.

Also consider how you are going to stop the canoe from floating away while you climb in. Do not be tempted to tether the boat to the bank, as this will make things difficult if you capsize. It may be possible to step into the boat while still holding on to the bank, just pick up the paddle beside you, and paddle away. Often, however, this is quite tricky. A useful technique is to place your paddle on the ground next to the boat, and keep one hand on it as you climb in. This is often easier than clinging on to a grass bank.

When the boat is afloat and you are holding on to it and the paddle, you are ready to get in. Place one foot in the bottom of the boat, and make sure it is right in the middle before you put any weight on it. Now gradually transfer all your weight on to that foot, and still holding on to the paddle if necessary, place your other foot right inside the footwell of the boat and gently sit or kneel down. Get comfortable and stable, and pick up the paddle if you have not already done so. Finally, get into your preferred sitting or kneeling position.

Getting into the Canoe

1 Put the canoe in the water close to the bank and keep hold of the nearside gunwale, so that the canoe cannot stray.

2 Make sure the canoe is floating freely, and that it won't touch the bottom when you get in. Lay the paddle across.

3 Holding on to both gunwales and the paddle, put one foot in the middle of the canoe and transfer your weight on to it.

4 When you feel confident that the canoe is balanced and stable, bring your other foot into the boat, still holding the paddle.

5 Supporting your weight on your hands, and holding on to the paddle, sit or kneel down in the bottom of the canoe.

6 Settle yourself into your preferred paddling position, still holding the paddle. You are now ready to set off.

Sitting or Kneeling?

Finding the right seating position is a fundamental part of canoeing. It is not just a matter of comfort, but a way of helping you control the craft.

You can sit on a seat in a canoe, or you can kneel in the bottom of the boat with your feet under the seat, resting your bottom against it. The latter is more stable because your weight is lower, and because you can brace your knees against the sides of the boat for better control. If you prefer to sit, find a way of bracing your legs because it is hard to balance the canoe if you are perched on the seat as if on a kitchen chair.

● *Kneeling correctly, with buttocks resting on the seat and knees apart.*

● *Kneeling down and slouching is very bad posture, and provides little control.*

Whether sitting or kneeling, you should always maintain good spinal posture, with your back straight. This is important for comfort, control and to prevent back pain or injury. It might seem easier to slouch at first, but this is a very bad idea.

Seating Position

The next step is called trimming the boat, which means sitting in the right position so that the boat performs well in the water. This means trying to keep the boat level or slightly bow up. A single paddler should sit in the middle, and two paddlers should sit so that the lighter paddler is in the bow.

The advantage of trimming slightly bow up is that less of the keel will be in the water, making the boat turn more easily, but you will sacrifice some speed. A level boat will be faster, but will be more difficult to turn unless it is flat-bottomed.

● *Sitting on the seat, with the knees against the sides, gives good control.*

● *Sitting off-centre on the seat, or with the knees together, should be avoided.*

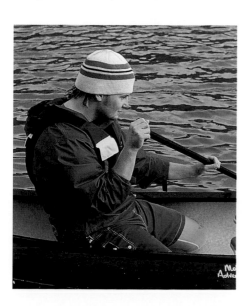

Capsize Drill in a Canoe

If you are going to paddle a canoe it is important that you know what to do if it capsizes. The ability to swim is obviously important, but how you get out of the boat and handle yourself from there is a safety issue that should be addressed as soon as possible.

With some skill and practice you will be able to salvage almost any situation without capsizing, but sometimes it is unavoidable. When it does happen, you have a surprisingly long time to react. The question is, do you get out of the boat as it goes over, or wait until it has capsized before getting out?

If you try to get out of a canoe while it is capsizing, you run the risk of a gunwale cracking you on the head, or getting in a muddle as you try to get out. It is far better to get out once upside down, when the boat has stopped

moving. Push away from the gunwale with your hands and, if possible, try to keep hold of your paddle. As soon as your head breaks surface, take hold of the boat and swim to one end. You can then either swim the boat ashore, or try to turn it over.

A reasonably athletic canoeist can often right the boat and get back in unaided. Get alongside the upturned canoe, and take hold underneath. Push it up until the gunwales are about to break the surface, keeping it level. Tread water to maintain upward force. Finally, allow yourself to sink into the water and, as you come up again, push up harder on one side than the other, flipping the canoe over with the minimum of water inside. With a really light boat it is possible to throw it into the air and land it upright. Having righted the boat, push down the

side nearest to you, and reach across to the opposite gunwale to haul yourself in.

The technique for capsizing, escaping and recovering is one every canoeist should learn, but there is an advanced method that can be used to avoid the danger of being caught under the boat. When you realize a capsize is otherwise inevitable, you can jump over the side; pushing off from both gunwales as you do so ensures that the boat levels out and remains upright. Your paddle, still held in the bottom hand grip, can be used as a brake; slap it down hard on the surface as you go in, and you should be able to keep your head above water, boat in one hand, paddle in the other. This is, of course, a very safe and controlled way to exit the boat. From this position, you can swim ashore or re-enter the boat as described above.

Capsize and Get Out

1 To practise the capsize sequence, start from your usual paddling position, sitting or kneeling upright in the canoe.

2 Let go of the paddle with one hand and take hold of the gunwale of the boat.

3 Lean over to one side until the boat overbalances. Continue to keep hold of the paddle as you go over.

4 Allow the boat to capsize, still holding on to the gunwale and the paddle.

5 Wait until you are completely upside down and the boat has stopped moving.

6 Kick away from the boat and surface – ideally, still holding the boat and paddle.

Jump Out of the Boat

1 When you realize the boat is going to capsize, reach across to the lower gunwale with your opposite hand.

2 Keep hold of the paddle in your other hand and jump out. Keep holding on to the gunwale.

3 By holding the paddle blade flat you can often prevent your head from going under the water.

TIPS
• If you know the boat is going to capsize, it is worth getting out if you have enough time.
• Only jump out of the boat if you are able to do so before it flips over.
• By kicking off from the high side of the boat, you can often stop the canoe turning over.
• If you jump out before a capsize, you will be able get back in without the difficulty of righting and emptying the canoe.

❯ *Watching experienced paddlers acting out a capsize situation is a very useful exercise. All beginners should learn to capsize as soon as they first start out on the water, and most paddle club instructors make this a priority.*

Go to the Front and Swim

1 Swim your way to the front of the boat, keeping hold of the canoe and the paddle if at all possible.

2 Take hold of the front of the canoe, leaving it upside down.

3 Using the paddle, if you can, and your arms and legs, swim the canoe to the shore or to other paddlers in your group.

Right Boat and Re-enter

The technique for righting the boat and climbing back in is well worth learning and practising until you are confident you can do it. The technique makes the canoeist fully self-sufficient and able to cope with almost any eventuality on the water. Once you are confident that you can do it in any reasonable weather (high winds and waves make it more difficult) you will be happy to jump out of the boat rather than to capsize, which is, in many circumstances, a much safer thing to do.

Beware, however, of becoming too reliant on your powers of self-rescue. With this technique, as with the ability to roll, there is a danger that you will simply give up and capsize or get out in a situation that may in fact have been recoverable using a decent support stroke. Obviously, you will be safer, drier and more in control if you can stay upright in your canoe.

● *Properly trained canoe paddlers can have great fun on white water, even when there is a risk of capsize.*

Although the open canoe is in a sense more vulnerable to capsize than a kayak and is far more likely to take in water, we can see from the solutions illustrated that the canoe is just as capable a craft as the kayak, and in some ways it is more versatile. Although it is possible to re-enter a capsized kayak, it is rare to see it done successfully, and the paddler nearly always has to contend with a boat that is full of water. The canoeist can quite often avoid this. The disadvantages of the open boat are that you cannot simply roll without bailing out, unless your boat is fully kitted out with airbags or similar buoyancy (flotation), and that a canoe loaded with gear can be almost impossible to right from the water.

If there are two paddlers, or another canoeist is able to assist, then have one person hold the gunwale down on the side opposite that on which you're getting in. The trick is to hold it firmly enough so that the canoe doesn't capsize or ship any water, but not to keep the boat so level that the person trying to get in cannot pull themlves up.

TIPS

• Lift the boat slowly. The pocket of air between the hull of the boat and the water surface creates some buoyancy, which will help to support you. This shouldn't be broken until the last possible moment.
• Focus on forcefully throwing the boat upwards, not on flipping it over.
• You will need both hands to right the boat, so leave your paddle on the water between you and the canoe.
• Put your paddle into the boat as soon as the boat is righted.
• Climb into the boat carefully: to mess up this part and fall back into the water is exhausting, and you need to preserve your energy.
• If you were paddling tandem when you capsized, one of you can hold on to the far gunwale while the other climbs into the boat.
• With every capsize you bring water into the canoe: remember to bring a sponge or a small bucket next time!

Right Boat and Re-enter

1 Practise the righting sequence from any starting position in the water. Swim alongside the middle of the canoe.

2 Treading water to keep yourself afloat, take hold of both gunwales in the middle of the boat.

3 Holding the gunwales, lift the boat as high as you possibly can, then push it up and away from you so that it rights itself.

4 Keep holding the boat up out of the water as much as possible. Be prepared for your head to go under as you put all your strength into holding up the boat.

5 The boat turns over and lands right side up, with a minimum of water inside. You will have had to let go of the boat to turn it, so now get hold of the gunwale again.

6 Hold on to the nearest edge and throw all of your weight on to it. This should tip the boat towards you until you can take hold of the far gunwale.

7 Holding on to the far gunwale, haul yourself across the canoe, trying not to tip the boat so far with your weight that you take on even more water.

8 Get all of your weight across the boat, with both hands on the far gunwale. Then, bring one knee up and inside the boat. This will level out the boat.

9 Flip yourself around so that you can get into your paddling position. If your paddle has floated away, ask someone in your group to retrieve it for you.

Holding the Paddle

It may look easy, but there is a definite knack to holding a canoe paddle correctly. If you think paddling a canoe means grabbing the nearest paddle and roughly holding it, you will have no hope of mastering canoe techniques.

You can only use a paddle properly if you are holding it correctly in the first place. This is because the correct grip enables the paddler to apply the maximum amount of force with the minimum effort. It is also important to hold the paddle in exactly the same way every time you use it. This is the only way for you to become familiar with – as quickly as possible – the feel of the paddle in the water, and how to learn to interpret the feedback you get from it. This is key to becoming a good paddler.

Canoe paddles have only one blade, with a T-grip at the other end. It is important to hold this T-grip with your top hand knuckle up and thumb under, and the shaft of the paddle with the other hand. If the paddle has a curved blade, you should grip the paddle with the bottom hand so that the blade has the drive (concave) face towards you. Hold the T-grip in one hand; place the other hand so that if the paddle is held horizontal in front of you, your hands are slightly further apart than your shoulders.

Which Side to Paddle On?

Early on in your canoeing career, you are going to have to decide whether you are a leftie or a rightie – that is to say, whether you will paddle on the left-hand

● Incorrect technique. The top hand is not over the T-grip and the bottom hand is upside down.

◐ Good paddle hold. The top hand is over the T-grip, the bottom hand is above the gunwale height (thumb at the top), and the paddle shaft is vertical and close to the boat.

side of the boat or on the right. Most people are able to paddle on either side, but have a preferred side. The only way to find out is by trial and error; whether you are right- or left-handed has very little bearing on the matter.

What is certain is that whichever side you are paddling on, you should try to keep to that grip. It is the principle of canoe paddling, as opposed to kayaking, that you should be able to do everything from one side of the boat, without changing sides. Expert paddlers use cross-bow strokes to put the blade in on the opposite side from their normal paddling side without altering their grip, although some purists claim that even to put the blade in the water on the "off" side is nothing short of bad form. Ultimately, do whatever works for you, but the easiest and most stylish technique is to paddle on the on-side where possible, using a cross-bow stroke or two if necessary.

Using the Paddle

Beginners often find what they imagine to be the easiest tasks actually the trickiest. Using the paddle is a very good example but, by following the guidelines below, and establishing good habits from the start, you should have no problems.

For all paddle strokes you should aim to put the whole of the blade in the water, but no more. There is no advantage to the blade being deeper in the water, and it will not work properly if it is only half in. Put the blade in until it is totally immersed; keep the paddle shaft visible.

When you make a stroke, you should lean forwards to give you as much reach as possible. This also means that much of the power for the stroke will come from your leg and torso muscles, leaving your arm muscles to provide control and react to feedback from the water. It is a misconception to think that canoeing is all about using arm muscles. If your technique is good, a vigorous paddle is more likely to leave you with tired, aching legs and stomach muscles.

The next point that a canoe paddler must concentrate on is head rotation. Before making a stroke, make sure your head is facing in the direction you want to move in. So, with forward paddling, you must look straight ahead at the horizon. If you want to turn the boat to the left or right, first turn your head and shoulders

to look that way. Such movements mean that the whole of your body is part of the stroke-making process. This also helps eliminate bad practices, such as looking at the blade or the end of your boat, neither of which will help your technique.

⊙ *Paddling with a correctly immersed blade. The whole of the blade area is completely covered but only just, and the paddle shaft is almost vertical. The hand is well clear of the water.*

⊙ *Blade not fully immersed. This will not give you enough grip on the water.*

⊙ *Paddle too deep. Never put the shaft in the water, and certainly not your hand!*

⊙ *Dynamic forward movement starts with good paddling technique. Holding the paddle correctly is a part of this.*

Forward Paddling

A correct forward paddling stroke is a basic requirement if you want to be a good canoeist, but it is not the easiest stroke to master. In addition to the technique for moving forwards, you will inevitably have to learn how to paddle backwards, stop and steer. Learning to combine these techniques is a useful discipline that teaches you control and the ability to respond to feedback from the water. In turn, this will help to make you a really good forward paddler.

The main aim of forward paddling is to propel the boat forwards. It is important to apply as little turning force as possible, since by turning you are making your forward stroke less effective. Normally, if you make a stroke on one side, the boat will move forwards but it will also turn away from the paddle blade that made the stroke. In order to minimize this effect, you should make the stroke as close as you can to the boat, with the paddle shaft as vertical as possible.

If you are paddling a canoe alone, you will also have to use a special technique to keep the boat in a straight line. This is called the J-stroke. If two people are paddling tandem, their paddles will be on opposite sides of the boat, and the J-stroke will not be necessary because their turning effects on opposite sides will cancel each other out.

🔽 *The lighter paddler should sit in the front of the boat when paddling tandem.*

Tandem Forward Stroke

Begin with both paddlers reaching forwards as far as they can, leaning from the hips without bending the spine forwards. Both should put the blade in the water as far forward as possible, with the drive face pointing back. When the blade is fully immersed, it should be pulled back firmly, using the shoulders and torso, straightening the top arm, and

🔼 *With a paddle on each side of the boat when tandem paddling, it is easy to propel the canoe in a straight line.*

keeping the T-grip on the side of the boat that the stroke is on. This will make the paddle as vertical as is comfortable.

Continue to pull the blade through the water until it is level with your seat. Try to resist the urge to pull with your bottom arm for as long as possible. When it finally does bend at the elbow, it will be to extract the blade from the water. Aim to keep the blade the same distance from the boat throughout the stroke.

As soon as the blade is out of the water, lean forwards smoothly to begin another stroke. The less time the paddle is out of the water the more control you have, but if you lunge forwards too sharply it will stop the canoe in its tracks.

Canoeists generally paddle on one side of the boat only. There is a stroke that involves reaching across to paddle on the other side, without changing grip, called cross-bow paddling, but this is usually the preserve of white water canoeists.

The J-stroke

This is the cornerstone of canoe paddling. Unless there are two people paddling the canoe on opposite sides, or you have an extremely straight-running craft, you will need this stroke to keep the boat going in a straight line.

The principle of the J-stroke is to perform a normal forward stroke but, at the end of the stroke, when the bottom arm is starting to bend, you must rotate your top hand outwards to point your thumb down. As a result, the drive face of the blade will then turn away from the hull of the canoe. This turns the stroke into a strong rudder, which arrests any turning force you may have inadvertently applied during the stroke. If you hesitate for a moment with the blade in this position, you will also be able to make fine adjustments to your course, by pushing or pulling the blade relative to the hull.

Although this may seem impossible at first, you should practise looking straight ahead in the direction of travel when making the J-stroke, rather than at the paddle itself.

It takes a while to master the J-stroke. Initially it may not seem to work, but persevere and learn to respond to the feedback from the blade. If, once you can do the J-stroke effectively, you find that some boats or conditions still make it difficult to paddle straight, there is a more powerful variation called the C-stroke. This is a J-stroke with a sharp pull of the drive face towards the hull at the very beginning, so that the blade creates a C rather than a J-shape. See the Draw Stroke for more help.

TIPS

• Practise the J-stroke for as long as it takes you to feel comfortable with it: it's key to the good handling and control of a solo canoe.
• Use the J-stroke to keep yourself in line when you are happy with your general direction.

❯ *This paddler is using a J-stroke to keep his white water open canoe on course as he moves downstream.*

J-stroke Technique

1 Put the paddle in the water as far forward as possible, leaning forward to increase your reach.

2 Push with the top hand rather than pull with the bottom, and use your body as well as your arms.

3 As the blade passes your body, twist the paddle shaft so that your thumbs are pointing down. Unlike this paddler, you should aim to look straight ahead of you.

4 Keep the pressure on the paddle until the end of the stroke or else it won't work. It's a stroke with a twist, not a stroke followed by a stern rudder.

Backward Paddling and Stopping

Paddling backwards is in principle no different to going forwards, but it is a bit more difficult. Beginners will often try to change their grip on the paddle, which is a mistake – always keep the same grip.

The first thing to note is that you back-paddle using the back of the blade. There is no need to turn the paddle around because any curvature actually helps you do the back stroke. It is bad practice to change your grip. It is not possible to keep the paddle shaft as vertical as you do for forward paddling, or to keep the blade so close to the boat, but you should try to do so as much as possible. Make a big effort to rotate your shoulders as far as you can to place the blade behind you; this also gives you an opportunity to look behind you to see where you are going.

Push your paddle forwards through the water with your arms fairly straight, and make the stroke as long as you can. Most boats will turn during the stroke, so you may have to turn the back face of the

○ *Paddling backwards presents few problems but look where you are going!*

blade out at the end of the stroke in a sort of reverse J-stroke, unless there are two of you paddling the canoe. Find somewhere safe where you will not crash into anything, and see how long you can keep going backwards in a straight line. It teaches you excellent control.

Don't be disappointed if you can't paddle backwards very far. It is a difficult technique to pick up, and can take a while to learn properly. Try to be as good at it as you can, but bear in mind that it is usually easier to turn the boat around and paddle forwards instead.

Stopping

Getting an open boat to stop in a straight line is almost impossible because the boat will always turn towards the paddle. If you have room to let the boat turn sideways this will be the safest way to stop. If not, stick the paddle in the water as a brake, and, when the boat turns, use a sweep or pry manoeuvring stroke to keep the boat straight. Repeat as many times as it takes until you are still. Once you have learnt the pries and bow rudder strokes, this will seem a lot easier.

○ *Rotating the shoulders as you place the blade behind you will help you make a more effective back stroke.*

Forward Sweep Stroke

The forward sweep stroke is the simplest and most useful manoeuvring stroke of all. It is used either to turn the boat on the spot, or to make adjustments to your course while moving forwards.

Unlike the technique for forward paddling, sweep strokes are intended to turn the boat as much as possible. Proceed by placing the blade as far forwards as you can, but with the shaft fairly low, and the drive face looking away from the boat. Then rotate your head and shoulders so that they are facing the direction you want to go. Now, keeping your bottom arm straight, sweep the paddle in as wide an arc as your reach allows. When you have turned enough, or the blade is close to hitting the back of the boat, lift it straight out of the water. It helps if you can edge the boat a little, using your legs, so that the side opposite your stroke is raised a little, just for the first half of the stroke.

Unlike a kayak, which can be turned through an angle of 90° or more on the spot, a canoe will only turn between 30° and 40° per stroke. It can also be used to change or correct direction while paddling forwards, by simply inserting one sweep stroke without otherwise breaking the rhythm of your strokes.

❯ *Here, the stern paddler is using a sweep stroke to change the direction of the boat on white water. The bow paddler maintains his forward stroke technique.*

Forward Sweep Technique

1 Place the paddle blade as far forward as you can, with the drive face pointing away from the canoe.

2 Look over your shoulder in the direction you want to go, and sweep the blade in a long wide arc.

3 When the blade gets to the back, lift it out of the water before it gets caught and your boat trips over it.

Reverse Sweep Stroke

As the name implies, the reverse sweep stroke is the exact opposite of the forward sweep. In fact, it is a much more powerful stroke, imparting more turning force, but it should not be used while moving forwards unless to turn around and head back in the other direction, because it will effectively arrest all forward motion.

Start with the paddle blade as far back as you can reach, on the side you want to turn towards. Rotate your head and shoulders in this direction. Drop the blade into the water with the drive face towards the boat this time, and then sweep the blade forwards in the widest arc you can make, until you are pointing the way you want to go, or until the blade is about to hit the front of the boat. Lift the blade out of the water.

Again, keep your bottom arm as straight as you can throughout the stroke. It helps to lean dramatically towards the stroke because it simultaneously lifts the keel and extends your reach.

It should be very easy to turn most canoes through more than 45° with one reverse sweep. You will find that once the blade is out of the water, the canoe will continue to rotate.

❯ *The reverse sweep is a powerful stroke. It turns the boat so well that it halts all forward progress.*

Reverse Sweep Technique

1 Begin the reverse sweep stroke by leaning back and placing the paddle blade in the water near the stern. The drive face of the blade should be pointing towards the boat.

2 Lean your body towards the paddle and sweep the paddle forward in a big arc towards the front of the boat. Use your body, specifically your torso muscles, not your arms to make the stroke.

3 Continue to lean over towards the paddle, and get all of your weight behind the blade as you push it forward to make the turn. Brace your legs against the sides of the boat to help keep your balance.

Draw Stroke

Few people learn to master this way of moving the boat through the water sideways. While you can manage without being very good at it, learning to do it well helps you master many other skills.

Begin by placing the blade in the water as far from the side of the canoe as you can reach, with the drive face pointing towards the boat. Push your top arm out as far as possible so that the paddle shaft is almost vertical. Now lift the edge of the canoe, using your legs, on the side you are making the stroke, and pull the blade straight towards your body. This should pull the boat sideways about 30cm (12in) in an all-purpose boat, less in a longer boat or one with a deep keel.

Do this gently at first because, as the blade approaches the boat, you need to cock your wrist back quickly to rotate the blade through 90°, and slice it away through the water back to its starting position. If you fail to do this and the blade hits the boat, you may fall in or become unbalanced. If you try to stop the stroke before it hits the hull, the same thing will happen. That is why it is important that you give yourself the time to execute the final part of the stroke.

When the blade has sliced out of the water, and is in the starting position, you can turn your wrist so that the paddle faces the boat as before. Then repeat the stroke. If the boat tends to turn rather

⊙ *The draw stroke involves pulling the paddle sideways towards the boat.*

⊙ *Applying a twist to a bow draw can turn the boat and move it sideways.*

than move sideways, it is because the stroke is being made too far towards the front or back of the boat. If the bow turns towards the paddle, move the stroke back a little, or vice versa for the stern. It will improve your skills if you make this happen deliberately; practise doing draw strokes, alternating with the bow or stern pointing forwards.

The draw stroke, also known as a hanging draw support, is very good for giving you support in the event of

a wobble or imminent capsize. When you have some purchase on the water with the blade, level the boat, and pull the boat into position beneath your body.

The technique needs to be practised over and over again, otherwise, by the time you will have thought about it, it will be too late to use it; you need to be able to use it reflexively. Being able to control your boat in three dimensions is very satisfying. Mastering these strokes will really set you on your way as a canoeist.

Draw Stroke Technique

1 Reach out as far to the side as you can, with the blade facing the boat. Bend at the waist to increase your reach. Leaning the boat away from the paddle actually helps, but it is very unstable.

2 Pull the paddle firmly towards you, keeping the blade fully immersed in the water. Continue to lean the boat away from the paddle if you feel confident enough to maintain your balance.

3 Lean the boat back towards the paddle. If your body weight is not inside the boat by the time the blade gets level with the hull, you could fall into the water. Twist the blade 90° and slice away from the boat.

Stern Rudder

The stern rudder, and also the bow rudder, will change the direction of your boat. Both strokes require the boat to be moving in order to be effective.

Sometimes it is desirable to make small direction changes, or to keep a canoe going in a straight line in readiness for a turn. For this, and many of the more advanced skills, the stern rudder is a very useful stroke.

As the term implies, the paddle blade is used as a rudder at the stern of the boat. Place the paddle in the water as for the start of a reverse sweep stroke, with the drive face pointing towards the boat and the paddle shaft at a low angle. Both your arms will probably be fairly straight. If the boat is not moving this will have no effect at all, but if you have some forward momentum the boat will probably turn slightly towards the paddle.

When you move the paddle away from the hull, the turn will become more pronounced; bring it closer to the hull and there will be less effect. By pulling it in towards the boat you may even start to turn the other way, away from the paddle. If you get up to speed, and then place your stern rudder in the water, you

● *The stern rudder is a passive stroke that is used to correct direction and to keep the boat running straight.*

can experiment with pushing and pulling, and get the boat to veer to and fro until it runs out of momentum, without taking the blade out of the water. You will find this a very useful way to get used to the feedback from the paddle.

A handy technique is to approach a landing place perpendicular to the shore, using a stern rudder to keep the boat pointing at the spot where you want to land. Seconds before the bow touches the bank, sweep your stern rudder forwards in a reverse sweep to turn the boat 90° and kill your speed. You will end

● *The canoe needs to be moving for the stern rudder to be effective.*

up stationary and parallel to the shore, close enough to get out with ease.

Always think about the next strokes you need to make. When going forwards followed by a turn, use strokes such as the forward sweep that will not impede your forward motion. If trying to stop and turn, the reverse sweep may be better. Note that the stern rudder does not propel you, and has little effect on your speed except to interrupt your paddling.

Bow Rudder

The bow rudder, unlike the stern rudder, is a very difficult stroke to learn. It is appropriate to mention it now, but you may find it difficult to make it work until you have mastered all the other strokes in this section. It relies on an excellent feel for what the paddle is doing in the water, and the draw stroke skills that have already been covered. The bow rudder is only effective if the boat is already moving forwards.

Place the paddle in the water about 30cm (12in) from the side of the canoe, about level with your knees and with the drive face pointing towards the boat. Experiment, rotating your wrists to turn the blade slightly, but resist any forces that act on the blade in the water. You will

● *A bow rudder while moving fast, requires commitment and a willingness to resist the force of the water against the paddle blade.*

● *Wrapping the top arm around in front of the paddle helps to rotate the paddle blade to face the bow.*

find that there is a position with the blade face almost parallel to the side of the boat in which the boat does not tend to slow or turn, and you cannot feel any pressure on the blade.

Next, turn the blade to face the bow, and the boat will start to turn towards the paddle. Bring your top hand and T-grip back until it is near your opposite shoulder. The more you roll your bottom wrist back to open out the blade, the more you will turn, but there will be a lot of force on the blade and the boat will quickly stop.

Bow Draw

You can increase the effect of the bow rudder by letting the pressure take the blade out, and then pulling it back towards the bow in a modified draw stroke. This is called a bow draw. It is a versatile canoe stroke whether you are moving or stationary. By experimenting, you will find that you can control the boat in many subtle ways, either by going with the water or by opposing it.

Sculling

The sculling strokes are refinements of the basic strokes, and will allow you much more subtle control of your boat.

Sculling Draw

The sculling draw, like the draw stroke, moves the boat sideways. It has the advantage, however, of being more useful in a confined space. For instance, when you are close to a jetty, and need to get even closer, the draw stroke may be difficult to execute. The sculling draw is also a lot less likely to tip you in.

Start with the paddle blade next to your hip, about 20cm (8in) from the boat, the shaft vertical and the drive face towards the hull. Cock your wrist back so that the blade face rotates 20° and opens out a little towards the bow.

Keep the shaft vertical and move the paddle forwards as far as you can, but keep it 20cm (8in) from the boat, and

◉ *You need to put the whole of the blade in the water for a sculling draw. A blade that is only half immersed just won't work at all.*

◉ *Sculling right next to your body, as here, will move the boat sideways. Sculling slightly behind you will turn the boat away from the paddle.*

Sculling Draw Technique

1 With your wrist rolled back, push the blade forwards through the water.

2 Take the stroke as far forwards as is comfortable for you.

3 Now, cock your wrist the other way and bring the blade backwards.

4 Push the blade back to the start position and repeat until the boat moves sideways.

resist its tendency to slice away from the hull. If anything, you will be pulling it inwards, which is where the sideways motion of the boat is generated. When the blade gets as far forward as possible, keep the shaft vertical, rotate your wrist the other way to angle the drive face 20° towards the stern, and pull the blade back as far as you can. At this point, rotate again to push forward, maintaining enough pressure on the blade to keep it equidistant from the boat at all times.

As you move the paddle, the boat will move sideways towards the stroke. It helps to lean towards the paddle and to lift the leading edge of the boat.

Sculling Pry

Reversing the blade angles, so that the pressure is on the outside (back) face, moves the boat sideways away from the paddle in a sculling pry. Like the sculling draw, the sculling pry exerts a continuous sideways force. Unlike the draw, the pry pushes the boat away from the blade. Sculling further forward will pull the boat bow-first in the direction of travel, while sculling further back will bring the stern around first. In this way, you can move and turn the boat at the same time.

Pry Stroke

A pry is a stroke that pushes the blade away from the canoe. It is so-called because it usually involves resting the paddle shaft against the gunwale of the boat, using it as a fulcrum or pivot as you lever the blade up and out. The basic pry is the opposite of the draw stroke, and pushes the boat through the water, away from the paddle.

Start with the blade next to the hull, the drive face in and the shaft in a vertical position. Then jam the paddle shaft against the boat and lever the blade away from you. As with the draw, when the stroke reaches the limit of its motion, you must rotate the blade 90° in order to slice it back to where it started. The sculling pry is a continuous version of the basic pry. It is used to push the boat sideways away from the paddle.

In the same way that a draw stroke can lend support, you can use a pry as a support stroke to lever the high (opposite) side of the boat down if there is going to be an imminent capsize on the side away from the paddle. This is very useful when you remember that you only paddle on one side, and you will not always capsize conveniently towards the paddle.

Using a pry. Although it may be difficult at first, try to look where you are going, and not at the prying blade.

Go carefully when you first start to use pries. Until you have learnt excellent edge control, using your legs and knees, there will be a tendency to overdo it and lever yourself right into the water. You need to balance the boat, so that the power of the stroke is turned into a lateral motion and not a capsizing one.

TIPS
• Proceed cautiously at first.
• Concentrate on keeping the boat level with your legs.
• Experiment with prying at different parts of the boat to get used to the turning effect.
• Look in the direction of the turn and not at the blade or you risk catching the blade on the boat.

Pry Stroke Technique

1 To begin the stroke, wedge the paddle shaft flush against the side of the boat. The blade should be just immersed in the water.

2 Lever the blade away from the boat, bracing your legs against the sides and edging the boat to keep the canoe level in the water.

3 Turn the paddle blade in the water through 90° to slice it back to the start point. Repeat until the boat has moved to face the direction you want.

Low and High Brace

The low and high brace are support or recovery strokes that are used to help you regain your balance when you are about to capsize. All support strokes require a willing suspension of disbelief. It is initially difficult to believe that you can trust most of your weight to a paddle blade, but this is exactly what you must do. The weight that you commit to the paddle is exactly how much support you will get in reaction to it.

Low Brace

The low brace gives support from the back of the blade. Place the blade on the surface with the drive face pointing up. If you are moving, angle the leading edge up slightly to stop it diving. It is usually easier to low brace with the blade just behind you, but the further it can be from the boat while staying fairly flat to the surface, the better the result.

Commit your weight to the blade and it will support you, and stop you from capsizing on that side, until the blade sinks too far into the water to keep it flat. When using the low brace to prevent a capsize, you must use your legs to level the boat before the paddle sinks, then recover the blade. If the boat is moving,

a low brace can be used instead of a stern rudder to turn the boat, while also providing some support.

High Brace

This works on the same principle as the low brace, but with the drive face pointing downward. Because of this, your elbows are below the paddle shaft, which implies that the water is higher than the boat, either because of a wave or because you are in danger of capsizing. In a canoe this means that water will be entering the boat, so it is an extreme measure. The high brace is a powerful stroke, but should be avoided if a low brace is possible because of the

The canoe has tipped over until it is in danger of shipping water, and the paddler will recover using the support of the blade in a low brace.

huge force it exerts on your shoulders, which can lead to serious injury.

As with any support stroke, keep your weight on the paddle until you can right the boat with your legs, then move your body back over the boat. Don't allow the paddle to take your weight if it is above your head because you risk an injury. It is better to capsize and recover by rolling.

Bracing in white water. The recovery is often so extreme that it is almost a roll.

Tandem Manoeuvres

Open canoes are ideally suited to being paddled by two or more canoeists. Tandem paddling removes a lot of the problems of steering and straight paddling. Communication is the key, however, and a constant dialogue is necessary to keep things running smoothly. Usually, the paddler at the back is in command because the back paddler can see what the front paddler is doing, and needs this information. The stern paddler will also have more effect on steering.

When forward paddling, both canoeists should paddle on opposite sides, so there is no need for J-strokes. Concentrate on keeping the strokes in time. This also applies when going back, when the stern paddler will have to look alternately over his shoulder (to check the direction) and back (to keep time with the other paddler).

Turning In Tandem

1 While the canoe is moving forward, the front paddler plants a bow rudder stroke in the water.

2 As the boat turns, the rear paddler uses a forward sweep stroke to maintain the momentum of the turn.

3 The front paddler keeps leaning on the bow rudder, and can if required turn it into a bow draw.

4 The rear paddler can either finish with a stern draw stroke, or can start forward paddling again, as appropriate.

⌃ A tandem turn towards the front off-side can be done while the boat is stationary or going forwards.

To turn a canoe in tandem, a rudder stroke at the back can be combined with a bow draw at the front to bring the boat around quickly. If turning on the spot, the front paddler can do a forward sweep and the back paddler a reverse sweep on the opposite side, or vice versa.

TIPS

• Agree who is in charge before you get into the boat: squabbling about it mid-route is guaranteed to cause you difficulties. If the bow paddler is making the turning decisions, the stern paddler should follow and complement those decisions, and vice versa.
• The strokes of a tandem pair need to complement each other. To understand the importance of each paddler's strokes, it is a useful exercise to spend some practice time swapping positions, so that both paddlers can be aware of the needs of their other half at the opposite end of the boat.

KAYAK AND CANOE ROLLING

Rolling is the art of righting a kayak or canoe unaided while still inside it. Only 20 years ago, any paddler who could complete an Eskimo roll would be regarded as an expert boater. Nowadays, rolling has become a basic skill learnt by almost everybody who goes out in a boat, even before they are very skilled at anything else.

It is possible to roll almost any canoe or kayak that you can grip well enough with your legs to ensure that you do not fall out, but clearly this skill is only of use if the boat will still be paddleable afterwards. There is little point in rolling an open boat without airbags, or a kayak without a spraydeck, because you will not be able to paddle (or indeed, balance) until you have emptied out the water.

Most paddlers learn to roll in a kayak, but there is no technical reason why you cannot learn with a single blade if canoe paddling is your one and only interest. The techniques may be quite different, but the essential principle is just the same.

◐ *An open-boat canoeist finishing a roll in turbulent white water.*

◑ *Preparing to roll an open canoe. This is the typical start position for a canoe roll.*

The History of the Roll

If it was not for the Inuit tribesman, who needed to right his boat without exiting to avoid swimming in icy seas, we might have had to wait a lot longer before rolling caught on.

Righting a capsized boat by rolling, without having to get out, was exclusively a kayak skill until the latter part of the twentieth century. It was invented by the Inuit tribes of sub-Arctic regions who paddled in such extremely cold seas that, had they tried to swim for safety from a capsized kayak, they would have almost certainly died. By wearing a kayaking jacket (tuvilik) of sealskin, laced on to the boat, with only hands and face exposed, the hunters could survive immersion if capsized, provided they could quickly roll up again. For this reason the skill was often called the Eskimo roll, though that term has now been abbreviated to the roll.

The first written account of rolling, by a missionary in 1765, lists about ten different techniques and drills, and is interesting because it cites a flick of the hips as the means used to right the kayak in each case. This trick is the key to effective rolling, and was overlooked by Europeans until as late as 1965.

The first non-Inuit paddler who learnt to roll was probably a curate named Pawlata, a Christian missionary to the Inuit in 1927. The Inuit had a wide variety of advanced rolling techniques that they would practise during the summer months to ensure survival in the freezing winter conditions. The skills Pawlata acquired were very basic and his technique was crude, but he took the idea of rolling back with him to Europe, and the method of kayak rolling known as the Pawlata roll is still used today as a stepping stone

to more involved rolling techniques.

Rolling did not become a viable skill for white water paddling until the mid-1960s and the introduction of the more robust kayaks. Until then, spending any time upside down in white water damaged the kayak. With the advent of fibreglass craft, however, reliable rolling became the goal for any adventurous kayak paddler or decked canoeist. Before long, airbags in open boats in white water made rolling also practical for open canoeists.

Now regarded as an essential skill for anything more advanced than placid water paddling, the roll has been refined to the point that it surpasses even the skills of the Inuit. The latest innovations in boat design have led to a degree of

◗ *Rolling up in a capsized sea kayak, using the screw roll technique.*

⬆ *Although the head should normally come up last, this paddler is focussed on the dangerous hole he is trapped in, and needs to see what is going.*

⬢ *Another very dynamic roll in super-aerated white water.*

control and body fit that could barely have been imagined even a decade ago, and this has aided the development of some of the rolling skills that follow.

In the chapter that follows, we look at how to learn to roll. The hip-flick concept is constantly reiterated because it is a key element in any roll. Described thereafter are a number of different rolling styles, in roughly the order of difficulty that dictates how they should be tackled. Conspicuous by their absence are many of the "extended grip" techniques that were at one time the most usual starting point. These are not so relevant now that better rolling methods have been developed.

Learning to Roll

The indispensable, essential roll may look quite daunting, and even dangerous, but once you have grasped the basic technique, it is actually surprisingly easy.

The best place to learn to roll is in warm, clean, calm water, where a helper or instructor is able to stand waist-deep beside your boat. A swimming pool is often the best place, although repeatedly capsizing in chlorinated water may become unpleasant. If it is possible to learn in warm sea or fresh water, do so.

Unlike the majority of paddling skills, rolling is not particularly reliant on feedback from the paddle. Instead, you must master a special sequence of actions that need to be timed correctly. As with learning to juggle, each action flows on to the next. With regular practice it becomes second nature. You just think "Roll!", and you are up.

There are a few key tips of which you need to be aware before you start to practise rolling. First, successful rolling is never about heaving yourself up with the paddle. Second, the point of the exercise

RULES OF ROLLING — 5 KEY TIPS

• Never try to get your body up out of the water first. Concentrate on righting the boat with your hips and legs.
• Your head should always be the last part of your body to emerge out of the water.
• Go with the flow. As a general rule, always roll up on the downstream side in moving water, or on the upwave side if you are sideways on to a wave in the surf.
• Have a sense of urgency, and roll quickly, as soon as you can. If it does not work, switch sides straight away because you are probably turning the wrong way.
• If you nearly succeed with a screw roll, it is the perfect moment to dive into a reverse screw roll the other way. The reverse screw roll is nearly always the best exit from a convoluted screw roll, but not vice versa.

is to right the boat, not get your head out of the water. Third, the more of you that is in the water, the more support you will get from your natural buoyancy, so right the boat first, then let your body follow. Your head will always come out last.

Initially, your desire to breathe and perhaps your determination to succeed will make you try to get your head up out of the water. This is quite natural. Your instincts and reflexes are programmed to get your head above water at all costs. You need to stop being a human in a boat, and imagine yourself as a different creature with a hull instead of legs.

The whole principle of rolling is that, with a little support from the paddle (in the manner of a high or low brace or a sculling technique), you will be able to turn the boat up the right way using your legs. Once the boat is righted, it is a simple matter for you to sit upright and paddle away. But you must right the boat before you can afford to worry about getting your body out of the water.

There are different ways of rolling, and which one you use should be decided by your position under the water, and where your paddle has ended up. It is definitely worth trying to learn all the techniques described here, but the best roll to master first is the screw roll. This is the one roll that no paddler can do without; in fact, many paddlers don't ever learn anything else.

⊙ A paddler sets up for a reverse screw roll to avoid a capsize situation.

⊙ Rolling up on the downstream side. The boat is righted with the hips and legs.

⊙ As the boat rolls up, the body barely moves and the head comes out last.

Kayak Rolling Drills

The best way to become proficient at rolling is to practise the following six drills. The drills are aimed at beginners, and will take you through each stage, building your confidence and improving your technique until you are ready to attempt the screw roll, which is the one key roll that no paddler can do without.

The fundamental principle of rolling is that you can right the boat by flicking it upright with your hips. This movement is known as the hip flick, or snap, and it is the most important part of any roll. In fact, the motion really comes from the waist. If you bend rapidly to one side, your body will stay still and the boat will twist the other way. That is the secret of rolling.

It is extremely difficult to roll a boat if you do not fit it properly. If borrowing a boat, try to acquire some padding in the form of foam or a purpose-made padding kit. Make sure there is a footrest, too, because it is difficult to brace without one. And do not forget your spraydeck!

Drill 1: Familiarization

This drill helps counter confusion when you are upside down, but you will need an experienced guide to assist you. The helper should stand beside the boat in waist-deep water. You sit in your kayak, and put your hands by your sides. Then capsize, and your helper will grasp the far side of the boat and pull you upright. Do this until you feel completely comfortable, and then progress to the next stage.

◔ *(Top) An underwater view of a screw roll. The paddler bends his trunk to get his head near the surface, but he stays in the boat until it is righted.*

◔ *(Above) An underwater view of a reverse screw roll. The paddler is about to start the roll by sweeping the paddle blade forwards towards the camera.*

Familiarization

1 Start off sitting upright with your hands on either side of the boat. Next, capsize towards your helper.

2 Once you are upside down, the helper reaches over the boat and flips it upright. Do not try to move your arms and legs.

3 After a few attempts, you will find that you are not disorientated by flipping 360°, and can progress to drill 2.

Drill 2: Hip Flick

The next step is to hold on to the pool rail or a partner's hands or paddle for support, and practise righting the boat with the hip flick. This allows you to concentrate on the flick movement, without worrying about holding your paddle.

Practise rotating your hips from side to side, making sure that you feel quite free and will not hurt yourself. Get a good grip on whatever you are using for support, capsize and relax your arms so that they are not supporting your weight. Bend your body up towards your hands as far as possible without using your arms.

You must now try to turn the boat up the right way using your hips and legs, without trying to lift your body out of the water. Remember, no matter what else happens, keep your head in the water until the boat is upright and capable of supporting your weight.

Hip Flick Practice Using the Pool Rail or Side

1 Holding on to the pool rail, position your body just under the water surface rather than hanging straight downwards.

2 Flick the boat upright with your knees and hips, leaving your head in the water. Repeat several times.

Hip Flick Practice with a Helper

1 Holding on to the hands of your helper, practise flicking the boat upright using your legs. Keep your head submerged.

2 At the end of the manoeuvre, the boat should be completely righted but your head should still be in the water, as here.

◔ *Practise the rolling drills as often as necessary to build your confidence.*

Drill 3: Using a Float

The next step is to repeat the same technique, using a swimming float or life jacket that affords much less support. This will show you whether you are really righting the boat with a hip flick from the waist, or whether you are relying too much on your arms. When you can right yourself using only a float, it is time to try rolling with a paddle.

TIPS

- Practise using whatever resources you have at your disposal on the day.
- Never practise alone: there should be someone to help in an emergency.
- If using a fixed platform, make sure you can't get stuck underneath it.
- If you are not able to practise with a swimming float you can skip drill 3, but make sure your other drills emphasize righting the boat only with the hips and legs, and not the arms.
- Do each drill perfectly ten times before you move on.
- If you are not proficient at one of the drills, go back two stages and start again from there.

Drill 4: Bow Rescue

This final confidence-building exercise is excellent rolling practice, and a useful technique when recovering from an accidental capsize if you fail to roll or lose your paddle.

First, capsize. When you are under the water, tuck your body forward into a safe position. Bang your hands on the bottom or sides of the boat to attract attention. Then push your hands up as far as possible out of the water on both sides of the boat, and sweep them forward and back to indicate that you are hoping to be rescued. A rescuer in a boat should now approach, their bow touching the side of your boat. One of your sweeping arms will make contact with the rescuer's boat. Grab it with both hands, and then use a hip flick to recover.

❯ *The bow rescue technique will save you from an uncomfortable swim in the event of a rolling mishap, which can happen to anyone from time to time.*

Bow Rescue Technique

1 The paddler is capsizing and unable to roll. This is a problem situation and the paddler needs to be helped.

2 Upside down, the paddler bangs on the boat to attract attention, then sweeps his hands to and fro on both sides of the boat.

3 A rescuer approaches and slowly moves the bow of their boat into the path of the sweeping hands.

4 On making contact with the rescue boat, the upside-down paddler grips the bow with both hands.

5 He then uses a hip flick to right the boat, putting as little weight as possible on the rescuer's boat.

6 The paddler then sits up, ready to retrieve his paddle and continue with the trip down the river.

Drill 5: Using a Paddle with an Instructor Helping

Now it is time to try to use one of the rolls described in the following pages. Some older books suggest learning to roll with a different grip on the paddle from the one you normally have when upright. This may have some advantages, but modern boats and paddles are not really suitable. And remember, rolling relies on the hip flick concept, not on the paddle. If you cannot roll using your normal paddling style, there is something wrong with your hip flick, and there is no point in practising a bad technique masquerading as a success.

Begin by asking someone to stand in shallow water and help you, and then decide which of the rolls you are going to try. For the screw roll, which most people learn first, place the paddle in the set-up position and capsize.

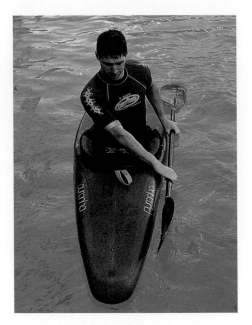

◉ *The set-up position for a screw roll. This is the position you will need to get into under water, from which to start.*

As you bring the paddle into position to start the roll, the helper will take hold of the blade and keep it on the surface while still allowing you to move it. You can then roll up according to your chosen method, with your helper's primary task being to ensure that you will make it if it goes wrong, and to work out whether the way you are moving the paddle is helping or hindering you. It is no use you trying to work out what you did with your paddle, because you were under the water, holding your breath, and you don't know what it is supposed to feel like anyway. An experienced helper will be able to tell you what to concentrate on. The most common problems are that the paddler is pulling on the paddle with their arms, which never works; or that the paddler is sweeping the blade correctly but the blade is angled in a way that doesn't offer much support.

Rolling with Help Using a Paddle

1 From the starting point of the set-up position, capsize with your helper standing on the other side from your paddle set-up.

2 The helper can give you a push to make sure you capsize quickly.

3 Bring the paddle into the start position. The helper takes hold of the paddle blade to add a little support.

4 Get your body as near to the surface of the water as you can without needing any support from the helper. Do not use the paddle for support.

5 Start your roll from this position, with the helper holding on to the blade but providing only as much support as is absolutely necessary.

6 The helper will be ready to catch you if you fall back into the water, but with a bit of luck you will finish the roll perfectly on your own, like this.

Drill 6: Using a Paddle Unaided

This is the stage that you are aiming for on the open water, but for now you still need to have a helper standing by to flip you up if required. Do not try to visualize the whole roll but get into the correct position, and then flick the boat upright. Everything else will happen naturally. If it does not, either your set-up is not right or your hip flick is not good enough: keep practising the early drills.

TIPS

• Get into the start position, pause, then do the hip flick: don't think about anything else.
• If it doesn't work at first, go back to basics and make sure you can do drills 1 to 5 in turn. Try drill 6 again.
• Ask your helper to guide your paddle blade through the sweep.
• If you succeed, well done, but make sure you are rolling using your body and not your paddle, or else the roll won't work when you need it.

❯ *Rolling an inflatable kayak, or "duckie", relies more on technique because the boat is less secure than a decked kayak.*

Rolling Unaided Using a Paddle

1 First you need to capsize, ready to roll on your own. You may find the capsize quite slow. Just keep the paddle close to the boat and wait.

2 Rolling up for the first time. The paddle has gone very deep without support from the helper, but the boat is coming up and the head is still in the water.

3 Completing the roll. Because the body language was good, the roll has worked despite the poor paddle action. This has been a very good first attempt.

Screw Roll

This is the most common practical roll of all. Many very proficient paddlers find they can get along using this as their only roll.

Begin the roll by placing the paddle in the water, along the side of the boat, with the water blade at the bow. The water blade is the blade in the water, used for the rolling stroke, while the other is the air blade. If you are rolling up on your right, the water blade will be the right blade. Tuck your body forward and up, facing the surface of the water on the side that the paddle is on. Next, push the air blade up out of the water as far as possible and then wrap your back arm around the hull of the boat.

This might push the water blade down below the surface, but it does not really matter. Try to keep the blade as near to the surface as possible. This starting position virtually guarantees you a good blade presentation as you roll.

◔ *Once underwater, tuck your body forwards and up, facing the water.*

Sweep the blade away from the boat, without pulling down on the blade. As the blade comes to the perpendicular, bend from the waist to throw your upper body into the water, and continue to sweep backwards. Continue with the bend – do not stop. You will come up leaning back, with the blade near the back of its arc.

◔ *Push the air blade up out of the water as far as you can.*

The screw roll is very reliable because the blade gives you plenty of lift for a long time. It is also a good roll to use if you are tired. However, the set-up from which you start is time-consuming and you rarely capsize with your blades in this position. The final position is not possible in a weight-sensitive, modern short boat.

Screw Roll Technique

1 To practise the screw-roll, set up with your top arm straight and the paddle along the side of the boat like this.

2 Capsize on the paddle side of the boat. Wait until you are completely upside down and the boat has stopped moving.

3 Wrap your back arm (which is on the left here) around the boat. You should still be holding the paddle with both hands.

4 Sweep the paddle blade in a big sweeping arc across the surface of the water, reaching as far as you can.

5 Arch your back to try to throw your head downwards, and right the boat with your legs only.

6 Keeping your head down in the water, continue to sweep the blade back until you are sure you are upright again.

Reverse Screw Roll

This is a favourite with freestyle paddlers and surfers because it begins on the back deck, which is where you will often end up after being hit by a big wave. Surprising as it may seem, you can still find yourself in the set-up position after falling over your blade while trying to do something dynamic.

Start by lying on your back as shown, and wrap your back (water blade) arm around in front of your face so that the paddle lies along the deck. Remember to keep your water blade to the stern and your air blade to the bow, which is the hard part of this roll. Now, capsize in that position so that you are lying face down in the water.

Next, twist your body out to that side, pushing the water blade out as far as you can, and try to get the air blade up and out of the water. Bending from the waist, use your body to sweep the water blade

forward. As this happens, snap your body downwards to the right of the boat. You will have to cock your water-blade wrist back slightly to stop the blade diving during the stroke. Continue the sweep forwards, and you will emerge on the front deck, with lots of support from the paddle, which will now be beneath you.

Since you may often find yourself in the start position by accident, you may as well use this roll. It is immensely powerful if you do it correctly, and you can get away with rolling at a bad time or in a bad place. Be careful, though, because this roll exposes your face to submerged objects. From a freestyle point of view, lying on the back deck in a big water feature will either ruin your manoeuvre, give you a good thrashing, or both.

❯ *Set-up position for the reverse screw roll. This is always your starting point.*

Reverse Screw Roll Technique

1 From your set-up position, wind your paddle up above your head and capsize on the paddle side of the boat.

2 Use your paddle to sweep the water blade away from the boat.

3 It helps to wrap the air blade arm around the hull of the boat like this as you sweep the water blade.

4 Drive the water blade forward using your body, and flick the boat upright with both of your legs.

5 Bend your head and body downwards as you come back up to the surface of the water.

6 When you come out of the roll you should be leaning forward with your head tucked down. You are ready to paddle off.

Put Across Roll

Also known as the combat roll, the put across roll is far more solid than the previous two rolls, but unfortunately you really need to learn the others first. Once you've mastered all three, you'll probably find yourself using the put across (combat) roll in combination with some elements of the others, according to your circumstances.

Begin by pushing the air blade out of the water. Swing the water blade away from the boat until it's as perpendicular to the kayak as possible. Do not lean forwards or back, just bend sideways until your body is as near the surface as possible. Now, do a hip snap – hurl your upper body down into the water, and snap the boat upright with your legs. Keep your head down, face down.

If your body was bent to the left at the start, you just have to bend it as far to the right as you can, and as fast as you can.

Do not do anything with the paddle except keep the drive face down, and do not move fore or aft. You will be up in a sudden snap, on a really solid brace.

It is quite hard to keep your paddle near the surface for this roll, but it does not matter. Even coming up on a vertical blade is acceptable, and often puts you in an excellent position for paddling again.

This is an exceptionally quick, powerful roll, and enables you to stay in the centre of the boat. It is good for a position in a hole, and means you are ready for another move if freestyle paddling. Since the paddle position is not critical, you can roll straightaway without having to flail around underwater. The power of the roll is especially suited to today's wide white water boats, in which you need to do the roll quickly or you will not succeed. You do need quite a bit of sideways flexibility, but with practice that is achievable.

You can modify this freestyle roll to make it a super combat roll. Just lean ridiculously far forwards, so that your nose is on the deck. Keep your arms and paddle forward, too, and do the roll across the front deck without sitting up until you are upright. It is more of an upper body snap than a hip flick, but if you can do the freestyle version you will not find it hard to master this one. It is nearly as powerful, and protects your face from any impact in shallow water.

If you are in a position to start a screw roll, the combat roll is just the same without the sweeping of the paddle, and with the body modified to move across the boat only. If, on the other hand, you are on the back deck, as for a reverse screw roll (this is much more common), then you can begin as for a reverse screw and convert to a put across roll as you get the paddle to the perpendicular.

Put Across (Combat) Roll Technique

1 Begin from the same set-up position as for a screw roll. Capsize with the paddle along the side of the boat.

2 When you are completely upside down and the boat has stopped moving, push the paddle up above the water.

3 Bend your body up sideways, so that you are as near to the surface as you possibly can be.

4 Plant the paddle so that the drive face is pointing down, then bend your body aggressively down on the other side.

5 Concentrate on levelling the boat by bracing your legs. Your head will come out of the water as the boat levels off.

6 Finish upright, and keep both your hands on the paddle if you are not practising in a swimming pool.

Hand Rolling

The following rolls are quite sophisticated, and can only be approached when you have acquired all the preceding skills.

The front and back deck hand rolls have a variety of benefits, the main one being that they will hone and fine-tune your paddling skills for more advanced future techniques. Hand rolls are a useful and advanced skill. Many instructors would claim that you should never have to use a hand roll, but it can save you a long and unpleasant swim if you are unfortunate enough to drop your paddle.

Furthermore, it is an excellent training exercise to ensure that your roll is not over-reliant on the paddle. This is a weakness in many people's rolling technique, and can mean that when tired or in very turbulent water their roll will fail them just when they need it most. It is a good idea, therefore, to work on a solid hand roll in both the forms described

here, thereby improving your technique for the main types of paddle rolls.

The best way to learn to hand roll is to build up to using less and less support. In the same way that you built up the six drills when you first learnt to roll, practise initially by holding on to the pool rail or a partner's hands, focusing on putting less and less weight on the hands and righting the boat just with your hips. Then try with a flotation device in your hands, and after that, a swimming float, until you can right yourself with your only support being your cupped hands in the water.

Back Deck Hand Roll

This is the easiest way to hand roll. Lean back and out to the side as you would for a reverse screw roll, and reach out to the same side with both hands, palms facing downwards. Bend up to the surface as much as you can. When you are fully

extended in this position, sweep your hands downwards to lend support, and simultaneously hip flick as hard as you can. Arch your body back as you do so, keeping your centre of gravity as near to the boat as you can. Since your top arm will not be able to remain in the water for the whole move, throw it across to the other side as you come up, and this will help balance the boat in the slightly tenuous finish position.

The back deck hand roll is easier to perform in many boats than the front deck variant, mainly because lying on the back deck gives you such a low centre of gravity. It is possible to succeed even if you are quite lazy about it. However, as with the screw roll, the finish position of the back deck hand roll is rather unstable, and the slightly more difficult front deck hand roll will be much more practical in a genuine emergency situation.

Back Deck Hand Roll Technique

1 Start the manoeuvre by capsizing into the water, leaning back a little, with your body leaning to one side.

2 Keep your body turned to face the water as you go over.

3 Maintaining this position under the water, reach out to the side with your cupped hands.

4 Sweep your hands downwards and keep them together, and use hip rotation to right the boat.

5 Arch your back and throw your top arm across the boat for balance as the boat rights itself.

6 Finish the roll by leaning back on the deck, with a hand in the water on each side of the kayak.

Front Deck Hand Roll

This very useful hand roll relies on the hip flick, mobility and timing. It utilizes the technique used for the put across roll.

Bend up to the side to bring your head as close to the surface as possible, but do not lean back. Rotate your upper body so that you are facing downwards. Reach out to the side as far away from the boat as you can, hands cupped and palms down. Then sweep the hands down into the water using your torso as well as your arms, and hip flick aggressively. This time you will come up with both hands still in the water on the same side of the boat, but it may help to switch one hand across right at the end to help you keep your balance.

With this and the back deck hand roll, even more than rolling with your paddle, it is essential that your head stays in the water until the roll is effectively finished. This demands commitment and a good

level of flexibility, but the roll will never work if you have to support the weight of your upper body as it gets out of the water – your hands simply do not provide enough lift.

It is fairly easy to hand roll narrow boats such as those used for slalom and polo, and some fast sea kayaks. However, the modern general-purpose kayak is wide and flat-bottomed, and is generally hard to right only using your hands. It is best, therefore, to learn in a pool using an easy boat such as the polo kayak.

With either the front or back deck hand rolls, you will find that the more complex hand movement is better than slamming the hands straight down. Imagine that you were swimming in a "doggy paddle" style: this helps you to reach out further and sweep a more efficient arc. In addition, if one hand paddles slightly after the other, this extends the amount of time that you have support during the roll. Try sweeping

◔ Underwater shot of the start position for the front and back deck hand rolls.

the top arm first, which makes sense, since as you roll up the top arm won't be able to reach the water. Alternatively, you can try sweeping the bottom arm first and getting in three strokes with your hands (bottom, top, bottom). Remember to hip flick as soon as the first stroke gets a hold of the water.

Front Deck Hand Roll Technique

1 Start the maneouvre by turning your whole body to one side of the boat to face the water and capsizing.

2 As soon as you are underwater, you need to reach out as far as you can away from the boat.

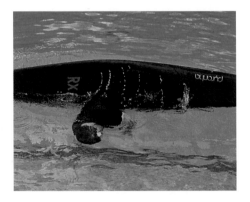

3 Sweep both your hands downwards and hip flick hard to rotate the boat.

4 Keep both your hands moving downwards and continue the hip flick for as long as you can.

5 Drop your head forward on to the spraydeck (spray skirt).

6 Complete the roll with your head and body tucked forward, as shown. Your arms should be wrapped around the boat.

Canoe Rolling

The technique for rolling a decked canoe would be essentially the same as for a kayak, but using a canoe paddle means you can only use the normal rolls on one side. Many canoe paddlers change their grip if they need to roll on the other side, but this has several disadvantages, especially in turbulent water. It would be very easy to lose the paddle, and a better solution is to learn a cross-bow roll. In this roll you flip over the paddle blade in mid-roll to keep it flat on the water, a useful skill that eradicates much of the vulnerability of canoe paddling. If you are learning to roll an open boat, some of the positions are a little different because it is not possible to reach over the hull of the boat. It is also difficult to finish the roll because the boat is very wide and unstable when it is on its side.

◔ *Underwater view of the start position for a canoe roll.*

Most open canoe paddlers use a roll that is somewhere between a reverse screw roll and a put across roll, because to finish leaning forwards is a more tenable position in an open boat. If you are paddling a decked canoe, any kayak

◔ *Rolling up: the canoe is on its side but the paddler's body is underwater.*

roll would be suitable. Once you are confident rolling on your "on" side, start experimenting with a cross-bow roll. Visualize the start and finish positions. You will have to flip the blade over at some point, or you'll get twisted up!

Canoe Rolling Technique

1 You can set up for a canoe roll with the paddle straight in front of you. Lay the blade of the paddle flat on the deck.

2 Capsize your boat and reach out to one side with your paddle. Extend the paddle as far as you can.

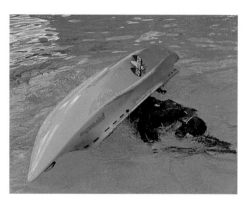

3 Use hip rotation to roll the boat upright. Keep the paddle extended as you roll the boat towards the surface.

4 Press down in the water with the paddle and lean forward as your body comes up out of the water.

5 Tuck your head down low and keep holding the paddle in the water in this rather unstable final part of the roll.

6 When you finish the roll you should be upright, with the paddle in your hand. You are ready to paddle off.

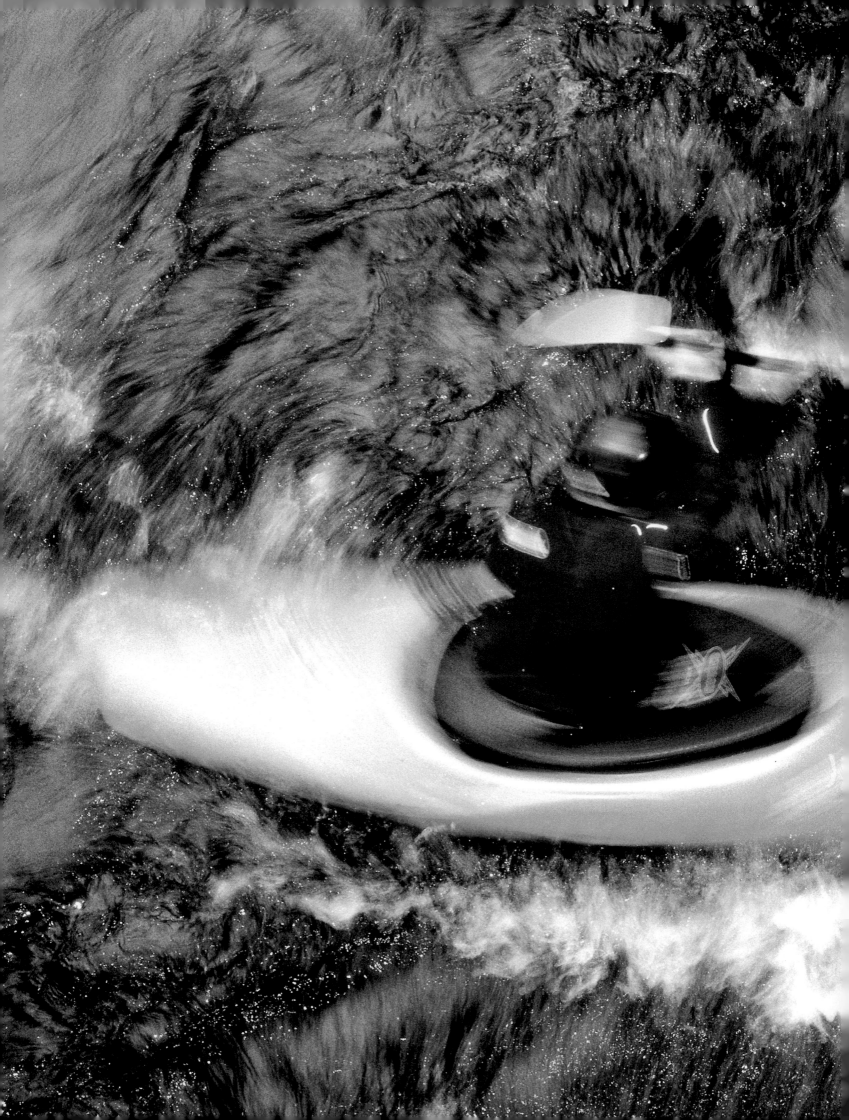

3 ON TO MOVING WATER

WHITE WATER PADDLING

Kayakers and canoeists with an adventurous streak gravitate towards white water paddling. The plastic revolution and the subsequent trend towards short boats have made the turbulent waters of steep rivers and creeks accessible to more people, and spawned the explosion of white water sport that emerged in the late twentieth century.

But what is white water, sometimes described as wild water? The terms describe any water, usually in a river, that has rapids with fast flowing sections where the shape of the river bed causes waves and currents that are chaotic and unpredictable. When the turbulence is pronounced, the water becomes aerated, as if air is being vigorously beaten into the water, creating its white and bubbly appearance.

A fairly mild current or a small wave is enough to cause problems for a paddler without experience of moving water. Once you understand the behaviour of the water, however, it is possible to cope, and indeed play, with white water rapids that look terrifying to the uninitiated. There is always an element of danger though. A moment's loss of concentration could prove fatal if the proper precautions are not observed.

White water river features demand concentration and proficient paddling skills.

An open-boat canoeist and two kayakers navigate their way around a white water river.

White Water Hydrology

Rapids have a relatively small number of components that always behave in much the same way. Once you can identify and understand these components you are well on the way to being able to master white water paddling.

When you look at a rapid, try not to see it as a whole. The non-paddler looks at white water as one big chaotic mass, when it is in fact made up of separate areas of water that are all fairly constant in their behaviour.

Currents

The water in a river flows predominantly downstream, but there are some parts moving faster than others, and sometimes water even moves upstream. Water in the centre of the river flows quite a bit faster

◉ *A medium-volume and steep white water rapid, Grade (Class) 4.*

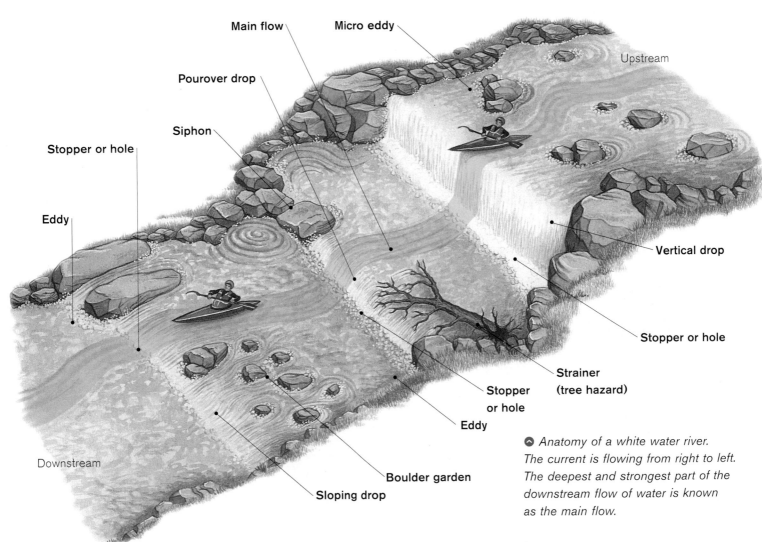

Main flow
Micro eddy
Pourover drop
Siphon
Stopper or hole
Eddy
Upstream
Vertical drop
Stopper or hole
Strainer (tree hazard)
Stopper or hole
Eddy
Boulder garden
Sloping drop
Downstream

◔ *Anatomy of a white water river. The current is flowing from right to left. The deepest and strongest part of the downstream flow of water is known as the main flow.*

than water near the banks because of friction with the bank, and because the river is generally deeper in the middle than the shallow margins.

As the river goes around a corner, the fastest part of the current will move towards the outside of the bend. There will still be a zone of slower moving water right next to the outside bank, but it will be narrower, and the slow zone on the inside will be consequently wider.

If the river goes round a very sharp bend, the water cannot flow smoothly around it. This means that the fastest part of the current will collide with the bank on the outside of the bend, and then rebound and continue downstream. Aim to stay in the slower part, which will move in a much more predictable way.

A kayaker reaches over a breaking wave and punches his way through.

Paddling in a large eddy on a pool-drop river. Although the paddler is in relatively calm, or slack, water, it still swirls and moves around him.

Eddies

If the bank protrudes, a rock breaks the surface, or there is a sharp corner, the water will flow around it and re-circulate upstream to form a sheltered area behind the protrusion or corner. This is called an eddy. It can be flat and calm, or it can rotate strongly, depending on the shape of the feature and the strength of the current. All but the most savagely swirling eddies are good places for kayaks and canoes to rest, regroup, or look for the best route downstream.

Green Water V-shapes

When you look at a rapid you can see that the water flowing between the rocks forms a green water V-shape with its apex pointing downstream. This shows you the path of the deepest and least turbulent current. You can paddle down these Vs, and they are usually the safest route. If this feature is a downstream V, then the V-shaped wakes caused by the rocks are upstream Vs. An upstream V has an obstruction or shallow water at its apex, and should usually be avoided by taking the middle of the downstream V.

The waves that form on either side of the V will meet at the apex and fold over each other to form what is known as a folded or V wave. Since your boat may capsize if you plunge directly into a folded wave, it is sometimes better to leave the V before you hit the apex.

Waves and Hydraulics

If the water flows over a ledge or rock on the bottom of the river, it will cause a disturbance on the surface. What this disturbance looks like to the paddler depends on the shape of the rock, and the depth of water flowing over it.

The more powerful the vertical re-circulation of a water feature, the more it will tend to hold a buoyant object, such as a boat, preventing it from passing through and carrying on downstream. Some people try to differentiate between wave types, but they are all similar phenomena with a profile that varies according to the velocity of the current and the resistance it meets.

When a hydraulic becomes powerful enough to hold a boat, it is often called a stopper or a hole. In extreme cases they can even re-circulate a swimmer. An unbroken wave can also stop a boat if it is big and steep enough, but because it has no component moving upstream, it will never hold a swimmer.

Sometimes the energy of a hydraulic water feature means that instead of one wave, there will be a whole series of them, getting progressively smaller as you go downstream. This is called a wave train, and is usually a bouncy but safe line to take down a rapid. The waves are nearly always pyramidal rather than river wide, and you will get a drier ride by paddling over the corners of waves, so avoiding the deeper middle.

Falls

These are a more dramatic example of the previous phenomena of waves and hydraulics. Where the river drops dramatically, the water will hit the bottom

and rebound upwards. What it does then is dependent on the depth and the steepness of the drop. The more re-circulation and the longer the towback, the more difficult it is for the boater to escape the clutches of the hydraulic.

Back-cut Drops

Certain geological features allow falls to erode in such a way that the water re-circulates behind, as well as downstream of the falls. This forms a double hydraulic from which it may be almost impossible to escape.

Cushions

Where the current rebounds directly off an object in its path, some of the water is forced upwards and some upstream. This forms what is known as a cushion (pillow). Far from being hazardous, these features will usually prevent you from colliding with rocks and walls. However, they can still capsize the unwary, and you should always approach them with caution.

Running a Downstream V

1 When approaching a rapid, look between the rocks and you will see a green water V shape, or "downstream V".

2 A downstream V is where the currents flowing around the rocks converge. This is the least turbulent part of the current.

3 The best route is usually to paddle down the apex of the V, as if it were an arrow pointing out the safest line.

4 There may be extremely turbulent water at the very apex of the V, if it is formed by two waves, as is the case here.

5 Even if the water looks fierce at the apex, this will still be your best route. The water at either side is much worse.

6 This paddler is safely through the V. Downstream Vs rarely point to anything nasty, but be aware that they can.

⏷ *On enormous white water the severity of water features is magnified.*

Boils and Seams

Water sometimes wells up from the bottom of the river as it rises to find its way downstream. This forms a feature that would look to a fish's eye like a mushroom, but appears on the surface as an area of elevated, bubbly water that moves outwards from the centre and down at the edges. This is called a boil. Where two or more boils meet, the join, also known as the seam, can be quite accentuated. It can be powerful enough to suck down a swimmer or even an entire boat, but in all but the biggest water this is usually only temporary, and both swimmer and boat will resurface without difficulty after a few seconds.

Whirlpools

The whirlpool is perhaps the most evocative white water feature, but it is also over-rated. It is not nearly as exciting or as dangerous as it seems: only on enormous white water will the whirlpool have the power to do anything more than snatch at the boat, and cause a bit of a wobble, although for paddlers new to white water they are best avoided. Whirlpools occur in areas of adjoining, extremely different phenomena, where there is a high current differential – for instance, along the boundary between an eddy and a strong current. Whirlpools are, unusually, rarely stable features, and they tend to appear at the top of such a boundary and whirl downstream for a few seconds before disappearing altogether.

TIPS FOR THE UNWARY

With the exception of whirlpools, the aforementioned white water features will be static on the rapid. The actual water is moving, but features such as waves, holes, and eddies will be standing still. If the river is higher than its usual level, it may begin to surge a little so that the features constantly change slightly in appearance in a rhythmic cycle, but they still will not move much. Because of this, a white water rapid is very predictable to an experienced boater, and in this chapter we will show how to make the best use of these static forms.

If the river has flooded badly and its course has completely altered, there may be some visibly moving features. Since the river bed and the banks will not have eroded to provide a smooth passage for the current, there will be some instability that causes waves to move around and to surge, explode and disappear. This is quite rare, however and is, in any case, a scenario that is best avoided because of its unpredictability and the likelihood of other dangers, such as trees, debris and low bridges.

⏷ *Probably one of the biggest whirlpools ever captured on camera.*

Grading Rivers

It is vitally important that you know how to accurately assess a white water river, and how to fully appreciate someone else's verdict on its safety level. In very extreme cases, it could be the difference between life and death. Always make sure you know your grades.

Grading or classifying white water rivers is essential if you are to assess their severity, and hence their suitability, for your level of paddling. There is a widely accepted international system

⊙ *A group of paddlers getting out to scout a Grade (Class) 4 rapid on an otherwise Grade 2 or 3 section of river.*

available to all paddlers. However, it is a subjective system that can be open to misinterpretation. As in other areas of paddling, what really counts is your own experience of rivers and your ability to judge a particular river for yourself.

Grades of River

Grade (Class) 1 This is flat water. If the water is moving at all, it has so little energy that the currents can be ignored and they will not affect the boat unduly. Grade 1 rivers are suitable for beginners unless extreme weather has affected the water conditions – for example, if heavy rain has caused flooding.

Grade 2 There may be water currents strong enough to prevent you paddling upstream, or through waves and eddies, but whichever route you take, the rapid will be safe if you have good basic paddling skills.

Grade 3 The waves, currents and eddies will be more pronounced, and there may be obstructions and/or drops that necessitate a particular route down the rapid in order to remain safe and in control of the boat. On Grade 3 water, the safe route should always be obviously visible to the experienced paddler while on his way down the rapid.

Grade 4 There is a safe route down the rapid, but it is not obvious from the boat. The size of the waves and the drops, and the complexity of the rapid, usually dictate that the paddler must first inspect it from the bank in order to plan a safe line and remain in control.

Grade 5 The size and severity of the features, and the complexity of the rapid, has increased to the point where, although there may be a best line through, even that route is not entirely safe, and the paddler can expect to lose control. The rapid is so turbulent and powerful that it is dangerous even for the highly experienced, skilled paddler. Often, swimming in this type of water would result in injury or drowning.

Grade 6 This has always been defined as the upper limit of practicality. There is no safe line to take through the water, and to swim would prove fatal.

⊙ *A big volume Grade 3 rapid such as this calls for experienced handling.*

This fairly straightforward rapid is Grade 4 because of the volume and severity of the water.

Is the System Perfect?

Over time, as boats and skills have constantly improved, many rapids that were once Grade 6 have become widely regarded as a less severe Grade 5; many Grade 4 rapids are now classed as Grade 3, and so on. These revisions make for some confusion in the system.

A number of paddlers have modified the international grading system in an attempt to improve it. Some use a + or − symbol to create more increments, so that 3+ means a difficult Grade 3 river and 5− means a relatively straightforward Grade 5. Some paddlers prefer to add a letter, so that the number indicates the difficulty of paddling the rapid and the letter the level of danger. So 5a would mean "Incredibly hard, but if you swim you will be fine," and 4d would mean "Fairly hard but any kind of mistake would be very dangerous."

None of these alternative, modified systems has gained universal acceptance, however. The original system may have its problems, but everyone understands it, and it gives a good indication of what you can expect to find. The most important point is that you are able to look at a rapid and accurately assess it, knowing the likely consequences of tackling it given your paddling ability and that of the rest of your group.

Tackling White Water

Before you attempt to tackle white water, you must understand the river grading system. If you are new to paddling rapids, do not attempt anything over Grade 2, particularly until you have learnt to roll. As you gain confidence, you can build up to more difficult rapids, but it should be a progressive development. You will also need all the strokes that will be outlined in this section. Being able to roll well is important as you are likely to capsize, but you are unlikely to roll successfully every time (initially, at least), so be prepared for a swim. Above all, be confident: an anxious boater is never a good boater. Facing and overcoming challenges is part of any adventure sport, but you should not attempt anything if you are not comfortable with the possible outcome.

This massive waterfall is ungradeable because of its power. To run it would probably result in death: the paddler's skill and route would make no difference.

WHITE WATER EQUIPMENT

The minimum equipment you need for tackling white water will include a boat, paddle, spraydeck (spray skirt), if paddling in a kayak, flotation device and helmet. You should also have a throw-line, and a knife that can be used to cut the throw-line in an emergency. Many people paddle with only the minimum amount of equipment, and find their paddling all the more enjoyable for not being weighed down with extraneous items, some of which they are unlikely to ever need.

On the other hand, there are many other pieces of equipment that can be useful, important or even essential, depending on the conditions you are likely to encounter on the water. In the following chapter, we outline the types of equipment that are commonly used by white water paddlers today, and discuss when they are required and why. Deciding how much equipment you need is a personal choice, and it should always be based on your own needs and experiences.

◐ A well-equipped paddler in a modern white water kayak.

◑ Airbags lashed in place on a modern white water open canoe.

Kayaks for White Water

A kayak for white water paddling will usually be made of plastic, unless it is designed for a specialist discipline such as slalom, white water racing, or squirt boating. It should have enough buoyancy to float well even when completely full of water. If there is any significant risk that, when full of water, you might end up swimming out of your boat (and there is a risk unless you are highly skilled), you should also fit airbags inside the boat to minimize the amount of water that can enter. Airbags are inflatable PVC bags designed to keep water out of the boat in the event of swamping.

Choosing a Kayak

Most people are now introduced to white water in a boat that is about 2.5m (8½ft) long, and fairly flat-bottomed. Many older books and some instructors still regard boats that are 4m (13ft) long and round-hulled as more suitable, but beginners and experienced paddlers alike will benefit from the responsiveness of a short boat. Also, the more volume the boat has, the better it will respond in white water, but it should not be so huge that the paddler can not properly reach the water when seated.

The boat must have strong footrests with some shock absorption system, and a back strap to support the back and maintain a spinal "S". The boat should also be equipped with end grabs strong enough to take a 1,000kg (2,200lb) load,

⊙ *A heavy-duty, reinforced white water paddle with a symmetrical blade. This is a good, affordable solution as a first white water paddle.*

and should be padded inside as much as is necessary to fit the paddler exactly. A boat that does not fit you is no fun at all.

Kayak Paddles

White water paddles are shorter than flat water paddles – a typical length is 1.9–1.98m (6ft 2in–6ft 7in). Many older books recommend longer paddles, and in 1975, white water kayakers were using paddles 2.1–2.2m (6ft 10in–7ft 2in) long, but they were also using 4m (13ft) kayaks. Things have changed since then. In today's

⊙ *A lightweight carbon fibre white water paddle with an asymmetrical blade. Lighter and stronger, this is the choice of the white water expert.*

short boats, shorter paddles mean faster paddle strokes and therefore more responsive paddling.

The paddle must be strong enough to survive being smashed against rocks, and it should be stiff enough to provide good feedback from the water. Good models can be expensive, but their superior performance and durability justify the cost.

⊙ *This boat has been fitted with thigh grips, a back strap and foam padding to ensure the paddler fits snugly and cannot move inside the boat.*

⊙ *A modern white water kayak suitable for beginners. However, an expert could tackle all but the most extreme white water in this boat with further outfitting.*

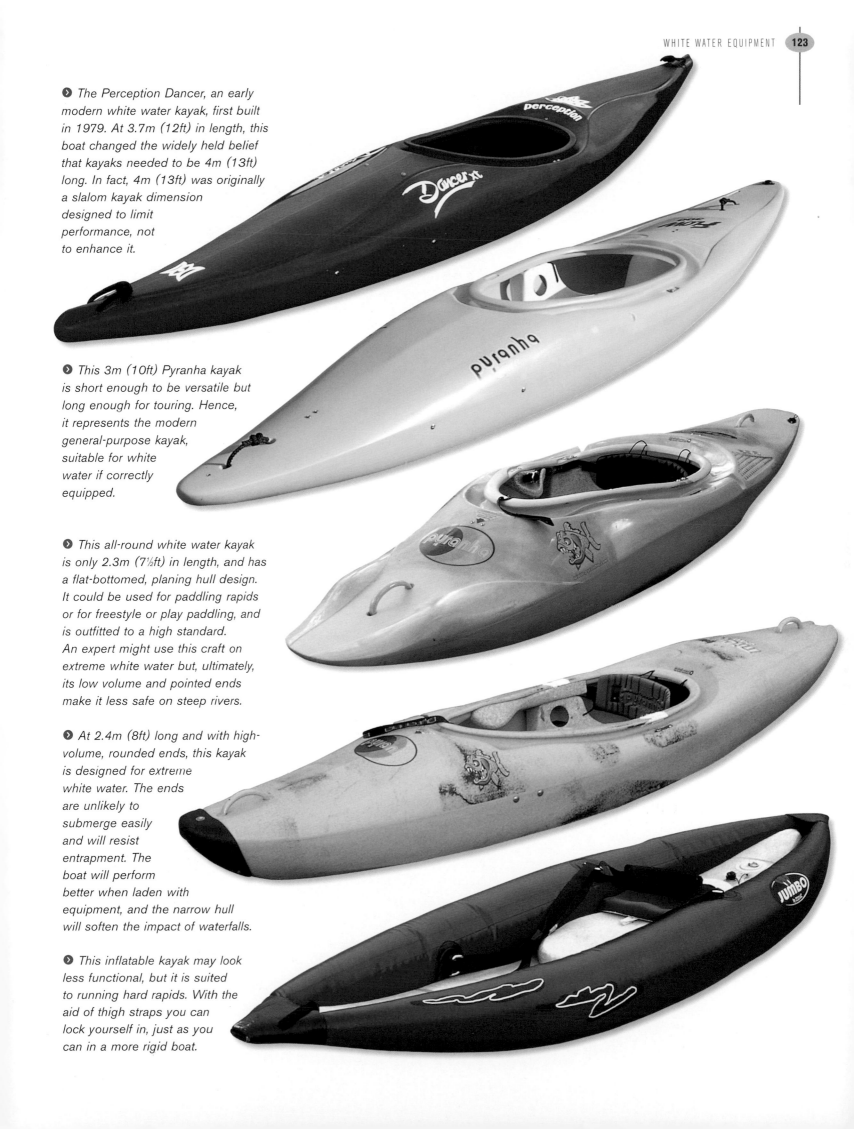

❯ The Perception Dancer, an early modern white water kayak, first built in 1979. At 3.7m (12ft) in length, this boat changed the widely held belief that kayaks needed to be 4m (13ft) long. In fact, 4m (13ft) was originally a slalom kayak dimension designed to limit performance, not to enhance it.

❯ This 3m (10ft) Pyranha kayak is short enough to be versatile but long enough for touring. Hence, it represents the modern general-purpose kayak, suitable for white water if correctly equipped.

❯ This all-round white water kayak is only 2.3m (7½ft) in length, and has a flat-bottomed, planing hull design. It could be used for paddling rapids or for freestyle or play paddling, and is outfitted to a high standard. An expert might use this craft on extreme white water but, ultimately, its low volume and pointed ends make it less safe on steep rivers.

❯ At 2.4m (8ft) long and with high-volume, rounded ends, this kayak is designed for extreme white water. The ends are unlikely to submerge easily and will resist entrapment. The boat will perform better when laden with equipment, and the narrow hull will soften the impact of waterfalls.

❯ This inflatable kayak may look less functional, but it is suited to running hard rapids. With the aid of thigh straps you can lock yourself in, just as you can in a more rigid boat.

Canoes for White Water

Canoes for white water paddling have more variations in design than kayaks. Open boats can be made from fibreglass, but are more usually polyethylene plastic or a sandwich of plastics with a core. The latter can give incredible durability with excellent stiffness and low weight.

On an easy stretch of white water, open canoeists might risk paddling without any special equipment, ensuring only that the boat has enough buoyancy to float when it is full of water. More often, though, every bit of the boat not occupied by the crew will be filled with airbags or rigid buoyancy barrels (very good for storing additional gear), which are lashed in place with cords or webbing. The conventional canoe seat or thwart can be replaced by a foam saddle, which might even have thigh straps to hold you in place. This enables the open canoe to be rolled like a decked boat should it capsize.

⊙ An open boat canoe is packed with air bags, which will keep it afloat when swamped with water.

⊙ A white water canoe paddle, made from Carbon-Kevlar™ and fibreglass.

⊙ A white water freestyle canoe. This boat is designed for play paddling, but could be used as well for running rapids.

⊙ A typical white water canoe is characterized by its short length, rounded ends and continuous rocker.

◔ *On white water, every bit of space in the boat is filled with airbags, which are lashed in place with cord.*

◔ *All white water canoes feature saddle seats, as well as footrests behind the seat for use when kneeling.*

Open boaters often carry throw-lines attached to the ends of the boat. In the event of a swim, which is very likely because open canoes are quite hard to roll, the paddler can swim to the bank holding the end of the line, and then brace himself until the boat swings into the bank. This can be better than trying to swim with such a large boat in the rapid.

Open or Decked?

The first decision is whether to choose a decked or open canoe. The decked canoe is basically a kayak with a seat, footrest, and its back rest replaced by a saddle and straps. There are very few purpose-built decked canoes today, except for hand-built composite slalom boats. Most recreational and freestyle white water paddlers use a kayak shell which they transform into a canoe.

Often the body position in a decked canoe is further forward than it would be in the equivalent kayak, because the paddler's legs are in a kneeling position and not in front of him. This can mean that the canoeist needs a special spraydeck (spray skirt) made with the body tube further forward. Always check that the hole for your waist is in the right place for the seat in your boat!

Canoe Paddles

Just like kayak paddles, canoe paddles for white water need to be strong, light, and stiff enough to provide good

feedback. A little flexibility is important because it allows the paddle to absorb shocks and prevent muscle strain; too much flexibility, on the other hand, will be counter-productive to your efforts.

Nowadays most canoe paddles are made from composite materials such as fibreglass, carbon or Kevlar™. There are traditionalists who prefer the warmth and feedback that comes from a wooden paddle, but wooden paddles are very high maintenance in a white water

environment. The cheapest paddles have ABS plastic blades on a metal tubular shaft. These will certainly do the job for a quarter of the price of some models, and would be suitable for beginners who may not progress far with white water. However, they don't deliver much power or feedback from the water. They can also snap easily, especially in cold conditions.

◔ *A tandem open canoe breaking into the current on a white water river.*

Accessories and Clothing for White Water

On white water you need heavy duty gear to keep you dry in turbulent water, and to protect you from injury and drowning.

Spraydecks

Spraydecks (spray skirts) for kayaks and decked canoes are absolutely essential in rough water. Spraydecks are invariably made from neoprene, the same material that is used for wetsuits. Fabric spraydecks used for flat water are splash-proof rather than waterproof, and will not be adequate for white water.

A good neoprene spraydeck will keep out every drop of water, and will not come off the cockpit rim unless you pull hard on the release strap, which is usually located at the front. Some basic spraydecks are available for the less confident paddler, which will come free if you kick and twist them, but that means they will probably come off in a roll or heavy waves. To see how secure the spraydeck is, put it on your empty boat, then put your hand in through the tube and under the deck, and lift up the boat by the spraydeck. If it stays on, it can be used on serious white water.

Whichever spraydeck you get, make sure that you can release it easily using the strap provided: practise doing this on white water as well as flat. When putting the spraydeck on, always check that the release strap is not trapped inside.

Flotation

Make sure that the flotation you use is intended for white water. For severe white water, some paddlers use special aids with a quick-release chest belt in case they need to be rescued. However, you should only get one of these if you know how to use one. Otherwise it is more likely to endanger than save you.

White water flotation aids can be minimal and slimline, as favoured by freestyle and play paddlers, or bulky and more buoyant, for tackling extreme rapids. The choice is determined by the likelihood of being capsized. The freestyle aids will allow more freedom, and you will be able to paddle better, but they might not afford you enough support if you are swimming in heavily aerated water.

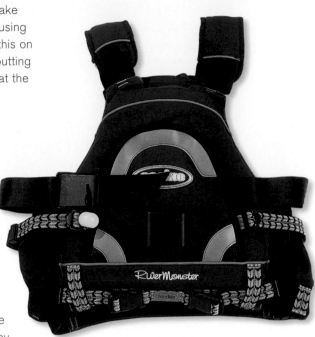

◔ *This reinforced white water buoyancy aid (personal flotation device) is fitted with a chest belt for use in a rescue situation. The belt should only be used by paddlers who have been trained in white water rescue.*

◔ *A white water play paddler equipped for summer: note the short-sleeved shell and wetsuit shorts. The flotation device, helmet and high-performance spraydeck (skirt) should be worn in all weathers.*

◔ *A reinforced white water spraydeck made from neoprene, the minimum quality material for white water paddling. The tight-fitting body tube is pulled right up to prevent water getting into the boat.*

◔ *A white water river running outfit. With the harness flotation aid, wetsuit trousers and a long-sleeved drytop, this paddler is equipped for extreme white water in any weather.*

Helmet

All white water paddlers are advised to wear helmets because of the high risk of finding yourself in the water, and knocking your boat or yourself against rocks. Choose a good-quality model that will protect your temples and forehead. Make sure the helmet fits well and will not come off, fall over your eyes, or expose the base of your skull to an impact. Remember, too, that the bigger the helmet, the more it can wrench your head around when you are upside down.

There used to be a fashion for having drainage holes in a helmet to let out any water that gets in during a capsize or roll.

● *Some people use all-in-one drysuits for cold weather paddling, but the zipper can be an encumberance and the suit lacks many of the features of the drytop.*

Many books still in circulation recommend that you only use a helmet with drainage holes. However, modern helmets are now padded with closed-cell foam. This stops the water getting in, and it means there is less chance of anything (such as an overhanging tree branch) poking through one of the holes. Foam-lined helmets are also warmer.

Clothing

In hot weather, the main purpose of clothing on the upper body is to keep water from entering the spraydeck tube, and protect you from the sun. In colder climes or on cold water, you may need several layers of clothing to keep warm.

Most boaters today use a specially designed paddling jacket, called a cagoule or cag. For warmer weather, there is a short-sleeve version. Cags usually have a seal at the neck and wrists to keep out water, the ultimate being an efficient latex dry seal. Good cags have a double waist system that sandwiches your spraydeck. They are made from a breathable, waterproof fabric, which will cut down on perspiration.

How much insulation you wear under your paddling jacket is up to you, but you will not need much. White water boating is extremely vigorous, and if you wear a thick fleece you will overheat in no time. One or two light to midweight layers should suffice, even in cold weather.

Wetsuits

Beginners to white water often wear wetsuits to keep them warm and protect them from knocks. A popular wetsuit is the long-john design, which allows the upper body freedom of movement. More confident paddlers may find this wetsuit too restricting, preferring wetsuit shorts, wetsuit trousers, or thermal leggings with dry or semi-dry over-trousers, according to the weather and water conditions.

Footwear

Your choice of footwear for white water paddling needs to have a good sole for scrambling about on wet, slippery rocks. Some paddlers choose wetsuit boots, some prefer special watersports shoes, and others wear technical sandals, with or without wetsuit socks. Be aware that anything that is not strapped firmly to your feet is likely to get sucked off during a white water swim.

FREESTYLE

Some freestyle boats are so slimline that you cannot get in wearing bulky footwear. Yet these boats are paddled on white water, so what do freestylers wear on their feet? The point here is that you would only be paddling the more vulnerable freestyle boat in the first place if you were an experienced paddler and within your personal limits. Freestyle boaters usually wear either wetsuit socks or go barefoot, with a pair of sandals or shoes tied in the back of the boat for when they are back on shore.

Safety and Rescue Equipment

There are a number of pieces of rescue equipment that are specially designed for white water use, and all kayakers who intend to paddle rapids should have a basic understanding of their use. There are four essential pieces of equipment that you require.

Throw-line

A throw-line is an invaluable piece of white water equipment. Practise with it until you are confident you could use it in an emergency: the throw-line is next to useless unless it is deployed correctly.

A throw-line is a rescue rope. It consists of a length of rope that will float tied to a bag. The bag will often have some foam buoyancy to keep it afloat as well.

In order to rescue someone who is swimming after a capsize, take your throw-line, open the bag and grasp the loose end of the rope, and throw the bag to the victim. Modern throw-lines are superbly designed so that they fly a

🔻 *A throw-line is attached to a rescue belt flotation aid using a karabiner.*

◀ *The throw-line is an essential piece of rescue equipment.*

long way with the rope running out smoothly behind. Aim to land the bag beyond the swimmer, so that the rope falls across him, and he can grab it and be pulled to safety.

In theory, this would appear simple, but it can be a tricky procedure when the water is moving fast, particularly if the victim panics. This is why it is imperative that all paddlers practise being both victim and rescuer, and are able to throw and catch the line. Always read the instructions that come with the throw-line.

Flotation

A buoyancy aid (personal flotation device) used for flat water is not appropriate for white water. White water models are sometimes fitted with a rescue belt, which can be an advantage to the trained user in extremely severe rescue situations.

The purpose of the quick-release rescue belt is to allow for a line to be attached to the back of the buoyancy aid, so that the wearer can attempt a rescue with someone holding the other end of the rope. Because the rescuer might also get into difficulties, it is essential that he can release himself using the quick-release buckle fitted to the front of the belt.

The line is attached to the back of the rescue belt. This is so that the wearer would remain the right way up, and able to breathe, if held in a fast-flowing current at the end of a line. Bear in mind that not all white water flotation aids are well designed. Take care when faced with a selection of models: choose one that you know works well for rescues.

Another common problem is that white water flotation aids often rely on the rescue belt to give them a good fit. Before you buy, make sure the aid fits well when the chest belt is unfastened. Otherwise, you may find yourself swimming in an ill-fitting buoyancy aid, just when you need it most.

Slings, Karabiners and Pulleys

A sling can be used as a towing aid and for securing boats. Made from reinforced nylon webbing, slings

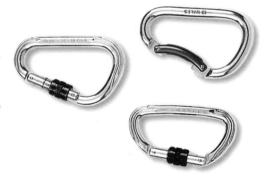

🔻 *Karabiners: the chunky screw-gate (here, the pink ones) and the quicker but less secure snap-gate (the blue).*

🔻 *Climbing slings are very useful for towing and securing boats and paddles.*

❯ *(Below) A pruning saw is a fantastic tool on the river. This cheap garden tool will cut through quite large branches and strong plastic with equal ease. Be careful to get one that can be locked closed, as the blade is a really nasty piece of work.*

❮ *A typical folding river knife. This one has a serrated part to the blade for hacking at difficult jobs, such as tree branches.*

are extremely strong but occupy very little space in the boat. If you also have a karabiner – a lightweight alloy coupling link – it will make the sling easier to deploy for securing and towing boats. Karabiners can have a screw-gate or a snap-gate fastening, and you should try to include one of each. Some karabiners are big enough to close around a paddle shaft: these are the most useful because you can use them to secure or tow paddles.

If you have a sling and a couple of karabiners you can use them together to make a pulley for your throw-line rope. In some situations, such as when a boat has become lodged between rocks after a capsize, a pulley system, operated from the river bank, will be your best chance of recovering the boat. Special pulleys for white water rescue are available, and they are more effective, but your boating will be turning into quite an operation if you get to this stage. For advice on how to work a pulley system, see *White Water Safety and Rescue*.

Knives and Saws

Whenever you take a rope with you as part of your safety and rescue equipment, you should also take a knife to cut it with. Small folding knives are the best because they are extremely sharp, but are still small enough to be carried in the pocket of most buoyancy aids. Some white water paddlers carry fixed-blade diving knives, but these can easily cause accidental injuries, and because they are much heavier they will quickly sink if you drop them in the water.

An ordinary garden pruning saw does not weigh too much, and is invaluable for cutting away branches of trees, which are the white water paddler's worst nightmare. They can also be used in more extreme cases – for example, to free a boater who has become trapped by a fallen tree branch.

❯ *(Top) The throw-line can be stowed inside the kayak or decked canoe.*

❯ *On an open canoe, the throw-line can be attached to the ends.*

Using a Throw-line

1 Get to the shore and out of your boat. Standing on the river bank, undo the bag of your throw-line and pull out about 2m (6½ft) of rope.

2 Identify where the swimmer is and throw the bag (NOT the rope) to them. Aim for somewhere behind them, so that the rope falls over their head.

3 Bring the rope from the swimmer, around the back of you and over your shoulder. Lean back and take the strain as the swimmer swings into the bank.

WHITE WATER SKILLS

This chapter provides a guide to the fundamental skills required to paddle through rapids. There are a few basic tips that can make a big difference to how well you cope with the transition from flat water to rapids. Having read the section on white water hydrology, you will understand that many forces are acting on the boat. Anticipation is the key to remaining in control. If you react to the water, your actions will always be too late. You must lean, edge and use the paddle, anticipating what the water will do. This comes only with experience.

Where you look is where you go. If you want your boat to change direction, rotate your body and look at your new goal to make it easier to turn the boat. The exception to this is rolling, when the body will follow the boat out of the water.

To be successful you also need to be aggressive. White water does not reward defensive behaviour. If you shy away from a wave or a rock, it will tip you in. Turn your shoulder and lean aggressively towards it, and you will survive the problem.

Finally, do not start doing something if you have not got a fixed goal. If you leave the safety of an eddy, you should know where the next safe place is, and be confident that you can get there. If you head down river without a plan, you are likely to run into trouble.

◂ *An experienced paddling group heads towards rapids on big water.*

▾ *Kayakers breaking into the current from the relative safety of an eddy.*

Planning your White Water Trip

Before you paddle on white water it is extremely important to know and understand what you are getting into. You can at best have a bad day, and at worst come to some serious harm if you misinterpret its nature and severity.

In the enthusiastic rush to get on the water, it is very tempting to overlook certain basic safety requirements. These include making sure everyone in the group knows the plan for the trip, who is carrying what in terms of safety and rescue equipment, provisions and maps, and where the dry clothes are at the end of the journey.

Pre-trip Preparation

Everyone going out on the water should understand the basic principles of white water hydrology and the international grading system. Someone in the paddling group (preferably everyone, but this is not always possible) must be experienced enough to be able to judge the grade of water, and whether it is suitable for everyone in the party. Finally, if parts of the river are too difficult for people in the group, will they be able to stop, get out and walk around the section?

◐ *Preparing for a trip on white water. Lay out the equipment on the ground, and check off everything you will need.*

◓ *Before you get afloat, make sure everyone knows the plan for the trip.*

Everyone should also know how long the trip is going to last, so that they can bring appropriate amounts of food, drink and equipment. It might be a quick 20-minute blast down an exciting section of river, or a trip lasting a few days with camping on the river bank. The type of provisions and extra clothing needed will also depend on the weather, so listen to a reliable daily weather report for the area before you set out.

Shuttles

A white water trip is usually a one way journey because the water flows too fast for there to be any possibility of paddling back to the starting point. Your group may be fortunate enough to be delivered to the put-in and collected from the take-out (also known as the egress), but more usually the group will have to give some thought to the procedure known as the "shuttle". Here is how it works.

The group convenes at the put-in to unload their boats and the equipment they will need on the river. All the dry clothes and anything that will not be required until the end of the trip, including towels and hot drinks, is loaded into one or more vehicles, which are driven to the get-out point. The drivers of these vehicles now need to get back to the put-in, so one extra vehicle will have to

accompany them and bring everyone back, unless you are lucky enough to have the help of a non-paddling driver, known to boaters as a "shuttle-bunny".

It may be practical to walk back to the put-in, which means that no vehicles are left at the top of the river and you won't need to return there afterwards. Otherwise, when the trip is over, someone will have to take the shuttle driver back to his car. Remember, all the dry clothes should remain at the get-out point until everyone has finished the trip.

If you don't have a shuttle-bunny at the get-out, it is essential that the paddlers carry with them the keys for all cars left there. It is all too common to leave the keys in the car left at the put-in, and then have to go on a long and arduous mission to recover them at the end. This can be extremely unpopular with a group of cold and tired paddlers whose warm clothes are safely locked away!

Safety Measures

Make sure that everyone knows the plan, and who is responsible for what during the trip. In a group of experienced paddlers who know each other well, there will not be any formalities because everyone knows what to do, but in a mixed-abilities group, it is important to have a preliminary talk before you set out.

An experienced group member must run through the procedure for the trip, emphasizing where you will re-group, who will go first and last, and who has the essential safety equipment. Typically the strongest and/or most experienced paddlers will go first and last, taking the basic items of rescue equipment. At least three members of the party (if not everyone) should carry throw-lines.

Finally, the entire group should warm-up and stretch at the same time. This means that everyone is ready together and you won't have some getting cold and stiff while others are still getting ready.

Communication

Hand signals can be used between paddlers for communication. This should not be attempted while paddling, but it is useful if paddlers have stopped in separate eddies because the noise of the river can preclude verbal communication. Some books describe a "correct" signalling procedure, but different groups use different signals. Discuss the signals the group will use during the pre-trip talk.

❯ *A group of paddlers get out of the water for a meeting in a remote gorge.*

❍ *These paddlers are discussing the plan for the next section of their trip.*

CHECKLIST
• What is the strength and ability level of the group?
• What is the aim of the trip?
• Will there be a support party?
• What equipment will the group need and who will carry it?
• Are there any special points to include in the group's briefing?
• How will the weather and water conditions be checked? By whom?
• Are any permissions required for access points or stretches of water?
• How will the group be organized on the water? Who will lead the group?
• What are the transport and shuttle arrangements?

Launching into White Water

There are several options when it comes to launching a boat, including techniques for entering the water from banks 10m (33ft) high. Build up your launching skills gradually. If you attempt an ambitious technique you are not ready for, you are likely to get hurt.

Getting into the water can be trickier than you might think. Unless there is an area of slow-moving flat water at the put-in, it will be impossible to get into the boat by the usual means. Kayak paddlers will find it difficult to put on their neoprene spraydecks (spray skirts) while afloat, and it will be difficult for anyone to get settled in the boat and not get swept away while trying to arrange their equipment. One of several techniques will be required.

Launching in an Eddy

If there is a convenient eddy at the put-in, it may be possible to put your boat in the water, get in, and put on spraydecks before pushing off. However, even the gentlest eddies are not usually stationary, and the water will be trying to carry you upstream and feed you into the current before you are ready. You will therefore need someone to hold your boat while you get in and put on your deck, making sure that your paddle does not float away.

❯ *Seal launching a kayak off a low river bank on to flat water.*

❯ *Getting into a white water open canoe on a section of slack water.*

Seal Launching

Because getting into the boat in an eddy is sometimes impossible, and since most paddlers prefer to be independent, it is normally better to get into the boat and get everything in place on dry land, and then launch yourself into the water. This technique is called a seal launch. No-one seems to know whether this refers to the way a seal slides into the sea from a rock, or the fact that the paddler is sealed in the boat as it is launched.

How you launch is determined by the bank, the depth of the water, and the nature of the river downstream. If there is a gently shelving slope into the water, you can get in the boat at the water's edge and push yourself into the water. If the water is moving fast, it may be better to launch backwards because the current will spin the boat around, pointing it upstream as you go in. This is a better orientation for getting away from the bank.

If there is a vertical drop from the bank to the water that is not too big, it is often better to shuffle to the edge sideways, and then lean out until you can bump the boat off the ledge with your hips, landing flat in the water. It takes practice to do this without falling in, so try it in deep, safe water at first. It is not comfortable or safe to use this method from a height of more than 1m (3½ft), unless the water is extremely aerated.

⬆ *A canoe can be seal launched off a bank as easily as a kayak.*

⬇ *Launching sideways off a low wall. This is a better solution if the water is too shallow for a vertical dive.*

⬇ *Making an enormous vertical seal launch. This kind of thing should only ever be attempted out of necessity.*

If the drop from the river bank is larger than 1m (3½ft) or not quite vertical you will have to launch forwards. This may involve free-falling, bow first, into the water, so you will need to make sure that the water is deep enough. Stick your paddle into the water to measure the depth: if it is less than 1m (3½ft) deep you risk injury from hitting the bottom. Push yourself to the edge using the paddle on one side and your free hand on the other, then launch yourself off the bank with a shove, bringing the other hand on to the paddle as you fall.

The push off is important because if you topple slowly you will over-rotate, and might land on your head. Sit fairly upright, and do not hold the paddle in front of your face in case it hits you in the nose. People have been known to seal launch safely from heights of up to 18m (60ft) this way, but try it initially from no more than 3m (10ft) because it can be difficult to maintain the correct posture while performing the manoeuvre.

⬆ *Getting a group into their boats on a rock ledge. When they are all ready to go, they will slide off into the rapid.*

If you have to launch from a great height but the water is not deep enough for a vertical entry, you still have a few options. You can either shove off hard from the bank, or get someone to give you a push, so that you enter the water at a shallower angle; this can be tricky. Or you can drop into the water sideways and land flat, provided you feel that your fitness or the aeration of the water means that you can exceed the 1m (3½ft) rule without injuring yourself; this is more risky. Or you can drop in sideways, letting the boat land on its side if you have the skill to do this. If you attempt this, do not land with a lot of force on your paddle blade. Even if the paddle does not touch the bottom you can hurt your shoulder, and you might break the paddle. It is better to capsize than to find yourself stranded or injured.

Breaking Out Techniques

The break out is a manoeuvre that allows you to move the boat out of the current and into an eddy whenever you want to take a break from the fast-moving water.

The eddy will be divided from the main flow of the river by an eddy-line. This is a distinct line or interface between the water moving downstream and the water in the eddy, which is stationary or is moving more slowly upstream.

As the boat crosses the eddy-line the current will try to spin the boat around and tip it over. In order to counter this it is important to lean the boat upstream, i.e. into the turn, as it crosses the line.

It is usually advisable to paddle into the eddy while pointing downstream, and allow the current to spin the boat to face upriver. This makes it easy to enter the top of the eddy, a relatively safe and predictable place, and to leave it again to proceed downstream. However, it is

Breaking Out using a Bow Rudder

1 Aim to get the bow into the top of the eddy at an angle of 45°.

2 Plant the bow rudder firmly in the eddy and lean the boat upstream.

3 Hang on the bow rudder until the boat is completely in the eddy.

4 Turn the rudder into a power stroke to pull you back up the eddy, if required.

◔ *Two canoeists negotiate their way down the river from one eddy to another.*

possible to paddle into the eddy across the current, or even while pointing upstream if necessary. The crucial point is to maintain that upstream lean once in the eddy.

It is best to approach the eddy at some speed, and to perform a powerful sweep stroke on the downstream side as you cross the eddy-line to ensure that you cross it properly and do not hang about at the interface, which can be a difficult place even for experts. As the boat turns into the eddy and you apply or increase your lean, you should support yourself with a low brace for stability, and to ensure that the boat carries on turning the right way. You should finish up well inside the eddy-line, facing upstream, and with the bow of the boat close to the top of the eddy.

With a good technique it is possible to enter the eddy without doing any strokes at all, just relying on the edges and carving performance of the boat to give you the necessary drive and turning force.

Exactly what type of stroke you use to break out is up to you. You should be

Breaking Out using a Low Brace

1 Aim the bow into the top of the eddy at 45°, and low brace on the upstream side.

2 As the boat begins to turn, lean on the low brace fairly hard.

comfortable with all the strokes by the time you venture out on to white water for the first time, so with any luck it will come naturally. Remember, though, that it is the difference in current as you cross the eddy-line that turns the boat and not your stroke.

The advantage of a low brace as you cross the eddy-line is that it will provide the greatest support. It is also an easy stroke to apply in what is (to the novice) an uncertain situation; as a result it is quite common to see paddlers new to white water using the low brace.

The advantage of using a bow rudder stroke is that it can be feathered to apply only as much braking force as required (which means it need not slow the boat), yet it still provides support to the confident paddler, and can feather into a forward stroke to take you deeper into the eddy as you come to a halt. The bow rudder would be the stroke of choice for experienced paddlers when breaking in or out of a current on white water.

To break out with no paddle strokes is good practice and helps you to feel the effect the water has on the hull, uncluttered as you are with feedback from the paddle. When you are entirely confident at moving around on a rapid, breaking with no brace can be used as a training exercise to maintain your concentration and control.

Breaking Out with No Brace

1 Attack the eddy at 45°, as when using a low brace.

2 Lean upstream a little before you start to turn the boat.

GO WITH THE FLOW

A white water river is primarily made up of water currents and eddies. It is up to the paddler to use these forces to manoeuvre and stop the boat. Entering currents, stopping the boat in case of a problem, to take a rest or to look at something interesting, and navigating your way across a river are vital skills that you need to learn to stay in control of your boat, and to enjoy your time on white water.

3 Hold the lean and keep believing it is going to work!

4 Finish facing upstream, and don't level the boat until you have stopped turning.

Breaking In Techniques

The technique for entering the river current from an eddy and proceeding downstream is known as breaking in. It is precisely the opposite of beaking out.

Paddle into the current while pointing slightly upstream, and with enough speed to ensure that you make it completely into the flow. As with breaking out, use a powerful forward sweep on the upstream side to drive the bow into the current and initiate the turn. Then use a low brace or similarly supportive turning stroke on the downstream side to complete the turn. Clearly, the forces here are acting the other way, so the current will be trying to tip you upstream. You must lean quite decisively downstream, again into the turn, supporting yourself with your turning stroke, until you are well into the current.

If there are waves in the main flow, you will do better to enter the current in a trough rather than on the peak of a wave.

As with the breaking out technique, there are a number of ways that you can achieve your goal of crossing the eddy-line into the current. The safest and most reliable way at first, when you are first learning to break in, is to use a low brace. Start off by paddling up the eddy fast enough to allow you to make it across the eddy-line: you need to do your low brace as, or slightly before, the boat

crosses the line and starts to turn. If you are paddling too slowly, you will spin around to face the downstream right on the eddy-line, and you will probably fall into the water. However, it is incorrect to paddle across the eddy-line and then turn. This feels all wrong, and it doesn't put you in a good position in the rapid either.

● *The important thing about breaking in is to make it into the flow, where you can establish a safe line downstream.*

More experienced paddlers tend to do exactly the same thing but using a bow rudder stroke in place of the low brace. This has the advantage that if you are not going quite fast enough, or if you

Breaking In using a Low Brace

1 Paddle up to the top of the eddy-line. Make your last stroke on the current side.

2 Your next stroke will be a sweep to drive you into the flow and start the turn.

3 Place the low brace on the downstream side for support as you make the turn.

turn too much, your paddle blade is ready for a forward stroke, sweep stroke or support stroke, responding to what the current is doing and making sure you complete the turn while making it into the flow of the current. The only difference is that you should reach forwards to place the bow rudder in the current because this stroke will not always slice cleanly

across the eddy-line without snagging in the water or tipping you right in.

Experienced paddlers may break into the current without using a turning/ bracing stroke. This is rather like the technique for breaking out with no brace, which is not a stroke but an exercise. In the case of breaking in, the paddler would appear to paddle across the

Breaking in below a small drop and immediately lining up for the next one.

eddy-line, which is bad technique. A paddler with excellent balance and control may be able to cross the eddy-line and turn, while appearing to paddle forwards, but do not attempt this until you have the skill and experience to do it well.

Break In using a Bow Rudder

1 Paddle out of the top of the eddy at 45°, lifting the upstream edge of the boat.

2 Make a bow rudder on the downstream side and lean on the stroke.

3 Hold the stroke until you are pointing downstream, then start paddling again.

Ferry Glide

Sometimes you will want to paddle across the current without turning downstream, often from an eddy to a point on the other side. This is known as a ferry glide, named after the ferry boats that used to cross rivers attached to a fixed wire. This does not involve a wire, but you have to paddle fast enough to stop being swept away. The skill of maintaining the correct angle is just the same as the ferryman's.

Ferry gliding is a very useful skill for crossing fast rivers, and for moving into a better position in the current. It can also be done in reverse, so that you move across the current while still facing downstream as you look for the best line down a rapid.

You need to keep the boat pointing upstream. The faster the current and the more its speed varies across the flow, the more directly upstream you will need to aim. Rather than keeping it on track by using forward sweeps on the downstream side to stop the boat from spinning around, you should lift your upstream edge. Use your knee rather than leaning your body downstream, and keep paddling hard enough so that you move across the current without being carried downstream. If you are entering an eddy on the other side, you will need to release your edge and lean slightly upstream as you cross the eddy-line.

If you find that the boat tries to turn downstream, you were not pointing upstream enough. Forward sweep the bow aggressively back into line to recover. However, anticipation is always better than reaction. It tends to go wrong only because you didn't set the correct angle of attack. Getting the angle exactly right only comes with experience. Initially, the rule of thumb is to set off pointing as directly upstream as you can while still allowing you to get across the eddy-line.

Reverse Ferry Glide

The ferry glide can also be done in reverse, so that you move across the current while still facing downstream, as you look for the best line down a rapid. The reverse ferry glide is an essential skill in white water paddling because many rivers have sections that can only be paddled in reverse. Unlike many reverse skills, it is actually easier in many ways to keep the boat tracking across the current than it would be when ferry gliding forwards, although all paddlers have less boat control when paddling backwards.

Ferry Glide Technique

1 As you leave the eddy, point as far upstream as you can while still making it across the eddy-line.

2 Lift the upstream – eddy side – edge of the boat as you cross the eddy-line into the main current.

3 Keep paddling, adjusting your angle across the current as needed.

4 As you reach the other side of the eddy, change edges as you cross the eddy-line by lifting the downstream edge.

5 Enter the other eddy in the same way as you would if you were breaking out.

6 You can now continue to paddle your way up the eddy.

S-cross

If the current is too fast to ferry glide, and the eddy-line is too difficult to negotiate, or the target eddy is a little downstream from your starting point, you can try a modified ferry glide called a cross. This involves letting the boat turn enough so that you ensure a fast transit across the current, at the expense of being carried downstream a short distance. In extreme cases this becomes an S-cross; the boat is allowed to break in until it is travelling directly across the current, then you immediately change to a break out to enter the target eddy, making an S shape across the river.

The S-cross as a set piece is used more for practice than anything else. However, learning to S-cross accurately from one eddy to another on a rapid will give you a lot of confidence in your ability to navigate white water, and will help you combine your repertoire of different skills and manoeuvres into a seamless flow. You will find this technique extremely useful when eddy-hopping your way down an unknown rapid, when you want to get from one safe eddy to another without having to think too hard about how to go about it.

If you attack the eddy-lines at speed, the boat can be made to plane and jet across narrow currents very quickly indeed. It will need practice and excellent reflexes to change edges at just the right time. If you cross a wider current like this, the boat will quickly stop planing and you will be in a conventional ferry glide. If this is not what you want, make sure you attack wider jets without too much speed, or at a less acute angle.

S-cross Technique

1 Break into the current at about 45°, using your normal breaking-in technique.

2 Start paddling fast before you are facing downstream.

3 Charge forcefully across the current, and keep leaning the boat downstream as you do so.

4 Cross the opposite eddy-line. Aim to keep the boat moving at speed as it crosses the narrow current.

5 Change edges, using your legs, and begin the break-out sequence. This relies on excellent timing: practice is all.

6 You should finish the manoeuvre facing upstream in the other eddy.

Eddy Use and Etiquette

Now that we know the basics of getting into, out of and between eddies, it is time to learn a little about how they should be used. As has been explained, an eddy is an important river feature and the right etiquette and protocol should always be observed when using one.

Eddies are primarily used as a place to stop, rest and look ahead before running rapids. They vary in size; many are large enough for a whole group to stop and chat, whereas others might only be big enough for a single boat. Some people call very small eddies like this "micro eddies". In fact, they might be so tiny that only an expert paddler would ever notice them, let alone be able to land a boat in one in the middle of a powerful rapid.

This means that paddlers must think about the whole group when entering and leaving eddies. If an eddy fills up, one or more paddlers might have to carry

Entering a Micro Eddy

1 Attack the eddy-line more perpendicular than you would with a normal eddy.

2 Brake to reduce speed as you go across the eddy-line.

3 Level the boat early so that you don't spin back into the rapid.

4 Finish as close to the banks as you can without bouncing off the current.

◔ *A paddler in a large eddy and another approaching from upstream. This eddy is so big that etiquette isn't really an issue.*

on downstream without a plan. Before leaving an eddy, therefore, everyone should know where they are next going to eddy out – i.e. make their next stop.

Whoever is first into an eddy should back down or move away from the eddy-line so that the next paddler can also enter at the top. It is much better for everyone to break out as high up the eddy as they can; if someone misses they still have a chance to catch the eddy further down. The trouble is, sometimes this means that the person who was first into the eddy has to be the last out. This is one of the many reasons for having your best paddlers positioned first and last on the river.

In a very safe place where paddlers are playing on the rapid, it may not be necessary or appropriate to back away from the top of the eddy. Sometimes, other paddlers will be queuing to leave the top of the eddy, and it would be rude and unnecessary to jump to the front of the line. If you see that this is the case, join the back of the eddy queue like everyone else. If, on the other hand, you are anxious or out of control, aim for the top of the eddy – it is up to more experienced paddlers to recognize your problems and make room for you.

When you are ready to leave an eddy, make sure that there is no one paddling downstream who will end up too close to you, or who might be aiming for the part of the eddy that you are leaving. It is too easy on white water to miss what other people are trying to do, but being considerate is very important.

Eddy-hopping

It is important that a group of paddlers leaves an eddy knowing that they will be able to catch one another within the distance that they can see (or know from experience) is safe. This way of running a river from one eddy to the next is called "eddy hopping". However, it may not be possible for everyone to make the same eddy, so before you leave, look ahead and consider where you and everyone else in the group will break out next. In small eddies, it may be necessary for the paddlers to swap the lead.

⬤ An open canoe joins the top of an eddy. The kayakers have made room at the top to give him safer access.

⬤ Group dynamics in an eddy. The expert paddlers at the top and back of the eddy will leave first and last.

Running Rapids

Many rapids have hydraulic and/or rock features that can be hazardous, and you need to know how to avoid them, or deal with them if they are unavoidable.

Waves and Holes

The nature of hydraulics changes with the depth and flow of the water. Unbroken waves are usually no problem because you can paddle over them. If they get very big or are really close together, it may be sensible to take a diagonal route over them. However, a wave that is breaking hard can stop and hold the boat. In extreme cases, it will hurl the boat end over end, disorientating the paddler. You will learn from experience whether you're likely to punch through a wave or not.

As the depth reduces, the drop into the breaking pile becomes more pronounced, and the re-circulating water pours back into the depression. This hydraulic will hold the boat, and it is only safe if you can see that the ends are pointing downstream to allow you to escape.

◔ This kayaker is on the towback of a powerful hydraulic, and the water is so aerated that his kayak barely floats. He must keep moving downstream to avoid being sucked back in.

◔ This rapid is full of big waves, although the water is too deep for them to form retentive "stoppers" or "holes", and the paddler's approach is dictated by comfort more than by safety.

Reducing the depth of the water further turns this hole into a pourover. Pourovers are nearly always unpleasant because they do not allow the boater to ride comfortably on the front of the pile – there is too much water falling on the upstream side of the boat. Sometimes you can jump over the towback by paddling right through the pourover, but it is better to skirt around it.

Whenever you look at a hydraulic, try to imagine what will happen to the boat if you are held sideways in its grip. It takes experience to read the water in this way, and there is no better test than watching what someone else does. You will quickly learn to spot the little tongues of water that can provide a passage downstream, and to recognize whether the pile helps you towards an exit through which you can escape, or constantly pushes you away from it. Practise as much as you can by playing in holes that are small and safe, gradually moving on to more difficult ones. Once you can go into a hole, and come out again unscathed, you are well on the way to confidently running rapids.

◔ *This is a particularly unpleasant scenario. A lot of water is falling steeply into a re-circulating stopper or hole. The white water is flowing back upstream from as far as 5m (16ft) downstream. A paddler or swimmer caught in this hydraulic would be swamped with water and would not be able to escape. In this example it is just about possible to sneak past the hole on either side, but the only sane route is on the bank.*

◔ *Although this stopper has a big breaking foam pile, it is friendly because the drop into it is not too steep. It is very powerful and will hold the boat indefinitely, but a skilful paddler can remain in control and can effect an escape by simple paddling out of the end of the pile. The hole is safe because if you were to swim, you would be flushed downstream. This feature is called an elevated pile.*

Running Drops

If you want to try paddling over a drop of any significant size, you need to know what the water below is like. It is likely that you will not have a good view of the water from your boat. Vertical drops have different characteristics from sloping drops, but both present significant dangers to the paddler. They should always be inspected to check for rocks or trapped trees. On a vertical drop you can often measure the depth with a paddle.

Sloping Drops

A sloping drop will usually have a big hydraulic at the bottom that you may have to paddle through. Look for any gaps in the pile, or any sign of a downstream V. This will be the best spot. If the water going down the ramp is not flat but consists of two or more flows crossing over each other, you need to be on the top flow. The other(s) would carry you under the top one, and might flip your boat as it goes over the drop.

🔽 *This man is using a kayak paddle to check the depth of the pool below a small 1m (3½ft) waterfall. He can also make sure that there are no trees or other obstructions under the water that might entrap the submerged kayak when he runs the drop.*

🔼 *A kayaker is attempting a meltdown on a sloping drop where he had no chance of jumping the hydraulic.*

🔽 *Running a sloping drop into an eddy. The kayaker can take a diagonal line across this drop to get to the eddy.*

● *Running any kind of drop can be a serious undertaking and should not be attempted without careful thought. A huge white water rapid such as this is for experts only.*

Vertical Drops

Waterfalls usually have a deep and very strong hydraulic re-circulation system at the bottom, but you will usually land downstream of it. If the fall is so big that you cannot do this, consider the sanity of the undertaking. If going ahead, the main consideration is the height of the drop. Can you survive the impact uninjured, and is the water deep enough? Whatever the profile of the fall, there are basically two ways of running it.

Meltdown

A meltdown is a way of taking the drop so that your hull stays in contact with the green water all the way down, and you then go through, or under, the re-circulating hydraulic. It was invented by squirt boaters in the 1980s, and has revolutionized vertical drops in all but the most high-volume boats. Just paddle normally towards your chosen spot on the lip of the drop, keeping your weight forward. As you drop into the pile, tuck your head right forwards and down,

and put the paddle along the boat as if preparing for a roll. You may well need to roll, anyway, but the main reason for doing this is to prevent the pile from snapping the paddle across your chest.

If the drop is vertical, do not paddle too fast; drop over the edge at your current speed, or a little faster to retain some control. This will ensure you do not go out too far. Do not lean back as you see the water below because the boat may

over-rotate, and this may hurt. However, if the drop is sloping, the faster you are going when you hit the pile, the better your chance of sliding through. Just make sure the nose of the boat goes under the pile, not up the face of it.

Boof

A boof is the opposite way of taking a fall. This involves paddling hard off the lip of the drop, and keeping the weight back just before take-off, so that the boat shoots downstream a long way and lands flat on the hull. It helps if you make your last stroke right at the lip, and use your whole body to heave back the blade. This means that the boat is projected forwards, and your weight will be at the back as you start to fall. Throw yourself dynamically forward as soon as you are in freefall because this keeps the bow up, which helps the boat land flat and prevents the nose from plunging deep into the pile.

Boofing allows you to remain dry and in control, and you can land in shallow water if you get it right. Never boof high vertical drops unless the water below is very aerated, or you risk spinal compression. On a sloping drop, it is only possible to boof diagonally into an eddy – generally, you cannot get enough speed to clear the hydraulic unless it is a vertical fall.

● *Launching out from a waterfall in order to boof into the water below.*

White Water Safety and Rescue

There are three main areas of risk that you need to protect yourself from while out on the water. Ultimately, the main threat is drowning, and you need to focus on the likely causes that can occur on white water.

Entrapment

The main killer of white water paddlers is entrapment. This can happen in rapids because they are typically fairly shallow, and filled with obstructions. The power of the water can easily pin a kayak against a rock, tree or even the river bed in such a way that you are powerless to dislodge it or escape from the boat. If you are trapped in this way with your head below the water, you will drown in a matter of seconds; rescuers do not have long to get you out and resuscitate you.

Fortunately, most people who venture on to white water are aware of this danger, while the relatively inexperienced will be strictly monitored by an instructor. There are many rapids on which you can practise where the danger of entrapment is minimal. As a general rule, note that entrapments are nasty and sudden, so take great care if you think there is the remotest chance of one happening.

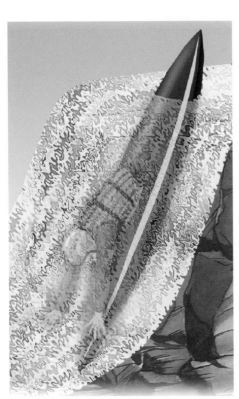

◐ If the bow of your kayak hits the bottom when negotiating a drop, you can get vertically pinned like this. The force of the water on your back makes it impossible to get out of the kayak. Sometimes you can shake the boat free or push off the bottom with your paddle, but the rule is, if you can breathe, don't move in case you make it worse. Rescuers can assist you by pulling the boat upwards to free the bow.

The upstream side of any rock is a potential danger spot, where you can be pinned against an obstruction, often one that is submerged under the water level. Sometimes, if the water makes a cushion wave, you will not be trapped, but you cannot rely on that happening. A fallen tree or any object that has become embedded in the river bed can be a fatal hazard: avoid at all costs.

◓ (Top) You can get into serious trouble if any part of your body becomes stuck between rocks on the river bed.

◓ (Above) If you hit the upstream side of a tree in moving water, this is how it can end. Even if you were on the surface when you hit the tree, the current will quickly force you below water level, and there is no escape. Avoid trees at all costs.

If you do hit some type of obstruction and you get pinned against it, you must act quickly. There will be a brief moment of just a couple of seconds before things may start to take a turn for the worse. Throw your weight downstream towards the obstruction, and use every bit of your strength to lift the upstream edge of the boat before the water flows over you. With luck, you may then be able to drag

◓ *This paddler has been swept into a rock in the middle of a rapid. By leaning on to the rock, he is holding the upstream edge of his boat above water, which saves him from disaster.*

yourself around the obstruction and release the boat from the pressure pinning it to the obstruction. If not, you are in trouble. If you can get right out of your boat and on to the rock or other obstruction, do it. These situations have a habit of deteriorating rapidly.

If you fail to hold the upstream rail up, the boat will angle down and become inextricably pinned. It may even start to fold up under the pressure of the water. You may be held in the boat by the force of the water, and might be unable to keep your head up. It is easy to say "Don't panic," but you have only got seconds to find a solution. Wriggle the boat around, and fight to get out. If you do get out, try to kick off in a direction that will take you around the obstruction and away.

Other entrapment dangers include vertical, shallow drops. It is possible to be rescued from this situation, but only if your fellow paddlers can get to you quickly, or are in position already,

◓ *If the paddler can't lean downstream quickly enough, the current will flip the boat upstream and pin it in a position from which there may be no escape.*

◓ *In this instance, things have gone wrong. The boat is pinned on the rock, but the paddler is able to get out and on to the rock to await rescue.*

◓ *If a boat is pinned to a rock by the current, you need to mount a serious recovery operation from the shore, using ropes, to get the boat free.*

◓ *Here, the paddler is using an elevated pull to lift the boat up from the rocks. The throw-line can then be used to drag the boat back to the shore.*

monitoring your progress. As a rule, a boat or person pinned to an obstacle by the current can only be released in the direction from which they came – usually upstream. If you cannot release the boat and have to extract the paddler, take care that the force of the water as he exits does not cause leg or other injuries.

Undercut rocks or cliffs are extremely dangerous. They are undercut because the current flows under them, and you can easily get trapped against the rocks. There may also be trees and other debris that has accumulated next to the rocks. If the water flows right up against a rock or bank, but there is not much of a cushion or pressure wave, assume that most of the current is flowing underneath the water surface: never paddle here.

Release and Recovery

If a boat is pinned by rocks, use one of the following pulls to dislodge it and/or drag it back to the shore.

A shoulder belay – in which the rope passes from the boat around your shoulders – is much more powerful than simply using your arms. The elevated pull is designed to lift the boat to reduce friction and water pressure while the boat is dragged away horizontally from the water. For the vector pull, tie a rope from the pinned boat to a tree or rock, then pull at 90° to the rope to reduce pressure on the boat and pull it free.

◗ *Using a vector pull to free a boat from entrapment on rocks in the water.*

Hydraulics

There are certain hydraulic wave features on white water that can stop and hold a kayak. In extreme cases, particularly on weirs and below waterfalls and pourovers, hydraulics are able to hold a swimmer and re-circulate him indefinitely. This is a potentially life-threatening situation.

The endless cycle of being submerged, surfacing, then being sucked upstream and submerged again rapidly leads to exhaustion. A swimmer in this situation can be rescued with a throw-line, or sometimes an experienced paddler can approach from downstream in a boat and pull him out. Self-extraction is extremely difficult, and impossible to practise safely. Prevention is always the best answer.

◔ *Wrapping the rope around your shoulders in a shoulder belay will make more effective use of your strength when recovering a boat from the water.*

White Water Swimming

Swimming down a rapid after a capsize has plenty of hazards besides the danger of entrapment. You are usually safer if you keep hold of your upturned boat because it will tow you through the hydraulics, and you can use it as a fender. If you have to make a choice between holding on to the paddle or the boat, choose the paddle: the boat will be easier to find later.

Position yourself so that you are upstream of the boat to avoid getting pinned. Face downstream and keep your legs up, pointing downstream, in what is known as the defensive swimming posture. You can use your feet to push yourself away from boulders, but be aware of the danger of getting your feet caught between rocks.

Keep holding on to your boat and paddle, and concentrate on conserving your energy. Wait for an opportunity to swim ashore, then head straight for the bank. If you still have the boat, ditch it if you are in any doubt about making it to safety. If you do not make it, the water will return you to the centre of the river and the attempt will have been wasted. You have limited reserves of energy, so choose your moment carefully.

❯ *A paddler caught in a hydraulic can be rescued with a throw-line from the shore, or by another paddler towing him to safety. However, the rescuer must be careful not to be sucked into the hydraulic himself.*

FOOT ENTRAPMENT

This is a very real threat. As soon as the foot is caught, the victim will fall down and the force of the current may hold him down and drown him. If you find your foot trapped, kick it upstream and upwards as hard as you can – yanking at it as you fall downstream will make things worse. To avoid foot entrapment, make it a rule never to stand in moving water less than 30cm (1ft) deep.

Using a Throw-line

A swimmer in the defensive posture can usually be rescued with a specialist rescue rope called a throw-line.

To rescue someone from the water, take your throw-line, open the bag and grasp the loose end of the rope. Throw the bag (NOT the rope) to the victim. Aim to land the bag beyond the swimmer, so that the rope falls across him, and he can grab it and be pulled to safety.

Throwing the bag and line can be tricky in fast moving water, particularly if the victim panics. All paddlers should practise throwing and catching the throw-line until they are confident they can use it.

⬇ *The defensive swimming posture. Float with your feet up and facing downstream to avoid entrapment.*

⬇ *When the time is right, turn on to your front and swim as hard as you can for the river bank.*

❮ *This man is trying to swim his way out of a powerful hydraulic after a capsize. Although the river is flowing from top to bottom in the picture, the man is being sucked back upstream by the re-circulating water and submerged again by the water pouring over the drop. The enormous force of the water means that with every attempt to move, the swimmer is becoming exhausted and less able to act decisively. If he can't find a way out of this re-circulating water (for example, by swimming to either end of the stopper or being pushed through by the main flow), this cycle will be repeated until he drowns or is rescued.*

4 OPEN HORIZONS

OPEN WATER AND SEA PADDLING

Kayaks and canoes are ideal for paddling over a great distance, or across exposed areas of open water. Indeed, both types of craft originated precisely because their builders needed to use them in this way, for hunting, trading and migration. The kayak is eminently suited to coastal and ocean travel, and the open canoe to exploring large rivers and great lakes.

The demands of long-distance paddling are quite special, and are unlike most of the other disciplines covered in this book. The main criterion is a need for speed because the distances covered can be quite long. Directional stability is equally important because one cannot paddle far in a boat that keeps veering away from straight lines. The boats also need to be very stable and easy to paddle. Long-distance boats need good storage space for food and water, and camping and survival equipment.

◀ *Riding an ocean wave. Surfing is now a hugely popular branch of paddle sport.*

◐ *Two paddlers in modern traditionally-styled sea kayaks explore a rocky coastline.*

Tides and Currents

Knowing about tides and currents is extremely important if you are planning to paddle a boat out at sea or on any large body of water. Ignoring them means possibly endangering your safety.

Tides

The tide is a familiar concept to anyone living or working near the sea, but it can be exceptionally confusing to others. All over the world, the sea and other large bodies of water are visibly moved by the gravitational effect of the moon, and to a lesser extent by the sun and planets. With only a few exceptions, this results in the water rising and falling twice a day – in any 24-hour period there will be two high tides and two low tides, with the water rising and falling fairly predictably from one to the next.

The size of the variation depends on two things: where you are in the world, and the date. Every month there is a cycle of tidal variation, which sees more extreme tides (highest highs and lowest lows) around the time of the full moon and 14 days later, reducing to less extreme ones (with a smaller change in height from highs to lows) in the weeks

◔ A sheltered estuary at high tide. Always remember that the tide comes in and out twice a day, with currents much faster than you can paddle.

in between. The extreme tides are known as spring tides, and the moderate tides are known as neap tides.

There is also a yearly variation. The biggest spring tides will be those that occur worldwide around the time of the equinoxes (when the sun crosses the equator) on 21 March and 21 September, and the smallest around the solstices (when the sun is furthest from the equator) on 21 June and 21 December.

It is useful to understand how tidal variations occur but there is no substitute for getting a tide table or checking the time of high and low tide on the day you

plan to paddle. If there is no appropriate information service available in the area, look for the information on the internet. Tides can vary by up to an hour between places only 100km (60 miles) apart.

◔ The same estuary as above, shown here at low tide. As well as the currents, you will have to contend with difficult access over deep mud banks.

◔ The high-tide level of this river is clearly visible. At low tide there is access to the grassy bank, but at high tide there is no accessible landing spot.

Currents

Although we describe the tide as rising and falling, there is a dramatic flow of water associated with it in many areas. The sea can exhibit strong tidal currents that are, in many cases, faster flowing than a river's. This is dangerous because you could set off when the water is slack at high or low tide, and find yourself a few hours later in a raging torrent like Skookumchuck in British Columbia, Canada, the Bitches in Wales or the Falls of Lora in Scotland, a situation for which you might be totally unprepared.

In most cases, the effects of a sea current are much the same as on a river. Good paddling technique will help you deal with the possible eddies and waves. There is, however, a special type of current called a rip that can be found in coastal areas. This can be dangerous to swimmers, but is a mixed blessing to paddlers who can use it to their advantage, as long as they know how.

The rip is a current most often found on surf beaches. The ocean swells breaking on the shore push a lot of water onshore, and this water has to run back

This exposed beach could be prone to strong currents. Find out about local currents before launching out to sea.

○ The directional pull of the current. A rip takes water out to sea, while the longshore drift moves around the land.

into the sea. Usually, it flows back in one or two spots, dictated by the shoreline, creating currents flowing back out through the waves. Anything in the area will be drawn towards the rip, and towed out to sea through the surf. You can see where they are from a cliff top, because the waves look flatter, but they are almost impossible to see at sea level. If you want to get out through the waves, a rip can

offer a welcome free ride. If you are in trouble or are trying to stay inshore, you must get out of the rip by paddling or swimming straight across it to water that is going inshore. Never try to fight against it, which is exhausting and futile.

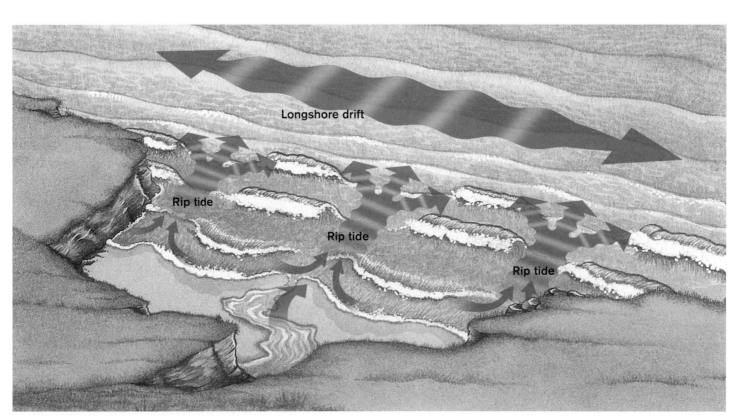

Longshore drift

Rip tide

Rip tide

Rip tide

Wind and Waves

When paddling on the open sea, winds and waves are important features, and they can have an immediate effect on what you are trying to do. It is crucial that you appreciate their power, and the way in which they work.

Wind Types

It does not take a strong wind to affect a boat. Even a light breeze, which you would barely notice on shore, can have quite a dramatic effect. Surprisingly, it is not paddling into the wind that causes most people problems, because this merely slows you down. A following wind is the one to look out for.

When it strikes, your boat will constantly try to turn around to face upwind, and most of your energy is used to keep the boat pointing the way you want to go. Kayaks suffer the worse from this; canoes a little less so, especially if a solo paddler is sitting in the back. It happens because the centre of drag of the boat (the deepest part of it, where most of your weight is) is usually quite far forward, and the tail half of the boat slews around quite easily. Boats are often designed this way to make them easy to

turn. The solution is to have a skeg, or rudder, at the back, or even to move your weight back if you can, to make the tail a little heavier. Some short boats as short as 3m (10ft) long, are very difficult to paddle in a following wind.

A cross-wind has much the same effect, blowing the tail away and making the boat turn towards the wind. It is less annoying and more predictable than a tail-wind because you know which way it wants to turn, but it is still very tiring as you constantly have to sweep stroke to

● *The wind has a huge effect on waves, which should never be underestimated.*

keep the boat on track. Many of the design features of sea kayaks are specifically intended to combat the effect of wind, but they can never eradicate it completely without rendering the boat impossible to manoeuvre.

When planning your trip, get accurate weather forecasts to see what conditions are likely, and remember that wind directions can change very suddenly. In warm weather, there is a tendency for winds to blow offshore at night as the land cools and the air over it flows out to sea. As the temperature rises through the day, the wind blows increasingly strongly onshore towards the warmer land. It is possible to experience winds swinging a full 360° in one 24-hour period. Mariners refer to a wind blowing onshore as lee shore conditions; an offshore wind creates a weather shore.

● *Waves without wind. This shore is catching a big ocean swell, but there may still be places to launch and land.*

Waves

On the open sea, waves are caused by the wind unless the water is moving quickly over submerged rocks. In the latter case, the effect is exactly the same as a white water river. Wind-blown waves are another matter, and they fall into two categories: chop and swell.

● *Onshore wind. Wind on its own isn't a danger, but the effect it has on the swell makes for heavy surf conditions.*

Chop

Random small waves, created by variable winds over a short distance, are known as chop. A calm sea can become choppy in a matter of minutes when the wind strength increases. Chop can be confusing for paddlers because waves seem to come at them from all directions. The best thing is to ignore the waves as much as possible – try to relax and trust your balance. Sometimes it can help to surf the waves, if only for a few seconds.

Swell

Winds blowing in the same direction for a long distance create a swell. The longer the wind pushes, the bigger the waves get. Winds blowing around the outside of a storm system commonly send 6m (20ft) waves radiating out across the ocean. Once these waves are made, they do not diminish unless they meet an oncoming wind, which reduces them. They will still be very large even after travelling 1,000km (620 miles) without any further power from the wind that created them.

Swell only ever occurs over oceanic distances, and is rarely a concern in small enclosed seas such as the Mediterranean.

Small swells of 1m (3½ft) can occur, for example, in some of the larger lakes in the North American and Canadian Great Lakes, but they do not rival the swells of the Pacific or Atlantic, which commonly reach 10m (33ft) high.

When paddling in the sea, you could experience chop and swell at the same time, and in fact this is very common. If you can think of the two as separate features, superimposed on each other and to be treated independently, you will not find them difficult to deal with.

Wind with Waves

A combination of wind and waves can occur in a variety of ways. Since choppy water is always associated with a local wind, you will have the latter to contend with as well. When the conditions become severe, with a 1m (3½ft) chop, you might find yourself in a trough, but when you go over a wave you will be hit by a savage gust that might even capsize you. Be ready for this. Anticipate, and lean into the wind, keeping your paddles low to stop the wind catching them.

Swells are affected by the wind direction. A following wind (onshore) will blow the tops off the waves and make them crumble rather than pitch. Offshore winds will steepen the faces of the waves, and make them rear up and crash down as they break.

One of the most notable effects of winds, waves and currents is the difference between wind blowing in the same direction as the tide and wind against the tide. If the tide creates a current flowing strongly downwind, the water might be smooth despite quite windy conditions. When the tide turns and the water is flowing against the wind, there might be a dramatic worsening of the conditions at sea until the area resembles a rapid, with large standing waves as well as chop.

● *The effects of swell and wind-chop superimposed on one another.*

Navigation and Distance

It is easy to think of touring and sea paddling as placid activities, far removed from the demands of white water, but a river flows in only one direction, and this makes it hard to get lost. On the sea there is a far greater chance of ending up in the wrong place, and the demands on your physical strength and stamina mean that you will tire more easily. No matter how confident a paddler you are inland, at sea you need to be able to navigate and chart your position, and accurately gauge how far you and your group can paddle without tiring.

Navigational Equipment
Different types of open water paddling call for different pieces of navigational equipment, but you should always take a compass with you whenever you paddle on the sea, on large lakes or on estuaries. The most important point with any equipment is that you know how to use it correctly, otherwise it will be useless.

○ Maps can be laminated to make them waterproof. Some spraydecks (skirts) have an accessory to hold maps in place.

Compass, Charts and Maps
If you are planning to spend the duration of your trip within easy reach of the shore, there is little need for sophisticated navigational equipment, but whenever you paddle on large lakes, rivers and the sea you should always have a compass with you, just in case. You also need to be sure that you know how to use the compass properly. At sea, a chart is extra insurance and will help you to identify onshore landmarks.

If you intend to make a significant open-water crossing, you must study basic nautical navigation. It is important that you can decide what compass bearing to paddle on to reach your goal, and that you can pay attention to it during your trip. It is rarely a case of pointing your boat where you want to go – at best this usually results in paddling much further than necessary, and at worst you might never get there.

If you are at sea and a fog descends unexpectedly (as it so often can do), a compass and a good knowledge of your locale make the difference between getting ashore safely and needing to be rescued by the emergency services. Paddling in the dark is great fun, and navigation at night can often be easier than by day if you can identify the onshore lights. Even so, you still need to be equipped with a compass.

Global Positioning System
For adventurous paddlers planning longer trips out at sea, more sophisticated navigational equipment is now available. The high-tech gadget known as the global positioning system (GPS) will provide you with a definitive position (a grid reference), and indicate which way you are travelling and how fast, which is invaluable information when the land is out of sight. The GPS is now becoming increasingly popular and affordable. If you can afford one, and want to use the very best navigational technology, it is a brilliant acquisition, although you will need a chart and a compass to use with it. Make sure you know how to use it correctly before you set out to sea.

○ A compass mounted securely on the front deck hatch of a sea kayak. This is invaluable equipment for open water.

Lighting
Not only is it important that you can identify your location with accuracy on open water, you also need to be well lit yourself. If you ever need the help of a rescue crew, they won't be able to find you unless you are visible. There is also a very real chance that you could be hit by a larger boat that cannot see your tiny craft. Always find out in advance what kind of shipping uses the water you are planning to paddle on, and plan the route of your trip accordingly.

Even if you are planning to paddle only 1 km (½ mile) offshore, you need to make sure you can be seen clearly. Many paddlers use chemical glow-stickers attached to their boats and their helmets and clothing to make them visible at night. Glow-stickers do not ruin your night vision, and they have the advantage of needing no batteries or precautions against soaking. They are available from most boating suppliers and some large DIY stores.

It always pays to be prepared for all eventualities, just in case you ever do need to take evasive action. If paddling out at sea, include a strobe light and flares as part of your safety and rescue equipment. For emergency use – for example, if you think a larger boat may collide with you – a strobe light is extremely bright and eye-catching, and your best chance of attracting attention. If you do not have a strobe, use a flare.

◔ Younger children can paddle in double boats with an adult; they should always wear a flotation aid.

◑ Your personal limits can vary. If you feel less than 100 per cent on the day, your stamina will be affected.

Know your Limits

It is important to know how far you and the rest of your group can paddle before tackling the open water. Bear in mind that your range on sheltered flat water will be greater than out at sea, where conditions are more demanding: paddling against a wind or current can make a big difference to your range, as can the roughness of the sea. Your response and strength can only be learnt from experience, so don't present yourself with too much of a challenge to begin with.

Children can run out of energy quite suddenly; when they do, they may refuse to co-operate, and towing them will be essential. The best solution is to have them in a double boat with an adult. This way they will not tire as quickly because the adult will do most of the paddling.

OPEN WATER EQUIPMENT

Open water, sea and long-distance paddling has special demands, and the boats usually differ dramatically from those used for inland day boating. There is also a variety of other accessories that can make touring in a kayak or canoe that much safer and more enjoyable. The key issue is self-sufficiency.

If you are likely to be away from any possible assistance for much of your journey, you will have to carry everything with you. You might end up using a fully equipped, expedition sea kayak. If, on the other hand, you are going to be a short distance from populated areas for the whole journey, your only considerations are comfort, and a credit card may be all you need.

Finally, it is important that you have everything you need to be safe and comfortable, but equally important that you can carry your boat. Do not attempt to take every gadget that could possibly come in handy. The emphasis should be on keeping it light. If you cannot carry the boat, how well can you paddle it?

❰ *Paddling on the open sea is awesome, but make sure you are sufficiently equipped.*

❱ *Open water gear can be stowed on the boat in waterproof compartments.*

Boats for Open Water

The range of open-water boats available can be divided into sea or inland, and kayak or canoe. Many of the key issues that need to be accommodated for by the boats' design are the same, whether it is a kayak or a canoe, to be used on inland waterways or the ocean. There are a variety of first-rate boats that can be used for both touring and open and sea-water paddling, and these will give you maximum flexibility.

Kayaks

Sea kayaks are intended for coastal and open-sea touring, but they can be used for touring inland and can negotiate simple rapids up to Grade (Class) 2 as easily as ocean waves. There are also light, fast, narrow sea boats suitable for day trips, and bigger, heavier ones aimed at trips and expeditions lasting several days. Both have waterproof bulkheads and hatches to contain essential equipment. They can be used with or without a rudder; purist paddlers object to

⦿ *An open canoe is an ideal platform for exploring marinas such as this.*

rudders because they think the kayaker should be able to control the boat without one, but do not let that put you off. Some boats have small, traditional cockpits, and others modern keyhole ones.

Double kayaks can be a faster and more sociable way to travel. Some have provision for carrying children in their mid-section. They have most of the features found in solo kayaks, but will also have a rudder because the boats are too long to manoeuvre without one.

⦿ *Open boats are a popular choice for one or more paddlers taking excursions on inland lakes and waterways.*

Touring kayaks are usually less comprehensively equipped than the sea boats, but often have many of the same features. The hull design tends to be the main difference, the emphasis being on manageability in more restricted conditions on inland water rather than sea-worthiness in extreme conditions.

● *Modern touring kayaks suitable for inland, coastal or open sea use.*

Canoes

Except for those canoes used on challenging stretches of white water, canoes tend to have fewer fittings and features than their counterpart kayaks. This belies the fact that subtleties of hull design can make a huge difference to the way the canoe behaves.

Touring canoes are built to cope with tracking and windage, which is the deflection of the boat off its route by the wind. They have a significant keel, and more balanced seating positions than other kinds of canoe. However, there is less specific provision for storage in a canoe than a kayak, despite its greater load-carrying capability.

Some canoe models have air tanks for flotation. These are usually small, forming seats in the bow and stern. They can be used for additional storage, and are reached through a waterproof hatch. However, they are not very common in touring boats, the very boats in which you might want to carry bulky camping or other equipment. Usually you will have to store gear in large dry bags or drums, which can be lashed to the seats to keep them securely in place.

Touring canoes are sometimes used for coastal paddling, but you should rarely venture far away from the shore in one because they are much more susceptible to the wind than sea kayaks, making

them less easy to control. However, they do have one advantage: even if you cannot roll a touring canoe you can still right it, re-enter it, and bail out in the event of a capsize. For a full description of this method of self-rescue, see the technique, *Right Boat and Re-enter*.

● *Paddling a sea/touring kayak. Note the waterproof hatches and the deck lines for attaching gear, safety and rescue equipment and spare paddles.*

Deck Fittings

Touring kayaks usually have deck lines, which are ropes running along and across the deck for handling the boat, and under which you can store equipment. Some of the cross-lines might be made from shock cord for securing a map or other item.

Canoes, clearly, do not have a deck on which to stow things but, if you need to lash down a lot of gear, a good solution is a cargo net, which can also be used for lying or hooking on quick-access items.

Pumps

Inevitably, you will ship water if paddling for a long time. A hand pump can be used to bail out a kayak or canoe. Some kayaks come equipped with hand pump and/or foot pumps, which means you can pump out water with your spraydeck still attached. As a rule, hand pumps move more water, but you need one or both hands free to operate them. The foot pump is a slower way to get the water out, but at least you can carry on using your paddle, which might be essential in rough seas. When choosing a pump, think about what you are likely to face in your paddling. After a capsize and re-entry (canoe or kayak), you will definitely have to pump out water, but this is an extreme case. If you're not going to be doing anything like this, the money might be better spent on a really good spraydeck to keep the water out, and a sponge for the annoying splashes you ship while getting in and out.

Paddles for Open Water

There is a wide choice of paddles for use on open water and the sea, from wing to split kinds. Paddles for touring and open water need different design features to paddles for general-purpose flat and white water paddling. Here we look at some of the popular advanced styles of touring paddles.

The most important issue when deciding which kind of paddle to buy is weight. If you are going to paddle for a long time, you need blades which are as light as possible. This means that modern high-tech composite materials are most people's first choice, but many paddlers still like wooden paddles, too.

Long paddles are also important to achieve a low paddling angle. This is especially true for kayaking, but even touring canoeists tend to use longer paddles with narrower blades.

Whatever paddle you choose, inspect it carefully before each use, and remember that your ability to move the boat, steer and roll relies on the integrity of your paddle. A damaged blade might break off just when you need it most.

● *Symmetrical bladed paddles work very well for touring and open water.*

Symmetrical Blades

The simple, symmetrical paddle is perfectly adequate for touring despite the undoubted benefits of more specialized designs. Make sure that your symmetrical blade is curved and spooned, or has a dihedral face, or it will flutter and will be difficult to paddle with over any distance.

Asymmetrical Blades

Paddle blades with an asymmetrical edge are more efficient than the equivalent symmetrical kind, and they make less splash in the water. The reasons for this

● *Asymmetical blades are less splashy and more efficient for forward paddling.*

● *A replica of a traditional Greenland paddle, as used by Inuit paddlers. It is so narrow that it gives little support, but it propels the kayak well.*

are clear when you look at how a paddle blade enters the water for a stroke. The disadvantage is that you must pick it up the right way round to get the full benefit.

Paddle Shafts

One notable feature of open water paddles is the shaft design. Many touring paddlers use bent paddle shafts. Kayak paddles are available with ergonomically curved shafts, which are very helpful in preventing some of the repetitive strain injuries that long-distance kayaking can cause. Canoe paddles are also available with these ergo shafts, or with a simpler

● *The bent paddle shaft is less likely to strain the wrists over long distances.*

⬆ *Though it is rare to break a paddle, the consequences can be dire if you are a long way from the shore. Split (break-down) paddles are carried on deck or stowed in the boat as insurance in case this happens.*

bend, so that the blade is at an angle to a normal, straight paddle shaft. The latter simply allows the blade of the paddle to address the water at a more efficient angle, rather than altering the ergonomics of your physical movement.

Wing Paddle

The wing paddle was invented for kayak racing, but many of its benefits make it useful for touring. The wing paddle is supremely efficient and it helps to stabilize the boat. The blade moves through the water in an arc, which

utilizes many more muscle groups than does a conventional paddle, thereby making each stroke far more powerful.

Greenland Paddle

The Greenland paddling technique is described in *Stroke Variations*. The actual Greenland paddle acquired its long thin shape because the Inuit peoples who designed it did not have the right materials to make wider, flatter blades. There are some advantages to the design, such as low windage (deflection caused by the wind), and the fact that you can use the paddle as a club, or can wind your fishing tackle around it, although these are dubious benefits for today's kayaker. Those who use this paddle do so because they enjoy using traditional equipment and mastering the same challenges as the Inuit.

Spare and Split Paddles

If you are planning to paddle a long distance, or a long way from the shore, you might want to take spare paddles with you in case any member of the group loses or damages their paddle. In a canoe it is easy to store a spare paddle under the seat, but this is a little more difficult in a kayak. The usual solution is to have a set of split (break-down) paddles that can be secured under the deck lines of your kayak, so that they do not get in the way of your paddling. By storing them here, it is possible to access them to roll with half a paddle if you lose your main paddle when knocked flat by a wave.

Spraydecks for Touring

These spraydecks (spray skirts) are not necessarily different to those worn for flat or white water, but few paddlers want to have a tight neoprene tube around their waist when paddling over a long distance and for several hours. Some paddlers choose to wear nylon spraydecks to avoid this, but these will let in water and allow water pools to form on the deck. A good solution is a combination touring deck. This comprises a neoprene deck with a fabric body tube, and will sometimes have braces to hold it up. With this deck you will have the advantages of both systems.

⬇ *This touring spraydeck features a neoprene deck with a fabric body tube and represents the best of both worlds for long-distance paddling.*

Open Water Clothing and Accessories

It is vital that you make the right choices with clothing for open water and the sea, not least so that you feel comfortable and warm. There is a wide choice of clothing available, and newcomers might feel slightly bewildered, but these guidelines will point you in the right direction.

Clothing for open- and sea-water paddling varies much more than that for white water because the emphasis is on versatility, due to the changing nature of the conditions. It is quite usual to take a choice of clothing with you in the boat.

Insulation

Though this is usually the same as for any other active sport, it is vital that you have a number of layers so that you can adjust your insulation level to suit the changing conditions. If you stop paddling you will notice a dramatic drop in your perceived temperature, unless you use a combination of fairly expensive layers.

Breathable Shells

It is usually necessary to have a wind- and waterproof shell garment with you, even if you do not wear it all the time. This should always be made from a breathable fabric that allows the vapour from perspiration

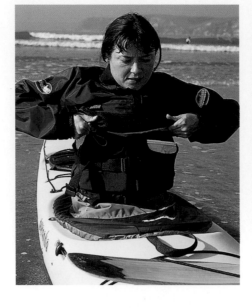

◔ A cagoule may not be necessary in fine weather but it is useful to have one with you if you become chilly.

◔ You may want to remove your cagoule, but you should always keep on the flotation device.

to escape, otherwise it will condense and you will become increasingly cold and wet. Some paddlers prefer a shell that they can put on over a buoyancy aid (personal flotation device) while they are afloat. Be aware, though, that capsizing with a cagoule over your head

can be a frightening experience: it would be very difficult to free yourself or to remove your spraydeck if you became tangled up in your garment underwater! In fine weather, a cagoule may be unnecessary, but it is very useful to be able to put one over your buoyancy aid if your thighs turn chilly. No matter how warm the weather, it is absolutely essential that you wear your buoyancy aid when paddling on the sea.

There are jackets and cagoules specially designed for paddlers. They are much better, and cheaper, than using a breathable walking jacket, which would fall apart very quickly if used for boating. In more extreme sea paddling conditions some kayakers wear cagoules. These are not quite as good as dry tops, but they have the advantage that they offer a little more adjustability and ventilation. They usually come with a hood, and are modern versions of the Inuit tuvilik or paddling jacket, which was made from sealskin. In Arctic and sub-Arctic conditions it is necessary to wear survival or drysuits because of the extremely short survival time should a paddler fall into the water.

❷ A good-quality kayaking jacket for use on open water and the sea.

Trousers

Many open water paddlers prefer salopettes, which are trousers with braces attached to hold them up, because they are more versatile, and provide a bit of upper body protection when worn without a jacket. Basic over-trousers are also popular, and these will keep the wind out when you are not in the boat. The choice of lower body wear for kayaking depends on how much time you will spend on land: whereas the canoeist will have his or her lower body exposed to the elements the whole time, the kayaker is relatively protected from the elements and has little need of extra insulation when paddling. Wetsuits are not appropriate for this type of paddling because they are fairly restrictive, can become hot and clingy, and are generally too uncomfortable to be worn for long periods.

◔ *Durable polyethylene containers, known as BDHs, are ideal for storing small items that need to be kept dry.*

◔ *A roll-top dry bag is useful for carrying items such as mobile phones and car keys.*

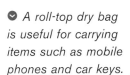

Headgear

It is unusual to wear a helmet while touring, but you may need to keep your head warm. It is well known that most of your body's heat loss is from the head so, if you are getting cold, wear a hood or a hat. Any hat will do; a woollen hat is a popular choice because it is very warm, but it can get heavy when wet.

In sunny conditions a hat with a peak or brim is invaluable. If your hat does not stay firmly on your head, you might want to tie it on, or attach it to your collar; if you don't, it is likely to blow away in a strong gust of wind. Of course, in colder weather you may be wearing a paddling shell with a hood, and this can serve the same purpose as a hat, without the likelihood of it falling off and blowing away.

◔ *Two sea kayakers appropriately dressed for the conditions. Despite the sunshine, sharp sea winds mean that warm headgear may still be needed.*

Additional Gear

Many items such as mobile phones, car keys and first aid kits need to be kept dry. The dry compartments of a sea kayak are not 100 per cent waterproof and, in any case, it is better to have really important items on your person.

Dry bags are a good way to protect your essentials from the water. There are different types, but the most common is the roll-top variety. For dryness and more protection, use screw-top polyethylene jars, known as BDH containers after the chemical company that invented them. These are available from paddling stores. They are only 100 per cent waterproof if used with a rubber seal inside the lid.

Safety and Rescue Equipment

You can meet all kinds of problems, from being injured and requiring a tow back ashore to attracting sharks drawn by your flailing legs as you attempt to swim for safety. The following equipment should help to guarantee your safety.

Flotation

The buoyancy aid (personal flotation device or PFD) should be worn at all times when paddling on open water or the sea. Styles of buoyancy aid vary but the emphasis for most sea and touring paddlers seems to be on having pockets in which you can carry certain essential items. Apart from this, the important thing is comfort. You will see many touring paddlers wearing a buoyancy aid that is incorrectly adjusted or unzipped, simply because it is not designed for long-term comfort. If they were to capsize, they would have difficulty doing up the buoyancy aid in the water, and would

○ *A typical buoyancy aid (personal flotation device) for sea paddling. It has bright panels and retro-reflective tape for visibility, and a selection of pockets for survival essentials.*

experience all kinds of problems through not being able to keep hold of the boat and paddles.

Many buoyancy aids have some retro-reflective material, making them and the wearer more visible in poor light. This safety feature is not so visible when you are swimming though, in which case consider retro-reflective cuffs on your jacket, or a strobe light.

Whistle

A whistle is very useful if you need to attract attention in open water. Sound carries a long way over open water, and it could be that it is the only way to alert rescuers to your position.

Strobes and Beacons

A specialist strobe light is essential for anyone going offshore. When switched on it will flash at a rate that is quickly recognized by the rescue services, and be visible over a long distance. If attached to the shoulder of a buoyancy aid it will be seen even when you are swimming. Some offshore paddlers also take radio or satellite

○ *Additional items for a sea trip might include a hand pump, knife, compass, VHF radio, transistor receiver, sunscreen and a mobile phone.*

beacons with them. When activated they send out a signal that is detected by special receivers, or even satellites, which alert the emergency services, giving them your exact position. The disadvantage is that they can be accidentally activated.

Flares

Flares are a common piece of safety kit to ensure that you can attract attention in case of an emergency. They can be

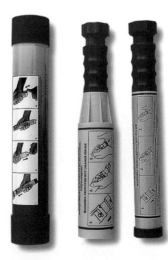

○ *Many types of flares are available commercially; these flares are a popular choice for offshore paddling.*

● *Using a waist-towline to recover a kayak after a capsize.*

● *The towline packs away neatly into a pouch worn as a belt.*

● *Pumping water out of a sea kayak using a hand pump. Excess water in the boat can be a real discomfort.*

spotted over greater distances than a strobe, and without many of the problems of radio beacons. You will need to carry a minimum of three flares. Always check that your flares are within their "use-by" date, otherwise they may not work.

Towline

A towline is a useful piece of equipment for helping other paddlers. You might need to tow a boat back to a swimmer, an injured or tired paddler ashore, or help a slower one keep up. The line is usually worn around the waist, but some paddlers have towing systems built into the deck of their kayak.

A simple tow can be attached to the front of the boat you are helping. If more paddlers are on hand to help, it is worth considering a husky tow, which means that two or more paddlers pull.

The most important point about towing is to ensure that you can release the tow, using the quick release buckle, if you get into difficulties yourself.

Bivvy Bag

This is possibly the best piece of safety kit ever made. If you have nothing else, an orange plastic bivvy bag can be a lifesaver. It is light, takes up little space, and can be used in four ways:

• To keep a victim warm when back on land: put them in the bag and, in extreme cases, get in with them to add your own body heat and increase their temperature.

• To keep yourself alive in the water. If you get into a bivvy in the water, it dramatically reduces the rate at which you lose heat. You can extend your cold-water survival time tenfold because while your body will heat up the water around you, you will keep the warm water in the bag, rather than constantly exchanging it for more cold water. You may also be less likely to get unwanted attention from predators such as sharks, because you will be big and orange and wafting gently rather than small, flailing and behaving like an injured seal.

• To attract attention by waving it around.

• To build a shelter from the sun, wind or rain when stranded ashore.

● *A waterproof first-aid kit suitable for all kinds of outdoor activities, including paddling. The orange plastic bivvy bag (right) is invaluable.*

OPEN WATER PADDLING SKILLS

People who only paddle canoes and kayaks on flat or open water often pay less attention to the basic paddling skills than those involved in white water or other specialist disciplines. This is understandable because they think that precise manoeuvring skills and technical strokes are wasted on flat water, or water with a lot of room to move around on. What these paddlers do not understand is that the better and more efficiently you can paddle, the farther and faster you will go on flat and sea water with the same amount of effort.

If you take up open water paddling or touring, having reached a level of proficiency in a general-purpose boat, you may well find that you have to modify your approach. In a short, simple kayak, many strokes are even more effective if done aggressively and explosively. But in a longer touring kayak, or when countering the effect of the wind, you may need more finesse and subtler leans to make the stroke work, and this can be very satisfying. The same applies to canoes – perhaps even more so. That is why it is so important that you respond sensitively to your boat and your paddle.

◐ Setting out to sea in a boat gives an overwhelming sense of freedom.

◐ Sea kayaks offer plenty of opportunity for camping and touring trips.

Stroke Variations

When paddling long distances in touring boats, or in the windy conditions often found on open water, you will need to adopt a different paddling style and in some cases learn new techniques.

Slide Hand

As we have already mentioned, kayak paddles for touring tend to be longer than a general-purpose or white water paddle. This is partly so that you can paddle with a lower stroke, reducing the effect of the wind, the chance of being blown off course or being capsized. A high paddle stroke is more efficient in still air, but a low stroke can be essential in a breeze, and is certainly more relaxing if you are paddling a long way.

One excellent low-stroke technique, called the Greenland slide hand, originated with the Inuit people of Greenland. They recognized the benefits of a narrow blade and a small overall paddle size in a strong wind. The technique involves holding the paddle with one hand, close to the middle, and the other near, or holding, the blade. You can then make a stroke with an extended reach, which allows a lower paddle angle, as well as more leverage to keep a wayward boat on track.

As the paddle goes across to make a stroke on the other side, slide the hands to use the same grip at the other end of the paddle. The action is almost one of throwing the paddle across, and catching it in the required grip just as the stroke begins. The technique can be used

continuously while paddling forward, or just to increase your reach in order to turn difficult boats more easily.

The picture below shows a paddler using a traditional Greenland paddle, but the technique can be used with any kayak paddle that does not have a bent shaft.

Assisted Turns

Another way to make a touring boat turn more easily is by using a dramatic outside lean. Whether moving forward or stationary, most straight-running boats, which have a long keel to assist tracking, will be much easier to turn if you lean them over to reduce the effect of the keel. Leaning to the inside or the outside might work, but an outside lean is better when going forward because you can then lean on your sweep stroke which, with an extended grip, can be very supportive indeed.

Sculling for Support

The concept of using a blade in a sculling action was described in the basic kayak and canoe paddling skills chapter. Sculling for support was deliberately

◄ Using a slide hand for forward paddling with a Greenland paddle. The top hand is holding the paddle at the blade. As the stroke ends, the paddle is slid across to be held at the other end. It feels odd but works surprisingly well.

◔ Sculling for support is a skill that can prove very useful in a long, narrow closed cockpit kayak.

omitted because it is a more advanced skill and much more difficult to achieve. In most general-purpose kayaks sculling for support is ineffective, and it is best avoided altogether in canoes. In a long, narrow boat such as a sea kayak, however, it can be very useful.

The sculling support stroke can help the paddler to avoid a capsize. It uses essentially the same action as the sculling draw, but the paddle blade is placed face down on the water. If the boat is at a dramatic lean angle, sculling can support it there indefinitely, whereas a low or high brace would only provide lift for long enough to recover to an upright position. An expert can scull with the boat laid completely on its side, provided his body is in the water and effectively supporting itself.

Many people find it easier to lie back while sculling for support, and this is recommended by many older books and instructors. However, it is safer and more effective to maximize your reach by remaining perpendicular, particularly once your body is immersed. The danger of lying back while sculling or high bracing is that it strains the shoulder, which can lead to injury, and the position makes it difficult to control the boat.

⊙ *Sliding the hands to one end enables the paddler to lean over for much of the stroke, which helps the boat to turn.*

Knifed-J and Figure Eight

These two strokes are peculiar to open canoeing, and though fairly obscure, they are worth mentioning because they are useful in windy conditions. Sometimes, particularly when paddling solo in a single-seater boat, it seems that every time you take your blade out of the water the boat blows off line. The solution is not to take it out at the end of the stroke, but to turn it flat to the hull and slice it forward to where the stroke started. In its simplest form this is called a knifed-J. The blade rotates at the end of the stroke and is ready to knife forward through the water, controlling the tracking without slowing down the boat.

A more complex version is the figure eight. It is a powerful stroke for controlling inside turns and is sometimes called an Indian stroke. It is similar to the knifed-J stroke, except that after the blade slices forward the T-grip is rotated in the palm of the top hand so that the next stroke is made with what was the back of the paddle. The figure eight is only suitable for fairly flat paddles.

Both the knifed-J and the figure eight are also very useful for sneaking up on wildlife, when taking the blade out of the water would make audible splashing and dripping sounds.

Re-entry and Roll

If you are paddling a sea or touring kayak on open water, this is a skill that will give you great confidence. If conditions are bad and you have had to swim, your companions may be struggling to rescue you. Or you might have ignored all advice to the contrary, and gone paddling alone. If you can re-enter your boat while it is upside down, and roll up, you will have the ultimate self-rescue skill at your disposal.

You may be tempted to right the boat first, and then try to climb in. This is possible in an open canoe, but a narrow kayak is too unstable. You will also find that righting the boat allows water into the cockpit. If you re-enter and put the spraydeck on underwater, you may be able to roll up with less water aboard.

The technique for re-entry and roll is non-specific. You need to try it for yourself and work out the best way for you, but obviously, being able to roll already is a pre-requisite.

RE-ENTRY TIPS

• Put your paddles through the decklines of the kayak sideways. This helps to keep the boat upside down as you get in.
• Get right under the boat before trying to put your legs in. Start off by facing the stern, then back somersault into the cockpit. Think of it as a capsize drill in reverse.
• Remain calm and move slowly, so that none of your actions are wasted.

Re-entry Technique

1 Hold either side of the cockpit rim, push yourself down under the boat, and allow your legs to float up between your arms.

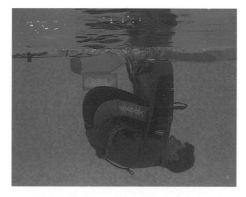

2 Push your feet into the cockpit, concentrating on staying directly under the boat. Try not to float up to one side.

3 Once your legs are in, get into the seat and put on your spraydeck (spray skirt). Grab your paddle and roll up.

Launching and Landing

Launching and landing skills are rarely required, but nonetheless are important because you are most likely to need them in an emergency situation. Practise them, and note the rules that apply in what can often be testing and difficult conditions.

While all paddlers should learn and practise how to seal launch into water from a height, touring paddlers will have less need of this skill, except in an emergency. Instead, sea paddlers need to be able to get afloat through waves on the sea, or a big lake or river that is large enough for the wind to produce some chop or swell.

In any type of boat it is important that you can launch and land effectively. In a touring boat, such as a sea kayak, that might be relatively fragile and

⌃ A double sea kayak setting out to sea from a public beach.

⌃ Even small waves require good technique and can upset the unwary.

heavily laden with supplies and rescue equipment, it is particularly important that you can do the job correctly. If a wave catches you sideways, you may lose control of your boat and capsize. Quite apart from it being a bad start to your fun day out, capsizing in very shallow water can cause you difficulties, and may even prove dangerous.

Launching Through Waves

Make sure that the boat is ready to launch, and that you have put in a drain plug (if required), secured the hatch covers, and tied down and protected your kit from the elements.

Next, put the boat down at the water's edge, pointing directly at it. If you are in a tidal area, remember that the tide might be coming in or going out, which could affect matters. If it is a heavy or tandem craft, make sure that you can move it towards the water without having to lift it, otherwise, once you get in, you might be stuck fast. And do not put the boat in

Launching Technique

1 Get into your kayak and attach the spraydeck when you are well above the waterline. Most paddlers find this easiest to do at the water's edge.

2 Move the kayak into the water, using your hands to lift yourself off the ground and push yourself along.

3 As soon as you are afloat, pick up the paddle and head out into the deeper water, propelling yourself forward with the paddle.

deep water where it can float because if you do it will be turned sideways by the waves, and can possibly knock you down or capsize. Once sideways to even small waves in shallow water, any boat becomes difficult to control. If you must manhandle it while afloat, stand on the seaward side.

Next, get into the boat quickly, and secure your spraydeck if you have one. Do not put your paddle down because it might be washed away. If you need both hands, secure the paddle under the deck-lines. If there are two of you, get into the boat one at a time.

Once in the boat, push it into the waves using your paddle on one side and hands on the other. Concentrate on keeping the boat at 90° to the waves, and then grab your paddle and get moving. Do not stop until you are so far out that the waves are not breaking. In particular, try to avoid capsizing in shallow water.

◉ *Holding sea kayaks stready in preparation for landing.*

◉ *This double kayak is preparing to land through waves.*

Landing Through Waves

The important point about landing a boat is to make sure you do not surf in on the front of a wave. Paddle in as close as you can while still allowing waves to pass underneath you. Even in small waves you might have to back-paddle to make sure they do not propel you shorewards, especially if the wind is onshore.

When you are as close to the shore as you can get, or are in danger of touching the bottom, paddle in on the back of a wave until your boat runs up the beach. Leap out as quickly as you can before the boat is sucked back with the returning wave, or before another wave comes in to turn your boat sideways. From here, you may be able to push yourself up the beach, using your hands, without getting out of the boat. Otherwise, jump out of the boat and pull it up through the shallow water on to the beach. Take care not to drop your paddle, or else it might be washed back into the sea.

Landing Technique

1 Wait for a wave to pass under your boat, then paddle in towards the shore on the back of the wave. Do not surf in on the front of the wave.

2 As the water gets too shallow for the boat to float, paddle on to the wave to get as far ashore as you can.

3 Push yourself safely ashore and jump out of the boat before any more waves come along. Keep hold of your boat, so that it doesn't get swept away by a wave.

5 ADVANCED PADDLING

SPECIALIST DISCIPLINES

Paddlers who achieve a high level of all-round skill and fitness tend to specialize in one or two disciplines: no one has the time to be an expert in more than a couple of fields. If you are looking for a speciality, the choice is wide – kayak or canoe, sea or inland, paddle or sail, freestyle or race. To help you make your decision, here are some key considerations. Two points to note are that, firstly, those disciplines with a competitive element are covered in more detail in the next section of this book. And secondly, with the possible exception of IC10 sailing, it will not be possible to attempt any of the following activities safely, with any hope of real success, until you are proficient at the skills covered so far.

◀ *Play paddling is the aquatic equivalent of skate-boarding on land.*

◉ *Using a kite to power a double sea kayak. This technology is still in its infancy.*

Extreme White Water Paddling

It is probably a lot more sensible to read about extreme kayaking than to try it, but if you really are tempted, the following gives a graphic description of what is involved. Danger is the key note, and the risks of serious injury are extremely high.

Extreme kayaking began around the 1970s, when paddlers first attempted white water descents so severe that if they fell out of the boat they were unlikely to survive. Usually listed as Grade (Class) 5+ or Grade 6 type waters, extreme paddling is characterized by large vertical drops or waterfalls.

The first practitioners were slalom paddlers because they already had the highly developed skills needed to tackle the difficult conditions. They were badly limited by their equipment, however. There was a limit to the volume of water or the size of drops they could tackle before their fibreglass boats disintegrated and pitched them into the water.

In retrospect, we know that the boats could have been made stronger then, but there was an obsession with light weight among performance-orientated paddlers. Perhaps this was justified

because they invariably used 4m (13ft) long kayaks that became increasingly unwieldy as they got heavier.

As more boats were made from plastic, there was a significant shift in the world of extreme kayaking. First, the paddlers were able to attempt much more difficult conditions knowing that their boats were strong enough to withstand the water. Second, the foremost extreme white water paddlers were freestyle paddlers who had honed their skills doing the three-dimensional white water acrobatics that smaller, stronger boats made possible.

Assessing the Risks

The modern extreme kayaker is attempting water on which drowning or serious impact injuries are a constant threat. To stand any chance of survival he must use a boat that has been reinforced to prevent it from collapsing under the enormous pressure it must withstand, and have plate footrests with shock absorbers. Usually the boat will be very short.

Most kayakers now recognize that acceleration and manoeuvrability are far more important than outright speed. The boat will tend to be fairly rounded, and able to withstand impacts and potentially lethal pinning to which more pointed boats are susceptible. Extreme kayakers sometimes wear full face helmets such as those worn by motorcyclists, and even elbow pads and reinforced gloves. For instance, paddlers attempting long vertical drops might wear back supports to prevent spinal injuries.

Usually, tackling water this extreme is a team effort. While it is unusual for the paddlers to be able to help each other on the water, a rescue and support team in place on the banks will provide invaluable safety cover. All members of the team should be trained in first aid, and usually there will be at least one fully qualified doctor on hand. Climbing skills and equipment are often required to get paddlers to the top of a descent in order

◖ An open-boat canoeist running an extremely large waterfall.

to inspect the river beforehand. In some of the more extreme cases, when the geography makes climbing too difficult, helicopter support is used to inspect and gain access to the location.

Using all the skills and support at their disposal, modern extreme kayakers have successfully negotiated Grade 6 rapids that were thought impossible only a few years ago, and have paddled waterfalls more than 30m (100ft) in height without injury. However, there is always a fine line between success and failure, and a number of paddlers have died in far less extreme conditions. It is, therefore, hugely important to understand that such extreme and dangerous kayaking is only for a talented few who are supremely skilful, athletic, experienced, confident, determined and well-equipped.

● *Steep and technical, this rapid holds all kinds of dangers. A moment's loss of control could lead to entrapment by the rocks or powerful hydraulics.*

● *This rapid looks so big and turbulent that even a big kayak is hurled end over end out of control as the kayaker battles with the might of the river.*

● *A Grade 5+ river with water seething over and around submerged rocks. To be upside down or swimming here would lead to certain injury.*

Play Paddling

As the name suggests, play paddling is the out-and-out playful side of paddling, where practitioners practise all kinds of fantastic tricks in what is the boating world's answer to roller-skating.

Play paddling began in slalom boats because skilful paddlers enjoyed trying to stand their boats on end in waves and stoppers. It was good practice for white water river running because it taught paddlers to cope with anything that the river could throw at them.

It was not until the plastic revolution of the early 1980s that play paddling gripped the imagination of the average recreational boater. Paddling these new and apparently indestructible boats, boaters were able to expose their craft to extraordinary feats and a level of pounding that had never before been possible. This was probably the most significant development in the history of paddle sport.

Today, play paddling and its competitive discipline, freestyle, means being so skilled at using a kayak or canoe in white water that all safety and survival considerations become second nature. In effect, the paddler is playing − frolicking in the waves and hydraulics, surfing, and performing acrobatic tricks using the power of the river.

Since the 1980s, nearly all white water paddlers have used play to exploit the power of the river. Their antics led to the development of kayaks and canoes that were specially designed for play paddling, and it subsequently transpired that experts could negotiate harder rapids in

these boats than they could in boats originally designed for more serious river running. This led to more people using play boats for all types of paddling and the development of new skills, spawning yet another generation of play boats.

This trend continued for the best part of 20 years. At the end of the twentieth century, play boats were relegated to what is known as park and play. This is a kind of extreme play paddling that revolves around taking your boat to a specific spot, playing there the whole time, and then going home without having run any rapids in the play boat.

⬧ *A play paddler makes a wave-wheel down a rapid. Acrobatic tricks such as this are the main focus of play boating.*

The core play paddling activities are surfing river waves, and using hydraulics to perform vertical tricks, flipping the boat from end to end. These are the key skills, but the range of manoeuvres the expert can perform is bewildering. Virtually every river feature now facilitates some form of boat gymnastics. Many of the tricks are influenced by skate- and snow-boarding, and there is a culture of kayakers with their own music, dress code and jargon.

⬧ *A twenty-first century play boat. This kayak is only 1.9m (6¼ft) long. It is designed to be dynamically unstable to facilitate aggressive acrobatic and aerial manoeuvres.*

Play Paddling Equipment

The essential equipment for play paddling is virtually the same as for any other white water routine. There are special park and play kayaks that resemble squirt boats, but they are made from plastic and have more volume in the centre to ensure that they are held by powerful hydraulics, while also having many of the safety features of a normal white water kayak. They are not terribly safe for general white water use but you can make good use of a general white water boat (especially a fairly recent one), for play paddling. A 1999 competition freestyle boat was still regarded as a good all-round white water kayak two years later, for instance.

It helps to have shorter paddles for play and freestyle paddling, but any strong white water paddle will do. A flexible shaft is a useful feature because this

❯ A big three-dimensional aerial manoeuvre, called a "kick flip", performed by the author, Bill Mattos.

❍ The open canoeist, European Freestyle Champion, James Weir, paddling a massive stopper wave.

⌢ *A play boater performs a cartwheel in a decked C1 freestyle canoe.*

type of paddling is quite hard on the wrists. Most play boaters use a 45° feather on their paddles (feather is the term used to describe the angle between the two blades on a kayak paddle), a good compromise between the higher feather angles for long-distance paddling and the very low angles used by squirt boaters. Play paddling tends to wear down the paddle blades from paddling upstream in shallow water, and constantly scraping them across the boat.

What to Wear

Clothing is an important consideration for play paddlers because you will be regularly rolling and getting fully immersed in the water. Most play paddlers have the best spraydecks (spray skirts) and drytops money can buy. Safety, on the other hand, is less of an issue. Despite the undoubted danger of white

water, the play paddler tends to wear a fairly minimal buoyancy aid (personal flotation device, or PFD) because anything more would interfere with the flexibility needed for the play boater's gymnastic body movements. Helmets, unfortunately, often err on the side of fashion rather than total protection because play boaters try to avoid being thought of as too serious. It would be rare to find a play-boater with a throw-line or any other safety equipment in the boat, and many remove the end grabs from their boats, perhaps to improve the hydrodynamics, but more likely just to make the point.

This is the less responsible side of the sport. The appeal lies in the absence of many of the restrictions seen elsewhere, and the emphasis is on fun and dare-devil feats. It is worth adding, though, that play boating has a low accident rate, perhaps because of the extremely high skill level of the participants. It is not for novice paddlers.

⌄ *Paddling into a stopper wave from downstream. The paddler's bib denotes permission to paddle on a commercial artificial white water course.*

Play Paddling Etiquette

There is an accepted etiquette among play paddlers that differs from some of the rules normally observed on the river. White water paddlers usually focus on safety, which means giving way to anyone coming downstream, and letting other people join the front of an eddy wherever possible. However, these rules don't work very well for play paddlers. If a boater is playing on a wave or in a hole, they will not want to get out when another paddler approaches, but will expect the other paddler to be able to go around them. Similarly, play boaters tend to queue in the eddies to wait their turn on the wave, so to join the front of the eddy is jumping the queue, and not acceptable.

These variations work fine among like-minded individuals, because play paddlers are usually highly skilled, and they tend to stick to familiar sections of water that they can handle easily. The problems arise when paddlers of a different standard play on the same stretch of water, and when confident paddlers become impatient with others who are finding it a challenge just to survive. Whenever this situation occurs, both parties should be aware of the other's needs and accommodate them as much as possible. If this can't be achieved, one of the parties should agree to move to another stretch of water. Confrontations in the water are never acceptable because of the risk that someone will be hurt.

◒ A canoeist attempting a cartwheel stopper. Open canoes can perform amazing acrobatics in expert hands.

◒ A play boater cruising around on a broken river wave before planning his next move.

Squirt Boating

Squirt boating is a radical and very special type of paddling which appeared in the early 1980s, and had a profound influence on all kinds of white water boating. It added new levels of fun, especially when dipping the end of the boat under water.

A squirt boat is an extremely low-volume, lightweight kayak or canoe. In fact, squirt canoes are fairly rare, but should not be ignored. Most of the development of the squirt movement took place in kayaks, but the slalom canoeists contributed perhaps the most important idea of all, that of sinking the end of the boat in a controlled manoeuvre.

How It Developed
Slalom paddlers learnt to dip the ends of the boat, usually the stern, so that they could squeeze under the poles when negotiating difficult gates in a race or practice session. They quickly realized that this technique could also give them a dramatically quicker brake, turn and acceleration. It feels as though the water is storing up the energy carried into the

● *This squirt kayak shows just how flat and surfboard-like these low-volume boats are. The paddler's feet fit in the two bumps near the bow, and the knees in the two either side of the cockpit.*

turn, which then feeds back into the boat as it accelerates away from the gate. And this is, indeed, how it works; the kinetic energy is stored as hydraulic energy, which converts back to kinetic energy. Paddlers quickly realized that swooping around the rapids, using these invisible dynamic forces, can be tremendous fun.

C1 (single-seater competition canoe) slalom boaters developed stern-dipping until they could easily get the bow above head height. Their K1 (single-seater

◀ *Bob Campbell, 1995 World Champion, surfing a wave on a cross-bow rudder. The unusual blade shape gives low resistance under the water.*

competition kayak) counterparts were not far behind, despite having less leverage and the weight of their legs in front of them. At the time, the move was called a pivot turn. In the United States in the 1980s, kayakers experimenting with cut-down race boats likened the feeling to a wet bar of soap squirting out of the hand, and the name stuck. From then on, any move that involved sliding the end of the boat under the water was known as a squirt, and boats specifically designed to do it became squirt boats.

The American Influence
Largely because of the influence of two American brothers, Jim and Jeff Snyder, who were experts at the sport, the boats rapidly became smaller until they had to be custom-built to fit the paddler. The Snyder brothers were convinced that, as long as you had the requisite skills, a squirt boat could be used on any stretch of water provided it was not trapped on the surface by its own buoyancy. They called this the dense boat theory, and they proved their point by running some of the roughest white

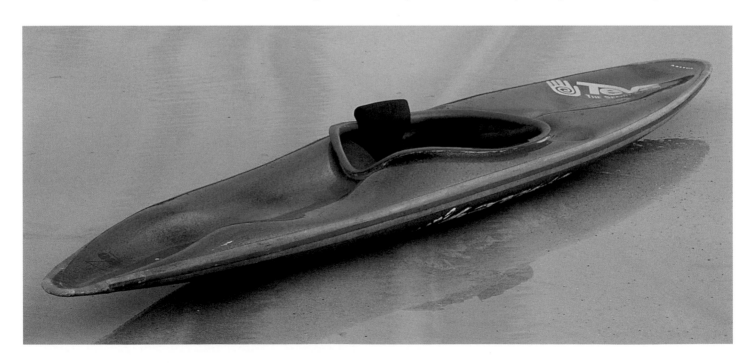

squirting techniques have been absorbed into the repertoire of the expert white water paddler.

These new techniques, and the evolution in boat design that they spawned, have been the driving force behind the transition from what is called old school white water paddling to the new school. They have made much of what was written or taught on the subject before about 1990 largely redundant. More importantly, though, it helped turn the sport of white water boating from one surrounded by issues of danger to one featuring fun, and for that we owe the founders a great debt.

Squirt Appeal

So why do squirt boaters choose to paddle these relatively dangerous boats. Why deliberately use a kayak that barely floats in green water, and take it into an aerated environment, where it will almost certainly spend most of its time underwater? This comes back to the aforementioned "dense boat theory".

A paddler who is comfortable with the white water environment finds that, so long as he can remain in control, a

◐ *Top British squirt-boater Hazel Wilson doing a past-vertical cartwheel in the World Freestyle Championships, 2001.*

◑ *A squirt-boater deliberately swipes at a rock in a flamboyant aerial move.*

water in the world in boats so small that they looked more like surfboards. They cartwheeled end over end on flat water, and performed the hallmark squirt boat trick, called the mystery move, where the paddler disappears completely below the surface to re-emerge at another place.

Shaping the Sport

Squirt boats are handmade in fibreglass or similar composite materials, and they have to be very strong to survive immersion in powerful water. Because of the way squirting has influenced white water boating, plastic play boats now bear a closer resemblance to squirt boats than they do to general-purpose boats from the pre-squirt era. Indeed, many play boats can now do cartwheels, and many

⊙ *A squirt boater resurfaces from the water after momentarily disappearing in the so-called mystery move.*

⊙ *Although squirt boaters invented the cartwheel, to perform one in a stopper like a conventional play boater, as here, is an extremely difficult feat.*

squirt boat is actually less likely to fall victim to hydraulics and other powerful water features. With minimal volume, the boat is almost "invisible" to aerated water, and responds only to the call of the green, allowing the pilot to navigate the solid currents of the river's heart without fear of turbulence and random transients.

to roll. Squirt boats are very sensitive to shifts in the paddler's weight, and this makes them prone to capsize. While squirt boats have performance advantages over other, high-volume designs, the consequences of any white water mishap are extremely serious. Entrapment, where part of your body or the boat gets stuck beneath the surface of the water, is the main danger for all white water paddlers because the strong currents can quickly pull you under. This is an even greater risk when paddling a squirt boat because

you are deliberately putting your boat in more precarious positions. These kayaks are physically difficult to get out of at the best of times, and to be seriously pinned in one would almost certainly prove fatal. In addition, the squirt boat is more prone to becoming pinned, and to planing to the bottom, by virtue of its wing-like shape. Drowned squirt boaters have been found still in their boats, with zigzag scratches on the hull a testament to their desperate attempts to lift an edge and unstick the craft from the bottom.

◉ *Vertical gymnastics are another hallmark of the expert squirt boater. The boats themselves are low-volume and are highly sensitive to shifts in the paddler's weight.*

◉ *The surfboard-like shape of the squirt boat lends itself to fast surfing and carving through the waves.*

Being made from stiff composite materials also makes the squirt boat a joy to paddle, compared to relatively soft and unresponsive plastic kayaks. The problem arises when things get out of control. To collide unexpectedly with a rock underwater is a nightmare for a squirt boater. Quite apart from the damage and injury it can cause, the loss of control can set off a chain of events that could end in disaster. So squirt boating is always practised in what are, for the expert paddler, extremely familiar and safe waters, so that the unexpected can never occur. Within the relatively safe confines of familiar rapids, the squirtists play unhindered by boat volume and the other limitations imposed on the more usual, surface-bound craft.

Squirting Safely
Paddlers should not attempt squirting until they are confident and quite expert at paddling an ordinary kayak. On top of this it is essential that they are able

Kayak Surfing

In the latter part of the twentieth century, the explosion in the popularity of all kinds of surfing has meant that kayak surfers need to put some thought into how they go about taking a kayak out in the surf. Undeniably exhilarating, kayak surfing carries risks, and before you rush in, you need to practise in safe conditions. You must also learn the surfer's etiquette that respects the enjoyment and safety of other paddlers. Incidentally, surfing is one of the few disciplines that is not practised at any serious level in a canoe, despite the fact that the concept was almost certainly invented by canoe paddlers, thousands of years ago in Polynesia.

Riding the Waves

In most cases a wave will start to break at one point, and this breaking part will rush along the face of the wave until the whole wave is broken. The surfer takes off next to the breaking part, and rides along the wave on the green, unbroken face of the wave. He attempts to ride in the shoulder, or power pocket, where the breaking wave is at its steepest. Riding here provides the energy that gives the surfer enough speed to remain in control. If you are too far from the shoulder, you will not be able to ride fast enough and will be overwhelmed by the break. If you are too deep in the pocket, the same thing might happen. It is a balancing act that can only be learned from experience.

An inexperienced kayaker cannot go out in the surf safely unless he can roll repeatedly and well, and there is no one to collide with. After a little practice you can learn how to get off the wave when it has broken, and avoid being carried ashore by the soup, which is the broken white water that tumbles shorewards after the wave has collapsed. However, even a good paddler may have problems,

◐ *A kayak surfer hurtling along a steep, barrelling wave-face. This is skilful wave-riding at its best.*

and while you are bouncing in the soup you cannot ensure the safety of anyone paddling through the waves. If you hit them, it can mean serious injury. Do not attempt to come ashore where there are other people until you are experienced.

Spin Sequence

1 The kayaker is riding in the shoulder of the power pocket of a small wave. The breaking shoulder is on the left, the green part of the wave to the right.

2 The paddler uses the paddle and his edge control (which in this case comes mostly from the legs) to spin the boat around without losing any momentum.

3 The kayak continues to ride along the wave, still in the power pocket but now travelling backwards, ready to perform another trick.

⊙ *An example of an aggressive top turn in a high-performance kayak. The wave is moving from right to left. The paddler is riding the power pocket towards the camera, and has turned (known as a cut-back) so as not to get too far from the shoulder of the wave.*

Tricks of the Trade

A good surf kayaker can get fantastic rides, every bit as good as most board surfers, with the possibility of trying more tricks. Early surf kayaks were, unsurprisingly, based on slalom boats, and there is still an international competition class which has a minimum length limit of 3.5m (11½ft). These boats can be paddled fast, out through the waves, and can race incredibly quickly along the face of a wave, and perform long, carving turns rather like long surfboards.

More recently, many paddlers have taken to using white water play boats in the surf. Typically about 2.5m (8¼ft) long, these boats are not very fast between waves, but they do have the advantage of being able to jump over some very large broken waves, enabling the paddler to get

more rides. The disadvantage of these boats is that they do not have enough speed to ride along the face of an ocean wave ahead of the breaking wave.

Wave Skis

Wave skis, a type of sit-on-top surf craft, had a spate of popularity in the 1980s. They were the first craft to provide spectacular leaping, aerial manoeuvres, but have now been replaced by the high-performance surf kayak – a 2.5m (8¼ft) boat which combines the best features of a wave ski boat, an international 3.5m (11½ft) boat, and a play boat. Surf kayaks often have surfboard-style fins to improve their grip and performance.

Essential Equipment

Kayak surfers use short paddles, usually about 1.85m (6ft) in length. They also need an extremely tough spraydeck (spray skirt) because the power of waves as they break is enormous, and will pull off all but the strongest decks. A helmet and flotation aid should be worn at all times, unless you are absolutely certain of your safety. They are recommended

because swimming in the surf is unthinkable. An empty kayak is a dangerous projectile that could seriously injure you or other water users. Airbags can be used to fill up any space in the boat in case of a spraydeck implosion. Airbags prevent sinking and will make it easier for you to get the boat ashore: a boat that is full of water is heavy and difficult to move when totally submerged.

Taking Up Kayak Surfing

The best way to start is by watching the experts. When you try it, remember that you need good all-round kayak skills, and the ability to roll well. It helps considerably if you can first become proficient at white water paddling on rivers because, contrary to appearances, they are a good place to learn the basic boat skills from others who can coach from the eddy. In the surf, no one can really help you.

Once you are good at controlling the boat, lifting your leading edge, and surfing small river waves, you can practise these skills at sea, building up the size of the wave as you progress. Aim for a quiet spot, where there are few people around.

🔼 *Twice World Kayak Surfing Champion Tim Thomas hurls a play boat into a spectacular exit manoeuvre.*

◀ *Riding in the shoulder of a wave in a long International Class 3.5m (11½ft) surf kayak.*

TIPS

• Do not go surfing in a kayak unless you can roll and have basic white water skills. Use a soft-foam wave ski craft to learn the principles.
• Notice how other surfers ride along the wave in the shoulder.
• Learn to get off the broken waves as soon as you can.

⊙ *A cut-back move in a play boat. These boats are widely used in the surf, despite being designed for river waves.*

⊙ *A classic surfing shot. The author, Bill Mattos, riding in the power pocket under the breaking lip of the wave.*

SURFING RULES

• Before you get into the water, sit on the beach and watch how other surfers ride it.

• Do not paddle out where other people are surfing. Wait until they have moved or paddle out elsewhere.

• Do not ride the soup unless there is no one between you and the shore.

• Do not take off on the same wave as someone else, unless you are on the other side of the break and you are sure you are going to ride away in opposite directions. Taking someone else's wave is called dropping in, and it is a surfing sin. The wave belongs to the first person to take off on it. If someone drops in on you, get off the wave, and afterwards explain the etiquette.

• If the surf is really crowded, go somewhere else, no matter how good a surfer you are.

Canoe and Kayak Sailing

Using sails on canoes or kayaks is a new and challenging aspect of the sport. Still in its infancy, there are few dos and don'ts, but what you will need most of all are strong arms and plenty of confidence as you get whipped along at high speeds.

It is perfectly possible to use sails either to assist paddling or as the sole means of propelling a canoe or a kayak. It is not a formalized discipline because it is still in its experimental stage but it does, however, have a long history. Many books and drawings from the late nineteenth century feature canoes and other narrow craft with a sail being used to help propel it along.

Sails for canoes tend to have a swinging gaff-type rig. This can emulate a square rig, but tracking is a big problem. Kayaks are often fitted with a small Bermuda-style Delta-sail, which can help to support a paddled kayak, but it does not offer any significant propulsion by itself. Some double sea kayaks are fitted with two of these sails. This is more effective because the sails are small enough that there is little likelihood of the craft being blown over by the wind,

⬥ *A traditional sea kayak with the mast and sail stowed along the deck. When required, the mast can be stepped in a recess just in front of the cockpit.*

and the double boats are so long that tracking is extremely good no matter what the weather is like.

Kites

A kite can be harnessed to a boat to support paddling. Kites are extremely powerful, and can pull a boat along at speed even in a light wind. Contrary to appearances, it is possible to sail at most wind angles provided the boat tracks quite well, but you need confidence in your ability as well as strength.

Now that two- and four-line kites have become commonplace, their use with canoes and kayaks has proliferated because the canopies have become more controllable. With a big 7.3sq m (24sq ft) kite or larger flexifoil design it is possible to make a double sea kayak plane along, but because the lateral force is considerable it would be very difficult to control a solo boat in this way. The advantage of a double is that one person can fly the kite, and the other can steer and brace with the rudder and paddle.

Experiments have been carried out with powerful kites and smaller, planing hulled kayaks. Still in its early days but demonstrating considerable potential, in kiting the emphasis is on excitement and aerial acrobatics.

Launching a Kite

1 When the wind is up, inflate the buoyant chambers of the kite.

2 DO NOT tie the kite lines to the boat or to yourself: this is potentially lethal.

3 Pay out the lines. This kite is designed to be launched from the water surface.

4 As the wind fills the canopy, hang on tightly. It could be a wild ride!

◒ *Two sea kayaks with small sails. There is a batten near the top, so that a square sail becomes more like a gaff rig with a mini topsail.*

◓ *Sailing downwind. The paddle is being used as a rudder here, but could equally act as a keel when reaching, i.e. sailing across the wind.*

TIPS

• Small sails can be used to assist while paddling a kayak manually.
• Larger sails will require that you concentrate on steering the boat using the paddle.
• Make sure that if the kayak capsizes, you will be able to unstep the mast and roll up.
• The sail can be rolled around the mast, and both mast and sail can be stowed on the deck when the kayak is being paddled.

Sailing IC10

This obscure and eccentric feature of the competitive canoeing scene is included here more for its historical than its contemporary relevance. Many people wonder why it counts as canoeing at all because the boat requires a sailing dinghy and paddles are not necessary. But canoeing it is, and if it is excitement that you are looking for, sailing IC10 really does have it all.

◔ *Two IC10 boats racing on Lake Windermere in England. The boat bears little resemblance to a canoe.*

What Is IC10?

The International Canoe 10 Square Metre was, until recently, the fastest single-handed sailing craft in the world. Nowadays, a variety of sail-boards and a handful of high-tech modern dinghies go faster, but it is still an amazing craft both to sail and to watch, requiring an incredible degree of skilful handling, balance, athleticism and agility. There is probably nothing else like it in the sports of sailing and paddling when it comes to the wide range of talents required for good control and handling.

The IC10, as it is sometimes known, is a sophisticated boat in a traditional form. Its name comes in part from its 10sq m (100sq ft) sail area, but how it resembles a canoe, except in the narrowness of its hull and consequent instability, is more of a mystery. The IC10 has a 5.2m (17ft) long hull weighing 63kg (139lb). The helmsman has a sliding seat on rails that can be extended up either side of the boat, allowing him to shift his body weight in and out. It replaces the wire trapeze system found on more modern dinghy designs. This, in combination with the narrow hull and relatively large sail area, allows the boat to reach speeds in excess of 30km per hour (19mph) in a stiff following breeze.

How It Developed

The sliding seat concept has its origins in the Native American open canoe. While there is no evidence that sailing these boats was ever commonplace, the paddling technique involved sitting outside the up-wind gunwale on a plank of wood, to stop the high-sided boats being blown over by the wind. The strength of the wind would be described as "it's a two-plank day" or a "three-plank day", depending on how many people had to sit out on the plank to keep the boat stable. This appears to be the tradition that led eventually to the development of the sailing canoe as we know it.

Perhaps not surprisingly, given its American origins, the sport of IC10 is especially popular today in the United States. In competitions in the United States, there used to be a so-called "paddling leg", in which the canoe would be sailed around the course for one lap and paddled for the next. The paddling aspect is new rarely included.

The shape of the IC10 hull is strictly determined by competition regulations, but competitors are at liberty to adjust the sail and rig design to optimize the boat's performance, as long as the total sail area does not exceed the stipulated 10sq m (100sq ft). In the latest high-performance sailing dinghies, the sail is usually fully battened from top to bottom.

● *A wooden sailing canoe. The sliding seat system can be clearly seen.*

● *Two IC10s on a reach. Note the narrow hull design, and the sailors with their weight right outside the boat.*

As a championship discipline, overseen by the International Canoe Federation (ICF), IC10 boats are sailed by men or women of 69–95kg (152–210lb) in weight, and of 19–60 years of age. To win, sailors must have all the skill and determination of motor-racing drivers, knowing how to use the wind and tides, while being tactically aware, and knowing how to prepare and tune the rig to give the best possible performance.

The racing of IC10 boats is governed by the ICF and national canoeing bodies. World Championships are held tri-annually, and national championships annually in many countries worldwide.

COMPETITION EVENTS

After World War I European skiing enthusiasts, who were starting to paddle white water for sport, came up with a new idea – the format for slalom and down-river racing that we see today. And much later, towards the end of the twentieth century, developments in boat design became the prime movers behind a whole range of more recent competitive events such as polo, kayak surfing and freestyle.

In turn, these events have led to an increasing emphasis on training, coaching and, in particular, psychology in order to improve performances. It would now be very difficult for even a talented individual to compete without attention to these issues. While theory is certainly important, there is no substitute for time spent paddling your boat as a way of increasing your experience.

What follows is general information on the nature of, and requirements for, today's major competitions. The best way to get involved in a competition is to approach your local kayak or canoe supplier, who will recommend a club that practises your chosen discipline. For all of the events mentioned in the following pages, you will need to be skilled with the paddle and, in some cases, will have to acquire better techniques and more experience before you can begin to compete, but do not let this put you off.

◐ A paddler performs his manoeuvre on a rapid while other competitors wait their turn.

◑ Competitive paddling makes excellent spectator viewing for the whole family.

Slalom

For plenty of spills and thrills, you cannot beat slalom. Racing downstream, through a series of gates, it tests racers on three levels, demanding great technical skill, strength to manage the boat, and superb concentration because highly accurate decisions about which stroke to make have to be made at fantastic speed.

Inspired by the sport of slalom skiing, which is a race downhill in which the skier must negotiate a large number of gates, European skiers came up with the idea for kayak and canoe slaloms. They needed something to replace their own sport in summer when the snow melted.

Racing the Clock

The sport is a time trial. One paddler at a time attempts to negotiate a predominantly downstream course on a white water river, marked out using gates through which they must pass. Each gate consists of two vertical poles suspended from wires. All the gates are numbered; green and white gates must be paddled in the downstream direction, while red and white gates must be paddled upstream.

The object is to paddle the course as quickly as possible without touching the gates or missing any. If you do either, penalty seconds are added to your time by the gate judge. Each competitor will

◗ *A British duo racing a double-seater competition canoe, or C2, in France.*

have one or more practice runs, and then two timed runs. The best of the two times counts towards the final result.

Competition Categories

There are a number of categories, including men's and women's kayak (K1) classes, and single and double-decked canoe (C1 and C2) classes. There is no separate women's class for canoe events. The kayaks must be 4m (13ft) in length and at least 60cm (2ft) in width; in the C1 class they must be the same length and at least 70cm (28in) wide. The C2s are 4.58m x 80cm (15ft x 31½in). Juniors classes use the same size boats as the adults. There is also often a team event in which a team of three paddlers negotiates the course at the same time. The team is timed from the first to start to the last to finish. All three paddlers must finish within 15 seconds of each other, and all their penalties are added to the time.

◔ *Manoeuvring skills and stamina are the key to the slalom paddler's success.*

◔ *A K1 slalom paddler. The bent paddle shaft is popular among slalom kayakers.*

Taking Up Slalom

If you want to become involved in slalom, you will need to join a club that has some members who are interested in this field. Not all canoe clubs have slalom paddlers as members, let alone a slalom coach. It would be very difficult to get to grips with it on your own, so seeking out the society of fellow slalomists is pretty essential if you wish to progress.

There are no skill pre-requisites, since the techniques for paddling a slalom boat are the same as for flat water paddling, and can be learnt in a competition craft, even if you have never paddled any kind of canoe or kayak before.

There are also divisional systems in most countries, which means you do not have to compete against national champions unless you are at that level!

Slalom Kayaking

Slalom kayaks are extremely lightweight boats made from carbon and/or Kevlar™. Hence, they are fragile considering the environment they are used in, but slalom paddlers are adept at dodging obstacles.

Slalom used to be the natural choice for anyone skilful at white water paddling and who had the urge to compete but, sadly, participation has declined since the introduction of plastic kayaks. The plastic boats have allowed more people, and in particular less skilful ones, to go paddling white water without fear of the consequences. However, slalom has been included in the Olympic Games intermittently since 1972, and it remains one of the few paddling disciplines to be well known to the general public. It is an extreme test of strength, skill and concentration, and is unlikely to be dislodged from its position as the world's premier canoeing and kayaking discipline, because of it's profile, status, and the fact that the whole family can enjoy watching the competition events in a controlled and safe environment.

⊙ *Using a stopper wave to help make the fastest line between gates.*

⊙ *This kayaker has exited a wave so fast that his lightweight boat is almost launched clear of the water.*

⊙ *A C2 slalom crew competing at World Championship level.*

Specialist equipment is not required - the same basic equipment that you would use when you first start paddling is fine for slalom initially, although you will find that most slalom paddlers aspire to close-fitting garments and gear that emphasizes light weight, and acquire such items as soon as possible. The boats themselves are relatively expensive compared to plastic recreational canoes and kayaks, but you do not need to have a top-flight slalom boat right away. In fact, you will usually be able to borrow boats for the first few seasons from a club that offers coaching in slalom. Contact your local paddling stockist for information.

◔ *This paddler has just cleared a gate but is careful not to touch the pole with his elbow or paddle blade.*

◔ *Note the intense concentration on the face of this Italian slalom competitor.*

SLALOM FACTS

• Slalom is the original white water sport, and is still one of the few Olympic paddlesport disciplines.
• The following arc the only classes available to the slalom racer:
    MK1 – men's single kayak
    LK1 – ladies' single kayak
    C1 – single canoe (unisex)
    C2 – double canoe (unisex or mixed).
• Top slalom paddlers train in the boat every day as well as gym- and cross-training.
• In an entire event, a racer might have only three two-minute runs down the course.
• Slalom boats are 4m (18ft) long, which makes them almost twice as long as a white water playboat. In addition, the slalom boat weighs only half as much as a modern plastic white water boat.
• A slalom course is designed to test all of the basic white water skills, such as breaking in and out, ferry glide, S-cross, and using currents and water features to full advantage. It is also a test of the fitness and power of the athlete.

River Racing

River racing, which includes wild water and rapid racing, is another competitive class that was first promoted primarily by European skiers. If slalom equates to slalom skiing, then river racing is the equivalent of downhill racing on skis.

Like slalom, the sport has strict regulations governing the design and dimensions of the boat, and the way the races are held.

Rules and Boat Shapes

Wild water racing (WWR) regulations are laid down by the International Canoe Federation, paddle sport's regulating body. These require the boats to have a maximum length of 4.5m (15ft) and minimum width of 60cm (2ft) for the K1 class, 4.3m x 70cm (14ft x 28in) for C1, and 5m x 80cm (16ft x 31½in) for C2. These maximum lengths are necessary because, generally speaking, the longer a boat is, the faster it is; similarly, the narrower the boat, the faster it is. These lengths in turn have led to homogeneous designs where all the craft are identical in dimensions and are extremely similar in overall shape.

River racing boats have a deep, vertical bow for slicing through waves, a narrow hull for speed, and a wide deck, which creates the minimum width while also

◉ A white water racing C1 and K1. The boats are extremely similar but for the kneeling/sitting issues and the paddles used. The easiest way to tell the boats apart is by the fact that the canoe has a smaller, rounded cockpit.

◉ These racers are preparing for a practice run. Note the high bow and flared hips of their boats.

providing the necessary volume to stop the boat rearing up when punching through hydraulic water. The wide back deck tapers rapidly again to a pointed, vertical tail to give a clean, turbulence-free passage through the water. That is why the racing boat looks very strange, and quite different from any other canoe or kayak around today.

⬢ *The downstream speed of the river racer is apparent in this photograph.*

They are usually made from high-tech composite materials such as carbon and/or Kevlar™, and are therefore extremely light and fragile. Some manufacturers produce plastic replica river racing boats that are suitable for learning and training in.

Handling the Boat

Wild water boats are quite unstable compared to slalom or play boats, but are not as wobbly as flat water racing boats.

⬢ *Breaking in and out of the current at speed is not easy in a river racer.*

They turn fairly responsively when leant to the outside of the turn, and can make dramatic changes in direction, using what is called a wave top turn, but with the full length of the hull in the water they are more directional than manoeuvrable.

Reading the water is an important skill for any white water paddler, but in racing it is absolutely essential to spot the fastest line down a rapid.

All steering must be done with leans, or with strokes that drive the boat forward rather than slowing it down. There is a rhythm to the forward paddling which attempts to make all the strokes when the boat is going up a wave, and not down. This helps a lot with speed and endurance, and stops the nose of the boat from getting buried in white water, and slowed down, any more than is absolutely necessary.

The most important part of river racing is to avoid both rocks and eddies. Hitting a rock in a lightweight Kevlar™ racing boat would almost certainly result in damage, and may well sink the boat. Clipping an eddy can cause the boat to spin round and out, which results in lost time. With practice and observation, you will find the best and fastest way down, and make no mistake, it is a wild ride.

River Races

Wild water races are run as time trials over a section of Grade (Class) 3, or higher, rapids. Rapids up to Grade 5 have been used for top-class events. The rapids rarely demand special skills, however, because of the length of the boats and their lack of manoeuvrability. The course takes 20 minutes to complete, and competitors start at one-minute intervals. This means that sometimes racers will overtake each other, which makes for extra excitement.

Rapid racing is identical to wild water racing, except that the course is more of a sprint, only one or two minutes long. It was designed for spectator appeal, and at some venues two boats at a time race each other. Rapid racing represents an attempt by the organizers of river racing events to attract interest, from the media and potential participants, to a sport which, like slalom, has declined dramatically since the growth of informal play paddling.

Taking up River Racing

The best way to get involved in river racing is to join a club that has a strong tradition of the sport. Get into a WWR boat and paddle it regularly to get used to the way these strange beasts behave.

Freestyle

Freestyle is the name given to competition play paddling. Originally called rodeo, it was conceived in the 1980s and has grown to be one of the biggest competitive canoeing and kayaking disciplines in many countries.

The original concept came from the common boating practice of taking turns to show off your best trick or ride in a hole, or on a wave. It was not long before informal competitions sprang up, with paddlers voting for the best performance. The skill level soon increased dramatically and more formal competitions were organized, with independent judges. For a long time it was not taken too seriously because the paddlers did not take themselves too seriously.

But, at the end of the twentieth century, freestyle became almost as rigidly formalized as other competition events, like slalom. There is now an accepted

● *A British Junior competing in the 2000 Pre-World Championships.*

● *An overview of an international competition scene. The competition stopper (hole) is clearly visible.*

structure – paddlers have a set period of time on a wave or in a water feature, and will attempt to perform as many complex tricks as possible in that time. The exact method for scoring these moves changes every year as the sport evolves, but the basic principle is as follows.

Technical Scoring
For every 180° transition (change of direction) from upstream to downstream, or vice versa, the paddler will be awarded technical points. If it is a flat transition (or spin) the score will be 1 point. An elevated transition (higher than 45°) will score 2 points, and a vertical transition will score 4 points.

It is worth noting that transitions from being sideways on in the wave to being sideways on facing the other way, or side-surf to side-surf, do not count because most failed moves will end up looking like that in any case.

The Classes

Freestyle has separate classes for Men, Ladies and Juniors, as do most other competitive disciplines, and it also has other classes for different boat types. Here are the main classes that you will usually find included in a freestyle event.

K1 (Solo Kayak) – Float Freestyle boats that are not squirt boats are usually called float boats because they float on the water, while squirt boats do not. Over the years, float boats have become more and more like squirt boats in their design, until the only discernible difference is that the float boats float.

A definition of a float boat is that you can get in one on flat water with no spraydeck (spray skirt), without the boat shipping any water. The cockpit area is usually the only part of the boat that has enough volume to remain consistently above the water. K1 float is usually the biggest class in any freestyle event.

Decked C1 These boats are usually identical to the competition kayaks, or K1s, except that they are propelled by a canoe paddle used in the kneeling position. The performance of these freestyle canoes is now so astonishing that they are outscoring kayaks. This is partly because the advantages of the paddling position outweigh the disadvantages for an expert, and partly

⬆ *A K2 crew competing in a freestyle event in Thun, Switzerland. These paddlers have missed the wave and are paddling for the eddy in an attempt to re-establish before their time runs out.*

⮞ *A competitor initiating a cartwheel in a stopper during a freestyle competition.*

There will also be a variety score. The judges have a list of tricks that are established moves and have names, such as the spin, cartwheel, splitwheel and blunt. Each additional trick performed in the ride adds to the technical score. The result is that the paddler tries to do as many transitions as possible in the ride, while incorporating as many different moves as possible. This ensures that you cannot win by simply cartwheeling (flipping the boat end over end) non-stop for the entire run.

◉ *An open canoe paddler in a freestyle event. He is surfing the wave, and uses his hand to initiate a turn rather than try a cross-bow stroke with the paddle!*

because practitioners can score so many clean moves (tricks performed without a paddle stroke), by virtue of the fact that they only have one paddle blade to use.

Open C1 The freestyle open boat is a controversial class. The rules ensure that the boat must be fairly close in design to a traditional open boat, and this makes it quite hard to do any modern freestyle moves. Many people feel that the open boat is being left behind as the other freestyle classes develop, but it still remains the most crowd-pleasing freestyle discipline because is it so simple and spectacular.

Squirt C1 and K1 The definition of a squirt boat is that it will ship water if you

sit in it on flat water without a spraydeck. Squirt boating is responsible for the invention of most of the moves we see in freestyle today, although sadly it is really quite rare to see one being paddled canoe style. Unfortunately the lack of volume, or buoyancy, in a squirt boat makes it less retentive in a hydraulic, which means it barely floats. However, these minimal-volume craft make up for that with their smoothness and style, and their signature manoeuvre, the mystery move, where the paddler disappears from view below the water surface and re-emerges at another place.

Freestyle — in Design and Competition

No other canoeing and kayaking discipline today has the profound and widespread influence that freestyle has. The vast majority of white water boats

sold today are identical to, or are based upon, the latest freestyle designs, even though they are unsuitable for their owner's activities. It is just like the heyday of slalom, when nearly all the boats used on white water were essentially based on slalom designs.

Unfortunately, it looks as if freestyle may suffer the same fate as slalom and become marginalized by its own rigid adherence to a competitive structure, deviating further and further from the latest thinking in general recreational paddling. As soon as it becomes a competitive discipline only, rather than a fun pastime, it will, like slalom, become a sport for a limited number of special enthusiasts. Many of the proponents of freestyle recognize this danger, and have begun to turn a new branch of the play paddling skills repertoire into the sport of extreme racing.

Scoring Freestyle Moves

Exactly how the judges award points for paddling moves will depend on the rules of the particular competition. However, there is a generally accepted score sheet. The following moves are given in ascending order, arranged by difficulty and hence technical score.

Surf

Planing in control on a standing wave or in a hole with the bow pointing upstream.

Backsurf

The same as surf, but with the stern facing upstream.

Spin

From frontsurf to backsurf, or vice versa. A 360° spin scores as 2 x 180°s.

Clean Spin

A 360° spin made with just one stroke will score higher than a spin.

Vert or "End"

A 180° direction change with one end of the boat elevated out of the water throughout. There are three scoring levels: up to 45, up to 75, and 75–105 (which would be called "past vertical"). A vert can be performed either on the bow or on the stern.

● *Paddlers in the eddy wait their turn. The paddler in the hole is either warming up or has commenced his run.*

◀ *These two paddlers are not actually competing, but are having fun during a break by crossing over one another as they surf in the hole.*

Cartwheel

This is a continuous transition from front end (bow) to back end (stern).

Clean Cartwheel

This is performed with the second end achieved without the paddle in the water. The boat is moved using the legs.

Superclean

A full cartwheel performed without making any use of the paddle at all for the duration of the move.

Splitwheel

A cartwheel with an edge change between the two transitions.

Pirouette

A 360° spin around the axis of the boat while it is standing on (either) end.

Loop

Somersaulting the boat end over end with the deck presented flat to the current (a cartwheel would be on edge).

Blunt

An elevated transition on a green wave.

Air Blunt

The same as a blunt but with the entire boat clear of the water.

Kickflip (or California Roll)

An aerial barrel roll.

Extreme Racing

Extreme racing is, at the time of writing, the newest form of specialist competitive discipline to gain widespread publicity. Though it sounds incredibly dangerous, it is not that alarming, though you will need high skill levels to try it.

Usually run over a section of Grade (Class) 4 rapids, extreme racing is a modern incarnation of what white water racing used to be – a race down rapids which, though extreme for an inexperienced paddler, is well within the capabilities of an expert. Perhaps because of its perceived danger level, it is now mainly practised by professional boaters. It is not, however, as extreme as the descents attempted by those who push the limits of extreme kayaking.

◔ This paddler's face shows the effort as he sprints a fairly flat section during an extreme race.

◔ The power of the hydraulic at the base of this fall makes the bow of the boat rear up, and the paddler has to fight for control of the boat.

History of Extreme Racing

Extreme racing as we know it today grew out of the shortcomings of freestyle as a media flagship for canoeing and kayaking. In fact, people had been racing down rapids for many decades, whether in specialist racing boats or in informal competitions using general-purpose craft. This probably attracted more media attention than most paddle sport events, but in the mid-1990s top freestyle paddlers, already established as the most skilful and extreme boaters in the world, began to look at the fun race events that often ran alongside freestyle get-togethers with renewed interest.

These events were more popular with the crowds and the media than any freestyler gyrating inexplicably in a hydraulic, so people began to organize races down what was, for them, quite manageable white water, but which could be billed as extreme. This 1990s buzzword attracted big crowds and advertising. At first, these races were by

invitation only, and just a few paddlers competed but, as the idea began to catch on, more people participated.

How to Take Part

To consider participating in extreme racing, you need to be totally confident at paddling Grade 4 and 5 rapids, and tackling waterfalls (albeit fairly safe ones) up to 10m (33ft) in height. There are currently no rules about the type of kayak you should use. Unlike white water racing, the emphasis is on what is possible and not the best time achieved by a boat

◐ *This paddler has taken an unusual and very risky line to try to stay on the top flow of this folded drop.*

◐ *Sprinting through turbulent rapids in a European extreme race.*

within set rules. Most paddlers use river-running or crossover play boats that are equipped for extreme paddling with full plate footrests, airbags, and plenty of padding.

The best extreme racers in the world currently seem to be top freestyle paddlers, but this may well change as more people begin to train specifically for racing. This is the likely trend because extreme racing seems the most likely kind of paddle sport to attract major sponsorship and prize money. In the meantime, however, you cannot simply go along to your local canoe club and tell them that you want to get involved in extreme racing. Instead, go white water paddling and freestyling, and get plenty of valuable experience. If you see an event advertised in the paddling press, you will have an opportunity to test out your skills.

Sprint and Marathon

Paddlers are always looking for new thrills and ways of racing, and sprint and marathon provided plenty of action. The two disciplines are accessible and attractive to all ages and abilities.

Paddling fast boats on flat water, or sometimes moving water has been a part of the canoe and kayak scene from the very outset. Pick any sports activity, and there will always be lots of people who want to adapt it for racing, and paddle sport is no exception.

Sprint racing is incredibly popular, and is a time trial over a fixed distance from a standing start. There are categories for K1 (solo kayak), K2 (double kayak) and the spectacular K4 (four-seater kayak), and races are over 500m, 1000m or 10,000m. The maximum for a Ladies race is 5,000m. There are similar categories for canoes with C1, C2 and C4, all paddled with a single blade in a high drop-knee position, which is half kneeling, on one foot and one knee.

Marathon is very similar to sprint, but the distance could be anything from 10km (6 miles) to the mammoth 200km (125 miles) Devizes to Westminster race, which is held every year in the United Kingdom, or the Arctic Canoe Race that is over 1,000km (620 miles) long.

● *An older and more stable K1 still shows a fair turn of speed.*

The fundamental difference between sprint and marathon is that sprint boats usually race on a lake and in a straight line, whereas the marathon is a journey, and might involve negotiating bends and getting out of the boat to carry it around weirs, rapids or other impassable sections of river. In some races, such as the British Exe Descent and the Irish Liffey, competitors might even tackle large drops and rapids in their wobbly racing boats in order to avoid walking around them.

Race Criteria and Skills
Single racing boats are about 5.2m (17ft) long and 50cm (20in) wide, although the double boats are longer to accommodate two paddlers, at about 6.5m (21ft).

● *A paddler holds on to the jetty as he adjusts the spraydeck (spray skirt) in his unstable racing kayak.*

You have to get in fairly carefully, putting your feet squarely in the middle of the boat and keeping some weight on your hands, but once you get moving it will be more stable. Marathon kayaks are fitted with a rudder, which is operated by the feet, because, while the boats are good at running in straight lines, nothing you do with the paddle seems to make much difference to the course. This is unlike most kayaks in which you expend a great deal of energy trying to make them run straight ahead.

While the rudder is effective at steering the boat, it does interfere with the rhythm of paddling, and is actually much more useful for offsetting a constant veer caused by a cross-wind, for example, than for making any changes in direction. Luckily the boats are responsive to slight leans: lean a little to the left, and it veers quite dramatically to the right, and vice versa. This allows you to do a lower, more sweeping stroke on the outside of the turn and a good high stroke on the inside. Because the boat is so narrow that it encourages a vertical paddling action, with lots of body rotation without too much effort from the arms, it is highly efficient for long-distance paddling.

The racing boat is quite unresponsive to most kayaking strokes apart from a really good forward paddling action. A low brace will be required to keep the boat balanced; placing the back of the blade flat on the water provides some support. Otherwise, you will not need to do much except paddle and lean, and anticipate when to turn, because large circles are the rule for these courses.

◐ *This K2 marathon crew uses the rudder to approach the bank for a portage. The stern paddler is trailing a low brace to keep them stable.*

Equipment and Safety

You need very little additional equipment except for the paddle, which should probably be a modern asymmetric design to facilitate a fast, long paddling action.

The usual test for paddle length is to stand the paddle up in the shop – you should just be able to reach and grip the top of the blade without having to stretch. It is worth spending a lot on a paddle to make sure that you get a good one that is light with slightly less than a 90° feather (the angle between the two blades of a kayak paddle). A full 90° will eventually place quite a strain on the wrists, but because much less causes a lot of wind resistance, settle for 70–80° if you can. The rule with paddles is try before you buy. Serious racers use wing paddles, a specialist type that provides high efficiency and lift, but these are initially very difficult to use and you will need a lot of practice before you can use one effectively.

A spraydeck (spray skirt) is sometimes used as small waves splash into the cockpit even on flat water, or you could simply opt for a decent sponge. And,

generally speaking, racers do not wear buoyancy aids (personal flotation devices) unless they are juniors, but this is because rescue is always at hand at the course. You should wear a flotation aid when training for a race because it can be fairly difficult to recover a swamped racing boat alone, and your friends will not be able to offer much apart from moral support. Furthermore, hardly anyone ever drowns while wearing a buoyancy aid. Unless you have taken other steps to ensure your safety, you should use one.

You should also wear shoes that you are not too heavy amd are safe to swim in, and take a drink of water or energy drink in the boat. You can end up quite dehydrated paddling a kayak, and when you are racing a boat it is very easy to forget how long you have been in the water. Being thirsty over a short period of time will not kill you, but it will negate many of the benefits of doing exercise.

The best way to get involved is to attend a club that specializes in sprint or marathon racing and training. Ask your local kayak supplier to recommend one.

Canoe Polo

Canoe polo is an aquatic ball game similar to water polo. Despite its name, it is not played in canoes but in kayaks that are known as polo boats. It is a fast, lively team game, nearly as good to watch as to play.

You need two teams of five players who endeavour to pass or carry a football-sized ball and throw it in the opposing goal, a square net that is 1.5m (5ft) wide by 1m (3½ft) high, suspended 2m (6½ft) above the water. The goals are placed at each end of a stretch of water, which is marked out to form a pitch, the dimensions of which can vary. The pitch can be delineated on any stretch of water, but will often be in a swimming pool. Canoe polo originated separately in a number of different places and in different ways.

Chasing and playing with a ball is an excellent way of learning good boat control skills while focusing on the ball rather than on the boat. This sub-conscious learning is a terrific way of developing and reinforcing the skills required to pilot a kayak successfully,

A polo player scoops up the ball to pass. Note the flotation aid and helmet.

Two players face off. The wire face guard is absolutely essential.

and because it was commonly used as a learning tool by instructors, it developed into a game, particularly in Britain, France and Australia. In 1989, the International Canoe Federation (ICF) accepted polo as one of its recognized paddle sports, and merged and adapted the different rules from various countries to create a set of international rules common to all ICF member nations.

Rules and Regulations

The game now has a strict set of regulations. Crash helmets are compulsory, as are buoyancy aids (personal flotation devices) that give the torso all-round impact protection. Although there are rules against dangerous play, quite a high level of

⌃ *Polo flotation aids have additional padding in the sides to protect the torso against injuries caused by heavy impact from other boats and paddles.*

⌄ *A polo player about to shoot for a goal. He has simply dropped his paddle across the deck to free both his hands.*

protection is necessary. Helmets have wire face guards, and paddles have a minimum blade thickness and radius to minimize injuries that might occur with a sharp edge. Ramming and other aggressive play is not allowed, although, like ice hockey, the game is a contact sport with plenty of pushing and shoving. Since the paddles and hands can be used to control the ball and to block opponents' shots and passes, it is inevitable that there will be firm contact and clashes of boats, paddles and heads. It is quite common to be pushed in by an opposing player while trying to play the ball, although there are strict rules on where on the body the player can be pushed (shoulders and arms only).

Being an explosive sport it is incredibly good exercise with plenty of sprinting, braking, accelerating, rolling and hand-rolling, as well as ball handling. Play

regularly and you will be incredibly fit. You do need to warm up and stretch before playing, though, otherwise the severe physical demands you place on your body may result in injury. The best thing about playing in an indoor pool is that it will be heated.

Although there are specialist polo boats, most clubs will have a selection of pool training boats and paddles, which are often used. If you join a local canoe club that plays polo, you will probably be able to take part without buying any gear. If you take only one piece of kit, make it a nose clip. You can only enjoy getting chlorine up your nose for so long.

For more information or the address of your local club, contact either your national governing body for paddle sport, or a local kayak or canoe store in your area that may be able to put you in touch with a relevant organization.

Dragon Boat Racing

The phenomenally popular sport of dragon boat racing dates back to early China. With boats powered by up to 20 paddlers they charge through the water, and make a fantastic sight when decked out in traditional colours.

How It Developed

Dragon boat racing originated in China more than 2,000 years ago. According to legend there was a warrior-turned-poet by the name of Qu Yuan. A loyal subject of the emperor, he was overcome with sorrow at the poverty and corruption that was then rife in the country. He protested by committing suicide, throwing himself into the Mi Lo River. When his followers heard of his death, they took to the river in their boats, beating the water with their paddles, and threw rice dumplings into the river to feed his spirit.

From that time onwards, the Chinese people commemorated the death of the heroic Qu Yuan by holding the annual Dragon Festival. Since then, dragon boat racing has become a widespread sport. In fact, some sources claim it is the

◔ *Dragon boating hosted as a fun event by the British Army's Royal Marines.*

second largest participation sport in the world, after soccer. This may be due to its enormous popularity throughout China, and its more widespread use as a commercial adventure sport in other parts of the world. Anyhow, the sport of dragon boat racing only really came to the West in the early 1980s. Since then it has grown steadily, and thousands of people now take part each year.

◔ *A ladies' dragon boat team in action. Synchronized paddle strokes are vital.*

Taking Up Dragon Boating

The first step is to find a club, or go to a session run by an outdoor centre. You can find them extremely easily on an internet search engine by typing in "dragon boating" for whichever country you are in.

Paddles for dragon boating are like canoe paddles, but they are shorter because of the lower sitting position. Serious practitioners use traditional wooden paddles, but centres and club boats more usually use plastic ones. Women often use paddles that have a thinner shaft and T-grip. With a really strong crew of 20 the boat practically lifts out of the water with every stroke, and can be powered at more than 4m (13ft) per second. In a race, there is always a drummer at the front who beats in time with the stroke paddler. This is an important job because if the drum is out of time the crew will be too.

For training and individual performance comparison, dragon boat racers paddle the racing K1s with an outrigger attached for balance, and they use a dragon boat paddle. Competitions are held in most countries, with national and world championship events held regularly.

Traditionally, a dragon boat is decorated with a colourful dragon's head and tail, and has scales painted all over the sides.

⊙ This team's optional warpaint matches the livery of their dragon boat and adds enjoyment to the ride.

⊙ A hard-charging dragon boat crew, with the drummer in the front and the steersman aft.

Kayak and Ski Surf Competition

If you want to go in for kayak and ski surf competitions, you have got to learn the special rules and techniques. Incredible fun, they are well worth trying on a good beach with first-rate surf.

Competitive kayak surfing is managed by national governing bodies for kayaking in many countries, and there may also be a governing body for wave-ski paddling. There are regular local and national events in many countries, and bi-annual world championships in both of these surfing disciplines.

Scoring System

Surfing is very much a freestyle discipline, but unlike freestyle kayaking in white water, points are awarded for riding a particular part of the wave rather than for tricks performed *ad hoc*. The usual format is for a heat of four paddlers at a time going out in the surf for a set period, usually of 20 minutes. Judges on the shore will award points (typically out of a total of 20) for the length and quality of the rides of each surfer on the wave. At the end of the heat, the two highest scoring paddlers out of the four will go through to the next round.

❤ *A short, high-performance class kayak charges a steep section of surf.*

❤ *A 3.5m (11½ft) International Class surf kayaker in action.*

Eventually, there will be a final heat of four paddlers, who will be scored in the same way as in the earlier rounds. Sometimes there will be a head to head, with only two paddlers going out in the water at a time, to make the competition more dramatic. This sort of drama is often added for the benefit of television.

To score highly in a surf competition, you need to be good at selecting waves that will give you the best possible ride. You then need to take off in just the right place to make your position in the power pocket as perfect and dynamic as possible, and use all your skills and manoeuvres to maintain that position throughout the ride, before exiting the fading wave with a flamboyant and impeccably-controlled manoeuvre.

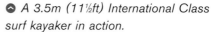
❤ *Straight take-off on a wave-ski. The paddler focuses on his balance.*

What the Judges Look For

On a wave-ski, you can carry on riding the wave after it has broken and the judges will carry on increasing your score for the length of ride, and for every impressive manoeuvre you make. In a kayak surfing competition, you will lose points for riding in the broken wave, unless you regain a shoulder and revert to riding in a power pocket. This reflects the different ways in which skis and kayaks handle the breaking wave; the finned and lightweight ski is a safer craft to ride in the broken wave because it is less inclined to go sideways out of control, and is easier to move off the wave.

To enter a competition you should be a member of the national governing body for your discipline (which will often provide insurance). You will be made aware of the regulations for your craft and equipment, which includes a leash for skiers, and a flotation aid and helmet for kayakers. Kayaks must be fitted with airbags, footrests and end toggles because end loops can be very dangerous in the surf.

🔺 *A women's ski competitor on a custom, composite wave-ski craft.*

🔽 *Driving a ski through a carving turn on a beautiful, glassy shoulder.*

PADDLING AROUND THE WORLD

Many paddlers see their boat as a way to travel and to explore areas that might be less accessible by any other means. Others see paddling as an end in itself, and travel in order to experience their sport in a different country, or in a different way. Travelling with a canoe or kayak is extremely fulfilling. You will often find that you are warmly welcomed by local boaters, who are usually only too pleased to show you the best paddling in their area. If you travel to a place where there are few indigenous paddlers, you will experience the ultimate fulfilment of being one of the few people who has navigated there. The canoe or kayak is accepted in most parts of the world, since it leaves no traces of environmental impact. With the right knowledge and preparation, you can paddle just about anywhere there is water.

The best way to get up-to-date information on paddling in any country is from the Internet. Just use a search engine site to find out about guidebooks, local tourism, rafting companies, and anything else related to paddling worldwide.

◗ Breath-taking scenery and exotic wildlife are some of the bonuses of paddling abroad.

◗ Travellers in search of white water need to be aware of seasonal water levels.

Europe

Broadly speaking, Europe consists of Scandinavia, mainland Europe, and the United Kingdom. The entire continent offers a mixture of white water rivers, inland waterways, open water (inland and sea) and reasonable proximity to coastal paddling and surf. In northern and central parts of Europe, the winters are snow- and ice-bound. In the far south, around the Mediterranean sea, it is extremely hot in summer and moderate in winter.

Scandinavia

In Scandinavia, which consists of Iceland, Norway, Sweden, and Finland, every kind of paddling imaginable is available, but the season is short since the whole area is ice-bound for at least half the year. White water paddling derives entirely from snowmelt, so the rivers tend to be biggest in the spring (April and May), dropping off to a low in August. The local geography is very rocky and mountainous, and tends to result in white water that is steep and full of waterfalls, but there is also a wide variety of more placid, mature rivers and estuaries (locally called fjords) for the touring paddler. Some of the Scandinavian lakes are enormous, resembling inland seas.

⦿ *A kayaker carries his boat down a tranquil street in a Swiss village.*

⦿ *A medieval bridge over Grade (Class) 2 white water in France.*

⦿ *Typical Alpine white water: the river is bouldery and not too steep.*

Mainland Europe

Central continental Europe is dominated by a number of large mountain ranges, which offer Alpine white water paddling in Germany, the Czech Republic, Austria, Switzerland, southern France, Spain, northern Italy, Croatia and Yugoslavia. This varies in character from generally small and technical rivers in most areas, to a few very high-volume ones in Germany and Austria. River guidebooks, which are kept up to date, are available in local languages and in English.

● *Paddlers navigate their way down a steep and narrow gorge.*

❱ *Entering a committing gorge, three paddlers line astern.*

The Alpine paddling here is almost entirely glacial or snowmelt, but it is often bolstered up in some areas by rainfall in the summer. The season therefore runs from April to August. In Portugal, exceptionally, the white water mostly comes from rain, so the season is October through May, although with luck there will still be decent white water during the summer.

The island of Corsica, off the coast of France, offers spectacular, big-volume and steep white water from April to June.

There is also an extensive network of very large inland waterways, which provide spectacular opportunities for the touring canoe or kayak. These are available throughout the Alpine countries and also in the low countries of Holland, Denmark, and Belgium.

Switzerland contains some huge and beautiful lakes, while coastal paddling in mainland Europe is plentiful wherever there is a coast. Surf, however, is mainly found on the west coast of Europe. France and Portugal face the best of the Atlantic swells. The Mediterranean does not provide rideable waves except after storm conditions.

United Kingdom

Considering its small size and maritime climate, it is perhaps surprising to find that the United Kingdom offers excellent paddling of all kinds, and has possibly the largest number of paddle sport enthusiasts per capita in the world.

White water paddling in the United Kingdom is entirely rainfall dependent, but such is the reliability of the British climate that the rivers are sure to be fast-flowing throughout the autumn and winter (October to January), and often during rainy spells in the spring (March to April). However, a peculiarity of British law dictates that, unlike most other countries in the world, it is illegal to navigate rivers without permission from the landowners. Luckily, most interesting sections of river have some sort of agreement negotiated on them, which means that paddling is allowed at least during the "closed" season for fishing. Nevertheless, it may still be necessary to apply for a licence, or some other kind of permit. The best way to find out about this is to contact the British Canoe Union (BCU), who have a comprehensive database and will tell you what you need and how to apply for it. Assume that white water paddling at least will be allowed only from October to March in most areas. This is the best time for the water anyway.

There are no such restrictions on Britain's extensive coastline, which offers excellent sea touring and estuary paddling, and the West Coast (Scotland, South Wales and Cornwall in particular) offers world class surfing. The sea is warmest in September and coldest in April.

North and Central America

The North American continent is the spiritual home of modern paddling. The traditional open canoe of course originated there, and the kayak as we know it today is descended directly from the Inuit craft that hails originally from the northern shores of what is now Canada, as well as from neighbouring Greenland and Siberia.

The United States and Canada together form an enormous continental land mass. The sheer geographical size of these countries means that there is inevitably a wide variety of paddling, but there are also great distances to cover. Whereas in Europe one might have a number of rivers within a few minutes drive of each other, it is common in the United States and Canada to travel for several hours, if not days, to find the water you are looking for. At least this way, you get to see more of the country.

⊘ *A big drop on the South Fork of the river Yuba in California.*

The United States

It is commonly believed that most of the white water paddling is restricted to the mountain ranges down the East and West coasts, but in fact almost every state in the United States boasts quality white water. However, the size of the country means that American paddlers tend to be either an East Coast paddler, or a West Coast one: zipping across the country from one side to another is not feasible for most people, and they prefer to stick to the coast nearest to where they live. This way, the United States even manages to field two separate teams for international competitions: one from the East and one from the West.

As well as its world-class white water, there is an enormous following for the more placid open water boating on flat water rivers and lakes. Open canoes are widely used for hunting and fishing as well as being recreational craft in their own right. It is probably true to say that open canoeing is bigger in America than

anywhere else, with whole families packing up their boat and heading down to the water, dog and all.

The coasts of North America are popular destinations for sea kayaking, and they offer good quality surf at most times of year. In particular, the Pacific coasts of California and Mexico are, perhaps not surprisingly, very well attended surfing locations. The east-facing Gulf of Mexico also catches some very good swells.

Central America

Guatemala, Belize, El Salvador, Honduras and Nicaragua all have spectacular white water and excellent surf on both the Pacific and the Caribbean coasts. However, these are not the safest or the most politically stable countries you could visit as a tourist. Further south, Costa Rica is a better bet, with world-class tropical white water paddling, great surf, and sea kayaking too. It is best visited from November through February, but

● *Huge white water: the National Falls, Upper Youghiogeny, Maryland.*

slowly through the summer. They are still supplying big-water fun into September.

There are many enormous lakes scattered across the Canadian landscape, as well as the almost Scandinavian coastlines of Newfoundland and British Columbia. Alaska, which is the northern-most state of the United States although entirely within Canada geographically, has much in common with Canada. It is dominated by the splendid Yukon river and the often ice-bound Bering Straits that separate it from neighbouring Russia.

The Canadian Great Lakes, Superior and Huron, border with the American states of Minnesota, Wisconsin and Michigan. These inland seas are bigger than a small country, and because of this, sea kayaking has a strong following in the area; the local paddlers often use full-on ocean kayaks. Sea kayaking in Canada is big business, and commercial trips are widely available. Adventure tourism is huge in Canada anyway, and opportunities to go paddling with seals, dolphins and killer whales are irresistible for tourists and paddling fanatics alike.

● *Running a sloping drop into an eddy on the Maryland National Falls, USA.*

is so popular with tourists that if you try to fly in around Christmas time it can be expensive, if not impossible.

Further south again, the narrow land-bridge that is Panama boasts some excellent touring in its beautiful National Parks, and sea kayaking on both of its coasts. From there we reach Colombia, part of the South American continent.

Canada

Canada is famous for big-volume white water. Although there are a variety of different rivers to explore, it is the mighty rapids of the Ottowa and St. Lawrence in the east, and the Slave, Peace and Fraser in the west that have captured the imagination of white water paddlers since the 1970s. These rivers are fed almost entirely by snowmelt, but because of the lakes, which act as reservoirs for the colossal amount of meltwater, the season is quite long – the water levels tend to be (too) high in April and May, dropping

South America

South America is a rather different place from its northern neighbour. Composed of 13 independent nations, each with a far less developed economy than the United States, it is inevitably less affluent, and this is reflected in the poor state of the continent's transport and communications network. Travelling with boats must be done mainly through bus travel, and anyone who has paddled here will have stories of epic ten-hour bus journeys in oppressive heat.

River Paddling

By far the largest of the countries is Brazil, which is dominated by the vast network of Amazon tributaries. The Amazon itself, the greatest river in the world, starts in Peru, in the west of the continent, and stretches right across to its equatorial delta in the east.

All the South American countries have great rivers and, with the exception of Paraguay and Bolivia, hugely interesting and extensive coastlines, but the popular kayaking destinations are Ecuador, Peru and Chile. Each of these countries has a mixture of indigenous native Indian cultures, and Spanish influence, courtesy of the medieval Spanish *conquistadores*. Living and travelling is inexpensive, but all three countries are dangerous places in wilderness areas, both medically and because of a widespread risk of theft, mugging and corruption.

White Water

Classic white water runs abound in Ecuador and Chile. The white water season throughout South America runs from October through to February.

There is more and more commercial kayaking and rafting in South America, especially in Chile. At the same time, however, many classic and beautiful white water runs are being dammed for hydro-electric power and are lost to paddlers forever. This is one of the problems facing white water rivers in developing countries.

🔼 *River gorges form beneath clear blue skies and steep mountainsides in Peru.*

🔽 *Casa Nova Falls and Land of the Giants, Rio Misahualli, Ecuador.*

Open Water

The Pacific coast features excellent surf, and is a popular destination for surfers. The sea kayaking opportunities, too, are plentiful, as one would expect from such extensive coastlines and tropical climate, but the infrastructure isn't really there to support anything more than the self-sufficient adventurer.

To the far south of the continent, the climate changes dramatically. By contrast with the tropical climes further north, the south of Argentina and Chile, culminating in the Tierra del Fuego and Cape Horn, are close to Antarctica. Severe bleak weather, combined with savage ultra-violet penetration because of damage to the ozone layer, make this an inhospitable place. The stormy seas around Cape Horn are famously the roughest in the world. They are not suitable for kayaking, although some intrepid expedition paddlers have rounded the cape and much of Tierra del Fuego in sea kayaks.

◉ *A team meeting on a river beach on the Rio Cassanga in Ecuador.*

◉ *Huge white water: the Lost Yak rapid on the Rio Bio Bio in Chile.*

◉ *Typical boat transportation in South America: the going is slow, but at least you have time to appreciate the sights.*

Australia and New Zealand

The enormous continent of Australia has relatively little in the way of white water, but with its incredible and extensive coastline makes up for it in sea kayaking and surf. The relatively diminutive islands of New Zealand, on the other hand, feature enormous paddling opportunities, and for this reason among others is beginning to be hailed as the adventure tourism capital of the world.

Australia

Of course, Australia does have its white water rivers, and the artificial white water course at Sydney, which was built for the Olympic Games in 2000, has done a great deal for the profile and the popularity of white water kayaking among Australians. But the sheer size of the country and the relatively large distances to be travelled between runs has dictated that Australia has not, as yet, become as popular a destination among white water tourists as neighbouring New Zealand.

The surf, on the other hand, is spectacular, and its close proximity to major cities makes it a very good reason to go there. Wave-ski paddling is far more popular than kayaking at the moment, although this may change as the global shift towards surf kayaks makes more

◐ *Horizon line: a kayaker about to take the plunge on New Zealand white water.*

◐ *The Australian coastline offers some excellent surf and wave-ski opportunities.*

exciting kayaks available to wave enthusiasts down under. Sea kayaking is big business in Australia, with such large sections of coastline commercially exploited, and tourism being one of the stronger industries in coastal areas.

New Zealand

From the point of view of an outdoor adventure enthusiast, New Zealand is an astonishing country. Not only does it boast some of the most spectacular white water on the planet (such as Huka Falls on the Waikato, North Island) but also some of the best play waves (Kaituna, Falljames) and famous surf breaks, such as Raglan point, one of the best left-handers in the world.

New Zealand has a great deal packed into a small country, but despite this and its enormous popularity, overcrowding and overuse of resources is not yet a problem. The relatively low population and the nature of the geography mean that, although you will always see and meet other paddlers, it won't be frustratingly busy. A lot of New Zealanders do paddle, but you will be surprised to find that many of the boaters you meet there are foreign visitors.

The white water rivers seem to run for much of the year, although most are primarily spring/summer rivers (from October through to May). Some of them, however, are dam-controlled and have year-round water. There is a wealth of information available on the Internet, because New Zealand is one of the most popular destinations for paddling tourism and a lot of help and guidance has been written and provided.

Commercial rafting on white water is widespread, as are jet-boat rides on the rapids and any other adrenalin-pumping activity the New Zealanders can sell to the tourists. Commercialism is one reason why there is an excellent infrastructure and information network for anyone who wants to paddle there.

Surfing and sea kayaking are equally well catered for by the commercial sector, but you will have no trouble getting off the beaten track and finding solitude if that's what you are looking for. New Zealand has more than its fair share of beaches and beautiful coastline, and sea touring in

particular is very popular. Inland touring is less available than in many countries, but what there is makes up for this with the beauty of its surrounding countryside.

Because of its maritime and temperate climate, New Zealand isn't particularly cold in the winter. The mountainous regions in the centre of the islands get snow, which provides much of the spring white water, but in low-lying areas and nearer the coasts the temperature is unlikely to be less than 10°C (50°F).

New Zealand is a relatively expensive place to fly to, even from mainland Australia, but in particular from the rest of the world because of its otherwise remote location. Once there, however, the cost of living and of travelling is one of the lowest outside the Third World. This makes for a tempting combination of a cheap trip with a highly civilized infrastructure and a truly excellent range of commercial resources.

◉ *A kayaker going deep on the Kaituna river, New Zealand.*

◉ *A kayaker makes a spectacular blunt on the Falljames river, New Zealand.*

Asia

This is rather a big place to try to describe in one small section, but in fact Asia is probably the continent whose paddling we know least about. Although intrepid expedition paddlers have penetrated almost every part of the Asian continent, there are still many rivers left to run, and all but a tiny minority of the vast land area is as yet untouched by adventure tourism.

If you plan to holiday in Asia, the Internet is by far your best way of finding out about the paddling possibilities. It is probably fair to say that this part of the world is changing faster than any other in terms of its potential for adventure tourism, although, with a few exceptions, it has a long way to go to catch up with countries such as New Zealand. However, the jewels in its crown are

● *Porters carrying kayaks towards a Himalayan river.*

◐ *Overnight stopover on the beach of the river Sun Khosi in Nepal.*

❯ *Enormous white water on the Indus, the river that gave India its name.*

Nepal for white water, and Indonesia for surf and sea paddling. Both destinations are unmatched worldwide in quality for their respective types of boating.

Nepal

This tiny, land-locked country is one of the most popular destinations in the world for white water kayaking. Extensively rafted and kayaked commercially, it is accessible and cheap, and until recently it enjoyed relative political stability. The surrounding countries all feature incredible white water, but it is less commonly paddled. India, Pakistan and Tibet have all enjoyed a fair amount of attention, but none of them are popular paddling destinations as yet.

South-east Asia

China is now a developing tourist destination, but although there are many white water rivers and beautiful coastlines, very few people have paddled there. Thailand has some white water that is commercially rafted, and is popular with a great number of inland and sea touring specialists: the Asia-Pacific region in general is tropical and has a tourist-friendly coastline.

Both kayaking and canoeing are huge in Japan. The number of Japanese people who regularly go white water, touring or sea paddling is enormous, although only a small number of foreign tourists paddle there. This is perhaps a result of the high costs associated with this small country, or it may be that the language barrier makes it difficult to get information about it. Most Japanese websites are in the Japanese language, and hence illegible to most foreigners.

Indonesia has white water that is now just beginning to be paddled regularly, although it is most renowned for its world-class surf. In fact, almost all of the Pacific island chains, Tahitian islands and Hawaii (which really counts as America) have the most fantastic surf imaginable, and these are key destinations for kayakers.

❯ *A Nepalese mountain gorge. Scenes like this make for exhilarating paddling.*

Africa

The enormous continent that is Africa is a hugely popular tourist destination because of its natural beauty and the sheer scale of its geography.

Almost all of Africa is either tropical or sub-tropical, so it is characterized by its extreme heat for most of the year. The continent is a good paddling destination: inexpensive and with a good infrastructure for tourism in many areas. Health issues must be considered – consult your doctor before you go, and explain what you will be doing there. It is a beautiful continent, but not one to be taken lightly.

Northern Africa

The desert countries of the northern sub-tropical areas (Morocco, Tunisia, Algeria, Libya, Egypt) have few paddling opportunities, although there is good surf on the west coast, and the Atlas Mountains have potentially exciting white water (though no-one ever seems to catch good water levels there).

Central Africa

The central tropical African nations have a wealth of rivers, both white water and mature. Access to these is fairly difficult, however, and the long-term political instability of many of these countries must be a concern. The Nile and Niger, Africa's biggest rivers, are still a draw for many tourists, and commercial paddling is available in many regions.

The white water of the Congo, Uganda and Zambezi is world-famous, and is becoming increasingly popular as a result of developing commercial tourism. This is enormous white water, and should not be attempted by the complete novice. However, there will often be expert guidance on hand in these areas from the local rafting companies and professional kayakers, and if you want to paddle the most amazing white water in the world, it should be possible – subject, of course, to adequate technical skills, fitness and strength.

◑ *Getting airborne in an African sunset. The scenery here is breathtaking.*

◐ *An absolutely colossal stopper (hole) in Uganda, Central Africa.*

Southern Africa

South Africa is a popular destination for all kinds of paddling, while neighbouring Namibia and Botswana are less popular. South Africa is sought-after for its surf and sea kayaking: wave-ski paddling is huge. The south-west coast of South Africa, around Cape Town, and Durban on the coast, are perhaps the two most popular and versatile location choices.

Coastal Areas

Africa is blessed with good surf. The entire west coast faces on to massive Atlantic swells, and Morocco, Senegal, the Ivory Coast, Cameroon and Gabon are all popular with surf fanatics. On the east coast, the waves are less consistent, but the Indian Ocean and Madagascar still provide some thrills and spills as well as beautiful coastal touring.

◔ *Playing on a big rapid. Central Africa has some world-famous white water.*

◔ *Play boating on white water in South Africa. The country offers good opportunities for all kinds of paddling, and is a favourite with paddling tourists.*

◔ *Safety kayakers with their raft on an eddy on the White Nile, Uganda.*

6 KEEPING SAFE

Safety and Rescue

While good planning and appropriate equipment can prevent many difficulties, accidents will still happen. This section is intended to tell you about the safety and rescue techniques that all kayakers and canoeists need to know, whatever type of water they are paddling on. More detailed advice, including essential equipment, aimed at specific types of paddling is given in the flat water, white water and open water sections of this book.

Practise the following techniques to a proficient level, and make sure you know how to use the equipment you have with you. In a situation where every second counts, it is vital that you know what to do.

Communication

The biggest part of safety and rescue on the water is communication. Make sure you know your paddling group's level of ability and experience, so that you will be better prepared if an incident occurs. If you come across a situation involving people you don't know, start a dialogue immediately. You can't bring your skills to bear on the situation until you have understood what is happening.

⊙ *Attempting a chase boat rescue to help a swimmer out of the water.*

Rescue and Recovery

If someone in your group is unable to re-enter their boat after a capsize, you may have to rescue them by paddling over and helping them to get back in. If they are unable to paddle due to injury or tiredness, you may need to tow them and their boat back to safety.

The following rescue and recovery techniques detail how to do this. Learn them all so that you can use the most appropriate for the situation on the day.

⊙ *Talking through the plans for the trip in advance can eliminate confusion later.*

Chase Boat Rescue

If a paddler is in the water and unable to re-enter their boat, you may be able to get them to hold the front or back of your boat, or even get on to or into your boat, so that you can carry them to shore. It is slow progress, and often better to get to shore and use a throw-line to pull them in.

When you attempt to rescue someone who is upset or panicking, they may be irrational and can unwittingly put you in danger by clinging to you or clambering on to your boat. Don't let a victim get hold of you until you have established verbal and eye contact, and you are sure they are not going to put both of you in more danger than you are already in.

SAFETY RULES
• Always wear a flotation aid, and put it on before you get into the boat.
• Learn how to capsize as a priority.
• It is more important to rescue the victim than the boat.
• Never undertake a rescue that puts you or the victim in more danger than you were already in.
• Only ever practise rescue procedures in a safe environment.

◔ *A shoulder belay is one way to pull a swimmer or boat from the water.*

Throw-line

A throw-line consists of a length of rope that will float tied to a bag. The bag will often have some foam buoyancy to keep it afloat as well. In order to rescue a swimmer when you are standing on the bank, take the throw-line, open the bag and grasp the loose end of the rope, and throw the bag to the victim. Aim to land the bag beyond the swimmer, so that the rope falls across him, and he can grab it and be pulled to safety.

Shoulder Belay

This is an efficient way to maximize your strength when using a rope to rescue a paddler or equipment from the bank against a fairly strong current. Wrap the rope around your back and over your shoulder to get your whole weight behind the pull. This way you can apply a force to the rope equal to about 110 per cent of your body weight. Pulling with your arms will only give you about 80 per cent.

Pulleys for Mechanical Advantage

If you are trying to recover a swimmer or a boat against a current that is too strong to resist manually, you can set up a pulley system from the bank to increase the strength of your pull.

Karabiners can be used with a sling to make a pulley. Karabiners are strong metal devices used for connecting ropes and slings to each other, or to boats and rescue equipment. They can also be used as improvised pulleys. You can attach a karabiner to a tree or rock with a sling, then put a throw-line through it to apply some braking to a swamped boat as it hurtles downstream. A boat full of water is a heavy projectile and you will not be able to control it otherwise. Karabiners are not as good as real pulleys because they apply a lot of friction, but this can be used to your advantage if you need to brake or control a descent or rescue.

If you use a pulley to double the force you apply to the boat, you will have to pull 2m (6½ft) of rope through the system for every 1m (3½ft) that the boat moves. With two pulleys, in a system called a Z-drag, there will be three times more force, but you will need even more rope. You also need to ask yourself whether you want to carry hardware such as pulleys every time you go on the river, and whether it might not be safer to abandon the boat and concentrate on rescuing only the swimmer.

Towing

A waist tow is a useful technique to operate from your boat. It can be used for towing a boat or a swimmer. It can also be used by two or more paddlers in a yoked or husky tow, which is invaluable for towing over long distances or in difficult conditions.

Using a proper towline, which will have a shock absorber to prevent spinal injury, loop the towline over your shoulder so that it can be quickly released if you become entangled with something in the water, or if you capsize, which would put you and the victim in further difficulties.

A simple 2m (6½ft) sling can be used in place of a towline for towing a boat or paddle. Put the sling around your elbow or shoulder. Never put it around your waist or body: you must be able to get rid of it easily if you capsize, even if the tow is keeping it under tension.

Modern flotation aids for white water incorporate a quick-release rescue belt as part of the design. This provides a stronger attachment for the towline.

Air Sea Rescue

Helicopters are often used to rescue kayakers from the sea or from remote wilderness rivers. You are unlikely to have experienced a helicopter rescue before, and it pays to know what to expect.

Helicopters make a lot of down-draught with their rotors. If you are afloat in a boat and one hovers overhead, it is like getting a trashing in a hole or in the surf. You will be blown over, and may not be able to roll up. It has been known for sea kayaks to be blown end over end across the water by the power of a helicopter's down-draft.

If a winchman or unmanned strop is lowered to you from a helicopter, you may need to allow for the strop to be earthed to ground on water before you try to grab it. Helicopters can generate a potentially lethal amount of static electricity which must be released to earth.

If an Air Sea Rescue helicopter is called out to recover you, they will not transport your kayaks and equipment. In fact, at sea they will deliberately sink your kayak to prevent potential false call-outs when an empty boat is spotted by shipping.

◔ *Most countries have an Air Sea Rescue service that will come to the help of paddlers in trouble at sea.*

Medical Knowledge for Paddlers

Kayaking and canoeing are very safe sports when compared to most other adventure activities, and much safer than team contact sports such as football, basketball, rugby or cricket. However, minor injuries are commonplace in all sports, and in addition to knowing how to cope with them, you must also be aware of problems that are specific to paddlers.

The skills required to tackle serious and/or life-threatening injuries in a remote environment cannot be learnt from a book. If you intend to paddle in situations where such threats are possible, it is vital that you go on a registered first-aid course to practise the techniques involved.

Of the few injuries that do occur, most happen while actually paddling, and not while capsizing, rolling or swimming.

The most common mechanism of serious injury is striking an object such as a rock, paddle or another kayak. The next most common are traumatic stress injuries caused by the impact of water against the body or equipment, and overuse injuries such as tendon problems, particularly in the wrists, and chronic back problems.

◗ *A bivvy bag can be used to retain heat and prevent wind chill. Note here the buoyancy aid being used as a pillow to stabilize the head position and maintain clear airways.*

Minor Cuts and Bruises

Cuts, bruises and splinters are far more likely than fractured limbs. Immersion of the affected area in cold water and/or wind chill ensures that minor cuts and bruises will not usually become painful until you get off the water. If there is an open wound, however small, be aware that it might get infected and decide whether to close or cover the wound before the wound gets wet, if you still have a choice. Clean water (fresh or sea), should be used to clean the wound, and this will temper any pain. If you suspect the water is dirty, keep the wound dry.

◗ *Rolling up with the head tucked on to the front deck can save you from knocks to the head and facial injuries.*

Hypothermia

If you become excessively cold you will slowly succumb to hypothermia unless you are able to warm up your body. The victim is unlikely to realize it themselves, but early symptoms may be noticed by other paddlers. These include:

• Irrational behaviour.
• Loss of co-ordination.
• Loss of communication skills.
• Memory lapse.
• Loss of motivation and will to move.

Hypothermia can be caused by sudden cooling, for example taking a swim in cold water, or by slow progressive cooling through the onset of exhaustion and/or inadequate insulation over a period of hours. The cause might even be a combination of the two. With the former, it is correct to warm up the victim quickly, when back on land, using a warm bath or shower, or switch on the car heater.

In the case of profound hypothermia caused by slow heat loss, this would be ineffective, extremely dangerous and could result in heart failure. Instead, get the victim dry and insulate them as much as possible with clothing, a hat, gloves, sleeping bag or anything else to hand. If you are carrying a bivvy bag as part of your first aid kit, you can put the victim into it. If necessary, you can get into the bivvy bag with them to increase the temperature. Check constantly that their air passage is clear, and get professional medical help as quickly as possible. The victim will not be able to do anything to help himself.

Remember that prevention is better than cure. If you or anyone in your paddling group is exhibiting the normal signs of getting cold, for example shivering, and loss of feeling in the extremities, while on the water, act immediately before hypothermia can set in. Get the person away from the water, and get them warm.

Hyperthermia

The opposite of hypothermia is heatstroke, also known as hyperthermia. The symptoms are loss of colour, a high temperature but not necessarily sweating, and shallow breathing. The victim will feel faint and nauseous. Cool down the casualty gently by moving them into the shade and giving them lots of cool fluids.

By far the most common cause of hyperthermia in paddlers is moving around off the water when it is hot, while still wearing all the insulation that was intended for the colder conditions on the water. The best immediate treatment is to remove as many levels of clothing as necessary to enable them to cool down before they overheat.

Shock

Traumatic injury or a frightening experience can lead to shock. Similar symptoms to those of hypothermia occur. The victim may be disorientated and not capable of looking after themselves. Shock can be treated as follows:
• Treat the cause if it is physical.
• Make the victim comfortable, and place them in the recovery position if possible.
• Keep the victim warm, and provide warm drinks if there is no reason to preclude this (if the victim is unconscious or has a head or facial injury).
• Watch the victim constantly in case they stop breathing or fall in the water.
• Provide professional medical attention as soon as possible.

Head Injuries

These can be caused by anything from low-hanging tree branches to rocks in the water when you capsize. Anyone suffering a severe blow to the head or who becomes unconscious for any reason needs professional medical advice as quickly as possible. If this happens when the group is out on the water, return the victim to the shore, and put them in the recovery position until help arrives. Do not move the victim unless it is absolutely essential.

🔽 *Improvise an effective stretcher using two kayak paddles and flotation aids.*

● *Warming up and stretching thoroughly before paddling is a good way to prevent injury and mishap on the water.*

Cramp

Cramp is a painful muscle spasm that occurs when the blood supply to the affected area is impaired. It commonly affects paddlers because of their sitting or kneeling position, especially in cold weather conditions.

The condition is not serious but the pain can be severe. The best treatment is to try to stretch the muscle, counteracting its contraction, and to massage the whole area to improve the circulation. Cramp can occur in any muscle but it is particularly common for boaters to get it in the calves and the feet.

Cold Hands

Paddling in very cold water can cause extreme discomfort in the hands and particularly in the fingers. Unfortunately, the instinct to stop and warm up the hands can prolong the time you are on the water and the discomfort. A good solution is to carry on paddling and getting wet, ignoring the fact that your

● *A group of kayakers venturing out to sea with a qualified instructor.*

fingers are getting cold, until they really begin to hurt. If, at this point, you continue to exercise quite hard, you can provoke a reaction from your blood vessels which, though initially painful, will after a few minutes stop the discomfort. You will then be able to use your hands normally and can continue paddling.

Surfer's Ear

Surfer's ear, also known as exostoses, is an increasingly common complaint among paddlers who regularly get

completely wet. The complaint is the growth of bony lumps in the inner ear as a result of the ear canal being constantly exposed to cold water and wind chill. After a several years of regular exposure, the lumps can impair the hearing, and will cause constant ear infections by preventing the inner ear from drying out as quickly as it normally would. The best preventative measure is to protect the ears whenever you paddle by wearing a skull cap or earplugs. These are available from most paddling suppliers. Consult your doctor if you suspect you might have surfer's ear.

Shoulder Dislocation

One of the most common traumatic injuries experienced by canoeists and kayakers is shoulder dislocation, and in particular anterior dislocation (where the upper arm is forced up and back beyond its normal range of movement until the shoulder joint is dislocated). In rare cases the joint is able to relocate on its own, but more usually it will have to be repositioned by an expert medical practitioner. The injury is extremely painful, precluding further activity of any sort, and usually requiring evacuation. All you can do is to try to stabilize the injury to prevent further pain and damage. It usually takes months to rehabilitate from a dislocation, so prevention is the way to go. Avoid high bracing, reaching too far behind you, and paddling without first warming up.

FIRST AID KITS

Always carry a basic first aid kit and include the following items. Look through the equipment in your kit, and make sure you know how to use it. Better still, attend a first aid course so that you can practise the theory.
• First aid manual.
• Sterile bandages.
• Sterile plasters.
• Sterile gauze and burn patches.
• Mild relief tablets for headaches, nausea, and bacterial infection.
• Surgical tape.
• Scissors and tweezers.
• Thermometer.

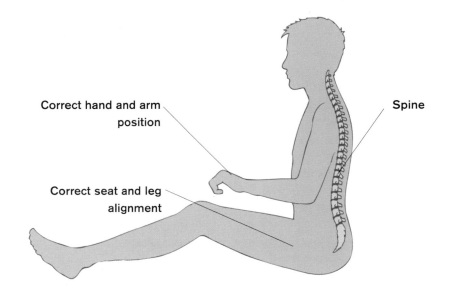

Correct hand and arm position

Spine

Correct seat and leg alignment

Tendonitis

Paddlers are prone to tendon problems, particularly in the wrists and elbows. This tends to be a chronic (ongoing) complaint, which can best be addressed by using paddles with low angles of feather, and simply not overdoing it. Gripping the paddle too tightly when anxious can exacerbate the problem, as can paddling aggressively with a poor or jerky technique.

Back Pain

Back pain is common for kayakers and canoeists alike. Back problems can be minimized by good all-round training,

◔ A dislocated shoulder or arm injury can be stabilized very effectively using a flotation aid in this manner.

warm-up and stretching routines, but you must also concentrate on maintaining a good body posture.

The spine needs to maintain a correct curvature, with particular attention given to the curve in the lower back. A kneeling canoeist can more easily maintain this posture while paddling, while a kayaker will find it almost impossible. Failure to maintain correct lower back posture while working hard can result in severe back pain. The problem is compounded if you get into a car without adequate lumbar support to drive home. Lying in the bath at home will further aggravate the condition, as the bath floor is sloping and not flat.

◔ An awkward capsize can easily lead to injury if there are any rocks or boulders beneath the water surface.

◔ Perfect posture, with the spine in the shape of a letter S, reduces pressure on the invertebral discs in the lower back.

Perfect Posture

All back pain should first be tackled by checking the posture. Perfect posture is the position of the seated spine when there is the least amount of pressure on the intervertebral discs in the lower back. Every spine has it own unique shape. When this shape is preserved the posture is perfect. However, the human spine is a vertical flexible column that was not designed to be seated. Perfect posture is nearly impossible to attain for long periods: it must be supported. Holding the spine in the shape of a letter S when kneeling, sitting or standing will support the spine and maintain perfect posture.

Glossary

Aft Toward the rear of the boat.

Asymmetric A type of paddle on which the top side of the blade is longer than the bottom side.

Back-cut drops Waterfalls with an airspace or cavity behind the curtain of water.

Beam The width of the boat.

Big water High volume rapids.

Blade The part of the paddle you put in the water; can be used as a word to describe the whole paddle.

Boater Common generic term for a canoeist or kayaker.

Boils Where water surfaces from below; it gives the appearance of boiling water.

Boof A technique for landing a freefalling boat flat on its hull.

Bow The forward most part of a boat.

Bow draw A stroke that pulls the bow of the boat sideways through the water.

Bow paddler The paddler in the forward position.

Bow rudder An advanced steering stroke that is used to turn the boat quickly while it is moving forwards.

Break-in Enter the current from an area of slack water.

Break-out To exit the current into an area of slack water.

Buoyancy aid A vest or jacket designed to give added buoyancy to a swimmer, but not buoyant enough to hinder swimming, or rolling. *See also* personal flotation device.

Capsize To turn upside down in a boat.

Canoe A small craft propelled with one or more single-bladed paddle(s), while sitting or kneeling and facing the direction of travel.

Canoeist A person who is competent at paddling a canoe.

Centre line Imaginary longitudinal line running through the boat from the bow to the stern.

Composite Made from a combination of more than one material, usually resin and a fabric (like carbon fibre).

Cross-bow Any stroke that is performed on one side of the boat using the paddle-blade normally reserved for the other side.

Cushions A type of pressure wave that tends to deflect boats and swimmers from the rocks that generated it.

Cushion wave *See* cushions

Deck The top of an enclosed boat; another word for spraydeck or skirt.

Delta Triangular type rig.

Depth The distance from the floor to the height of the gunwale measured at the boat's centre line.

Downstream Towards the sea.

Draft The vertical distance from the waterline of the boat to the lowest point of the boat.

Draw stroke A stroke that pulls the boat sideways through the water.

Drop Any pronounced change in the water level.

Dropping in Attempting to surf a wave or hole that another person is already using.

Dry-top A special type of cagoule designed for paddling, which has efficient seals to keep the water out.

Eddy An area of slack water moving upstream.

End grabs Handles at each end of a boat for use when carrying or towing the boat.

Falls Any distinct drop in the river level, but most often a vertical or near-vertical step down.

Feather To angle a paddle blade; the term usually refers to the angle between the two blades of a kayak paddle (an angle of between 30° and 90°).

Feedback (from the water) Kinaesthetic awareness of forces acting on you, the boat or the paddle.

Ferry glide A technique for crossing a current without moving up- or down-stream.

Flare The amount the sides of a canoe curve outward from the perpendicular; can also mean an illuminating safety device that can be used by paddlers in distress to attract attention at sea.

Flat water Water that does not have waves or currents that are strong enough to affect a canoe or kayak.

Flotation Material encased beneath the bow and stern decks that allows the canoe to float when swamped.

Forward Toward the bow of the boat.

Forward sweep stroke The most basic form of turning stroke, which can be used while the boat is stationary or in motion.

Free blade Any paddle or propulsion device that is held in the hands and not attached to the boat.

Freeboard The distance between the waterline and the gunwale of the canoe.

Frowny Any hydraulic with the ends (and

hence the exits) upstream of, or higher than, the middle of the hydraulic.

Gaff A type of sailing rig wih a boom-like support at the top of the sail as well as the bottom.

Grade/grading The name given to the accepted system for describing the severity of rapids.

Green water Unaerated – but not necessarily flat – water.

Grip The way in which you hold the paddle, or the specific part of a paddle shaft that rests in the hand.

Gunwale A strengthening rail, running the length of the canoe on each side, which is attached to the top edge of the boat sides.

H or HI rescue A technique for emptying another person's boat with help from another boater, while afloat.

Hand-roll To right the capsized craft using only the hands, without having to get out.

High brace A more advanced support stroke that is to be avoided if possible since it carries a risk of injury.

Hole A retentive (recirculating) wave capable of stopping and holding a boat or swimmer (also known as a stopper).

Hull The underside of any type of boat.

Husky tow Two or more paddlers towing a third paddler who may be tired or injured and experiencing difficulty on their own.

J-stroke A special canoe stroke that keeps the boat travelling in a straight line without the need to paddle on both sides.

Karabiner A metal connecting device designed for climbers but much used by white water paddlers.

Kayak A small craft propelled with one or more two-bladed paddle(s) while sitting and facing the direction of travel.

Kayaker A person who is competent at paddling a kayak.

Keel A longitudinal V-shape to the boat's bottom, on its centre line, to give strength, protection, and added control.

Leeward From the boat, the direction toward which the wind is blowing.

Low brace A basic support stroke.

Meltdown Deliberately putting your boat underneath a wave or hydraulic.

Oar A paddle-like propulsion device that is attached to a boat when in use.

Offside The side of the canoe opposite that on which the blade is normally used.

Open water A large expanse of usually flat water, typically a sea, lake, or very large river.

Onside The side on which a canoe is normally paddled (left or right according to personal preference).

Paddler Common generic term for a canoeist or kayaker.

PFD (personal flotation device) US description of a buoyancy aid or lifejacket.

Pocket/Power Pocket The steepest green part of the wave, usually right next to the shoulder.

Pin spot A place where there is a natural danger of physical entrapment.

Pontoon A tethered, floating platform.

Port The left side of the boat as you face forward.

Portage The carrying of a boat or its contents over land from one body of water to another.

Pourover Anywhere that water pours over a distinct drop in the river bed, but most usually water pouring over and around a boulder to form a nasty, retentive hydraulic.

Prys Strokes that are performed by levering the paddle shaft against the side of the boat (usually a canoe).

Rapid An area of turbulent water.

Recirculate To be repeatedly carried upstream and submerged by the towback

of a hydraulic water feature, such as a stopper wave.

Reverse sweep stroke A basic turning stroke that can be used while the boat is stationary or on the move.

Ribs Frames on the inside or outside of the hull to give additional strength.

Rocker The amount a boat's hull appears to be curved upwards at the ends.

Roll To right a craft after a capsize without having to get out.

Saddle An open canoe seat that is straddled by the paddler.

Sculling Imparting a force using a continuous to and fro action with a submerged blade.

Sculling draw A technique that propels the boat continuously sideways towards the paddle.

Sculling pry Like a sculling draw, but the pry propels the boat sideways away from the paddle.

Seal Launch To slide or drop into the water while seated in the boat and holding the paddle.

Seams Where two currents converge they often fold downwards to make a seam-like feature on the surface.

Shaft The cylindrical part of the paddle, also known as the loom.

Shoulder The edge of the breaking part of a wave.

Shuttle The vehicle used for, or the practise of, transporting paddlers or equipment by road to the opposite end of a paddling trip.

Siphon Anywhere the current goes under an obstruction, such as a tree, with no airspace.

Ski A sit-on-top surf craft.

Skirt *See* spraydeck.

Smiley Any hydraulic with the ends (and hence the exits) downstream of, or lower than, the middle of the hydraulic.

Spraydeck (spray skirt) A device that is worn around the waist to keep water out of the cockpit.

Spray rail Longitudinal rails running slightly above the waterline on the outside, to deflect waves and chop.

Starboard The right hand side of the boat as you face forward.

Stern The rearmost end of the canoe.

Stern paddler Paddler seated in the rear of the boat (kayak or canoe).

Stern rudder A steering stroke to be used while moving forwards.

Stopper A retentive (recirculating) wave capable of stopping and holding a boat, swimmer or any buoyant object hitting it from upstream (also known as a hole).

Strainer An obstruction through which the water is forced, forming a sieve-like effect.

Surf Breaking waves (noun); to ride in control on the face of a wave (verb).

Symmetrical Of a paddle, that the blades are a symmetrical shape; it does not mean that the blades are the same.

Tandem paddling Two paddlers paddling the same boat.

Technical water Usually low volume rapids with a lot of rocks and much manoeuvring required.

T-grip The handle on top of a canoe paddle shaft.

Throwline A proprietary rescue device carried by most whitewater paddlers.

Thwart A support or seat extending across width of canoe from gunwale to gunwale.

To ship water To accidentally take on water.

Touring Travelling the countryside by boat.

Towline A proprietary rescue device commonly used by instructors.

Tracking The term used to describe how well a boat tracks (keeps its direction) under the influence of currents and wind.

Trim To load the boat so that it is level or slightly stern-down.

Trimming Making the boat float level by redistributing the weight of paddlers or gear.

Tumblehome The amount the sides of a canoe curves out and then returns inward from the perpendicular.

Transom The square stern in canoes designed for stern-mounted outboards.

Upstream Towards the source of the river.

Volume The amount of air trapped inside a boat; also refers to the volume of water moving down a rapid.

Wave-wheel A cartwheel-type manoeuvre performed going down the back of a wave.

Wet exit The procedure for bailing out from the boat while under water, following a capsize.

Whirlpools Whirling vertical vortices with a core of air that carry anything that falls into them down to the bed of the river, lake or sea. Similar to the way in which water swirls down the plughole of a bath.

White water Water that, because of the wind or the current, has become turbulent enough to become aerated and appears white and frothy.

Wilderness paddling Paddling far away from the resources of civilization.

Windage The degree to which a boat's sides are exposed to, or tend to catch, the wind.

Windward From the boat, the direction from which the wind is blowing.

X-rescue A technique for emptying another person's boat single-handed while afloat.

Further Reading

Books

Canoeing: A Trailside Guide
Gordon Grant/Norton (1997)

Outdoor Pursuits Series: Canoeing
Laurie Gullion/Human Kinetics Publishers
(1994)

The Canoe Handbook
Slim Ray/Stackpole Books (1992)

Canoeing Handbook
Edited by Ray Rowe/British Canoe Union
(1997)

Teach Yourself Canoeing
Ray Rowe/Hodder & Stoughton
(1992)

**Kayaking: White Water and Touring
Basics/Trailside Guides**
Steven M. Krauzer/Norton (1995)

**Kayak: The Animated Manual
of Intermediate and Advanced
Whitewater Technique**
William Nealy/Cordee (1990)

White Water Kayaking
Ray Rowe/Hodder & Stoughton (1988)

Sea Kayaking
John Dowd/Douglas & MacIntyre
(1988)

Squirt Boating and Beyond
James E. Snyder/Menasha Ridge Press
(2001)

The Art of Freestyle
Brymer, Hughes and Collins/Pesda Press
(2000)

Weather Forecasting for Sailors
Frank Singleton/Hodder & Stoughton
(1981)

Magazines

Canoe Kayak and **Playboating**
Gunn Publishing
179 Bath Road, Cheltenham
United Kingdon GL53 7LY
Tel: (01242) 539 390

Paddles
Alexander House,
Ling Road,
Poole, Dorset,
United Kingdom BH12 4NZ
Tel: (01202) 735 090

Canoe & Kayak
10526 NE 68th Street,
Suite 3, Kirkland,
WA 98033 ,
United States
Tel: (800) 829 3340

The American Canoeist
P. O. Box 1190,
Newington,
Virginia 22122
United States

Kayak Session
3 Rue de la Claire
69009 Lyon
France
Tel: (472) 19 87 97

Useful Addresses

National Governing Bodies

British Canoe Union
Dudderidge House
Adbolton Lane
West Bridgford
Nottingham NG2 5AS
United Kingdom

American Canoe Association
8580 Cinderbed Road
Suite 1900
Newington
Virginia
United States

Canadian Canoe Association
333 River Road
Vanier City
Ontario K1L 8B9
Canada

Australian Canoe Federation
Room 510 Sports House
157 Gloucester Street
Sydney
NSW 2000
Australia

New Zealand Canoe Association
P. O. Box 3768
Wellington
New Zealand

French Canoe Kayak Federation
17 Route de Vienne
69007 Lyon
France

German Canoe Association
Berta-allee 8
4100 Duisberg 1
Germany

Training and Education
United Kingdom
Royal Lifesaving Society
Mounbatten House
Studley
Warwickshire B80 7NN
United Kingdom
Tel: (01789) 773 994

British Waterways
Melbury House
Melbury Terrace
London NW1 6JX

International Long River Canoeist Club
Catalina Cottage
Aultvullin
Strathay Point
Sutherland
KW14 7RY

Advanced Sea Kayak Club
7 Miller Close
Newport
Isle of Wight
PO30 5PS

For details of canoe and kayak clubs
in your area, please contact the British
Canoe Union.

United States
Rescue 3 International
9075 Elk Grove Boulevard 200
P. O. Box 519
Elk Grove
California 95759-0519
Tel: (916) 685 3066
Customer Support 800-45-RESCU
www.rescue3.com

American Rivers
801 Pennsylvania Ave S. E. Suite 303
Washington DC 20003

Nantahala Outdoor Center
US 19W Box 41
Bryson City
NC 28713
Tel: (704) 488 2175

A directory of state and local clubs can
be found in the *ACA Canoeing and
Kayaking Instruction Manual.*

Index

Acknowledgements

The author, photographer and publishers would like to thank the following individuals for their valuable contributions to this book:

Kevin Andriessen, Pete Astles, Duncan Eades, Nathan Eades, Rob Feloy, Rodney Forte, Paul Grogan, Dino Heald, Darren James, Graham Mackereth, Malcolm at Mega Kayaks, Mark Potts, Jason Smith and Martin Tapley.

Thanks also to the following companies who supplied clothing and equipment for photography:

AS Watersports
Kayaking and canoeing accessories.

Nookie Xtreme Sports Equipment
Kayaking clothing, accessories and safety equipment.

Pyranha Mouldings Ltd
Canoes and kayaks.

River Dart Country Park
For photography locations, logistics, hospitality and bank support.

System X
Werner and Schlegel paddles.

Thanks also to the following models, canoeists and kayakers:
Alec Ashmore, Steve Balcombe, Nikki Ball, Duncan Browne, Owen Davies, David Dean, Tim Denson, Rob Feloy, Mark Harvey, Roger Hopper, Mariano Kälfors, Beki King, Tom Klamfor, David Manlow, Bill Mattos, Tim Maud, Jon Miles, Lee Pritchard, Jason Scholey, J. Simpson, Howard Smith, Tank, James Weir, Steve Whetman, Hazel Wilson and Paul Woodward.

PICTURE CREDITS
All photography by Helen Metcalfe except for the following.
t = top; b = bottom; c = centre;
l = left; r = right

Action Images 203t, 204b, 205t, 205b, 214b, 215b.

Kevin Andriessen 230t.

The Art Archive 12t, 12b.

Duncan Eades 234t, 234b, 235t, 235bl, 235br.

Rob Feloy 161t, 177tr, 196tr, 197t, 197b.

Rodney Forte 13cr, 13bl, 13br, 126t, 128t, 128cr, 128br, 129ct, 168bl, 169bl, 170bl, 170br, 171br.

Dino Heald 26bl, 147b, 212t, 213b.

Martin Ording 224bl.

Mark Potts 29tr, 115b, 117t, 117b, 118bl, 119t, 119b, 133t, 133b, 135bl, 139t, 146br, 147t, 183tc, 183tr, 183b, 209t, 2210t, 226b, 227t, 227b, 228tr, 228bl, 229t, 229bl, 229br, 232t, 232b, 233t, 233b.

Jason Smith 4 (background), 6t, 7t, 7b, 186t, 186b, 187t, 187b, 190tl, 190br, 191tl, 224t, 224cb, 225t, 225b, 230bl, 231t, 231b.

Max Spielman 198, 199t, 199b.

Jono Stevens 220t, 220bl, 221t, 221b.

Martin Tapely 182, 185b, 209b, 212b, 213t.

Dan Trotter 196 (sequence), 239b.